Body Variations

ADVANCED LABANOTATION SERIES

EDITOR
Ann Hutchinson Guest
Director, Language of Dance® Centre, London, UK

Vol. 1, 1:
Canon Forms
by Ann Hutchinson Guest
and Rob van Haarst

Vol. 1, 2:
Shape, Design, Trace Patterns
by Ann Hutchinson Guest
and Rob van Haarst

Vol. 1, 3:
Kneeling, Sitting, Lying
by Ann Hutchinson Guest
and Rob van Haarst

Issue 4:
Sequential Movements
by Ann Hutchinson Guest
and Joukje Kolff

Issue 5:
Hands, Fingers
by Ann Hutchinson Guest
and Joukje Kolff

Issue 6:
Floorwork, Basic Acrobatics
by Ann Hutchinson Guest
and Joukje Kolff

Issue 7:
Center of Weight
by Ann Hutchinson Guest
and Joukje Kolff

Issue 8:
Handling of Objects, Props
by Ann Hutchinson Guest
and Joukje Kolff

Issue 9:
Spatial Variations
by Ann Hutchinson Guest
and Joukje Kolff

Issue 10:
Body Variations
by Ann Hutchinson Guest
with Andy Adamson and
Raymundo Ruiz González

Body Variations

BY

ANN HUTCHINSON GUEST

WITH

ANDY ADAMSON

AND

RAYMUNDO RUIZ GONZÁLEZ

DANCE
BOOKS

First published in 2022 by Dance Books Ltd.,
Southwold House, Isington Road, Binsted, Hampshire. GU34 4PH

www.dancebooks.co.uk

ISBN 978-185273-185-4

This book was written and produced at the Language of Dance® Centre
        17 Holland Park
        London W11 3TD
        United Kingdom
        T: 44(0)207 229 3780 Web: www.lodc.org
        e-mail: info@lodc.org

PHOTOS

Ann Hutchinson Guest
LHD, DHu, MBE

Andy Adamson
B. Mus

Raymundo Ruiz González
MA

Contents

xi

Preface

Having published *Spatial Variations*, Advanced Labanotation, Issue 9, it seemed logical to follow it with detailed presentations of variations in Body Movements. Inevitably there has been some overlap with material given in previous books, but the point of view, the focus, is often slightly different thereby providing a different aspect or understanding. Other valuable information has also been included. The more widespread use and development of Motif Notation has contributed to general movement descriptions as well as specific statements, and how these are presented through the notation symbols. Unusual descriptions have, as their source, the explanation and imagery used by chorographers to get their ideas across to the performers. Some images may not be physically possible, but striving for them will produce a different energy, a subtle expression that is closer to what the choreographer aims to achieve.

Acknowledgements

When **Raymundo Ruiz González** completed his Choreomundus examination in June 2019, to my delight he was free to accept my invitation to be involved in the production of this book. With his advanced level notation knowledge, his belief in the importance of Labanotation, and his dedication to advancing knowledge of this valuable tool, it was splendid that he agreed to be my assistant.

Because many symbols in this book were not available in LabanWriter, we turned to **Andy Adamson**, the inventor of CALABAN (computer aided Labanotation) a system which is more flexible in creating symbols and detailed notation. Fortunately, he agreed and was able to devote his expertise to this project with excellent results. In addition, he has taken on the role of editor for this volume. Thanks also to Clare Lidbury for assistance in final proof reading.

The arrival of Covid19 in March 2020 inevitably affected our work, making life much more difficult. Details on the problems encountered will obviously not be given here, but I must express my great appreciation to both Ray and Andy for consistently carrying on as best they could.

I must next give credit and much appreciation to each of the Senior Labanotation Specialists who agreed to be a Reader, checking each chapter and sending in comments and corrections, as needed. They were, alphabetically: **Sandra Aberkalns**, **János Fügedi**, **Leslie Rotman** and **Lynne Weber.** Of particular value was that each had a particular focus, an awareness or range of knowledge and experience. The time they devoted to this project, the thought they gave to each detail and the lengthy responses we received were all very valuable. We were so glad that Janos, our Hungarian colleague, was able to take part; he had been the protégé of our much-valued colleague, the late Mária Szentpál.

The source of this book was the many notes collected over the past decades, particularly reports on technical discussions at the New York Dance Notation Bureau, letters from colleagues abroad, and from similar sources. Most of these discussions were dated in the 1980s, although some came later.

Participants in Labanotation Discussions, circa 1980s

In the following alphabetical list of people involved in these discussions, either in person or by mail, an asterisk identifies those most involved:

Sandra Aberkalns,* Jill Cirasella, Bryce Cobain, Ray Cook,* Mary Corey, Tina Curran, Virginia Doris, Ilene Fox,* János Fügedi,* Jen Garda, Doris Green, Carla Guggenheim, Peggy Hackney, Richard Haisma, Angela Kane, Mira Kim, Billie Mahoney, Sheila Marion, Jane Marriett,* Jan Moeckle,* Leslie Rotman,* Gretchen Schumacher, Mária Szentpál,* Muriel Topaz,* Judy Van Zile, Irene Wachtel, Charlotte Wile*.

Body Variations

Chapter 1. Body Parts

1. Limb and its surfaces

1.1. The sign for any body part, that is any body area or limb, is **1a**. The sign for 'a limb' is **1b** with **1c** being any limb. The front and back surfaces for the arm are indicated in the illustration of **1d**, while **1e** illustrates the front and back surfaces of the leg. In the chart of **1f, i)** is the front (outer) side, and **v)** the back (inner) side; **iii)** refers to the right big toe-thumb side and the little toe/finger-side for the right limb; **vii)** follows the same logic for the left limb. The in-between points are shown by combining these signs, as in examples **ii), iv), vi)** and **viii)**.

2. The Arm as a Limb

2.1. The arm is the limb below the shoulder; **2a** indicates both arms, **2b** states either arm while **2c** is the left arm and **2d** the right. The indication of either side; **2e**, can be applied to the elbows, **2f**, to the wrists, **2g** and to the hands, **2h**. This indication can also be applied to the legs and its parts.

2.2. The upper arm is the limb above the elbow, **2i**, simplified to **2j** for the left upper arm, while **2k** and **2l** are for the right upper arm. The lower arm is the limb above the wrist, **2m,** which is simplified to **2n** for the left side, and **2o** for the right.

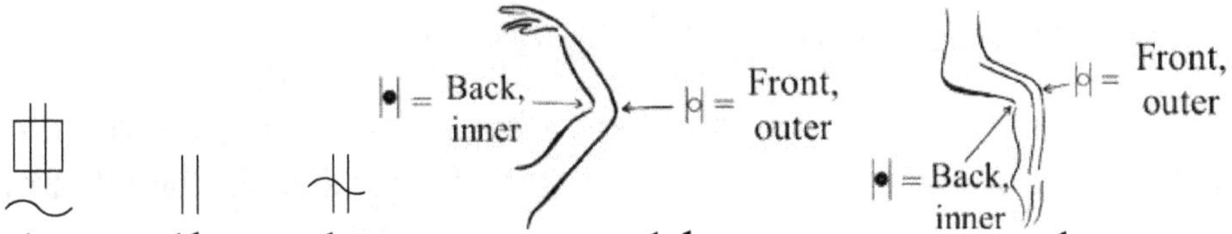

1a 1b 1c

= Back, inner

= Front, outer

1d

= Front, outer

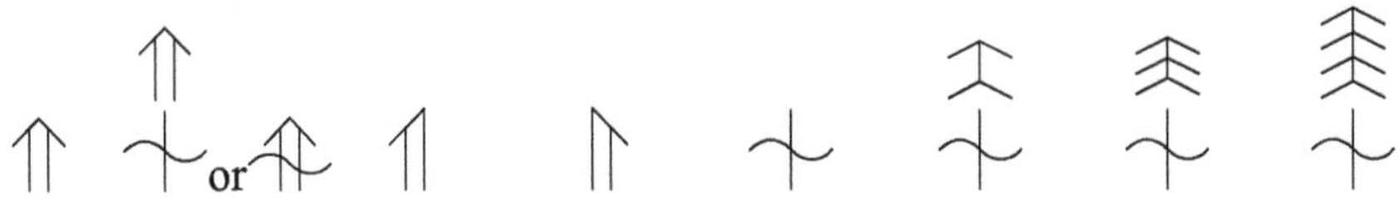

= Back, inner

1e

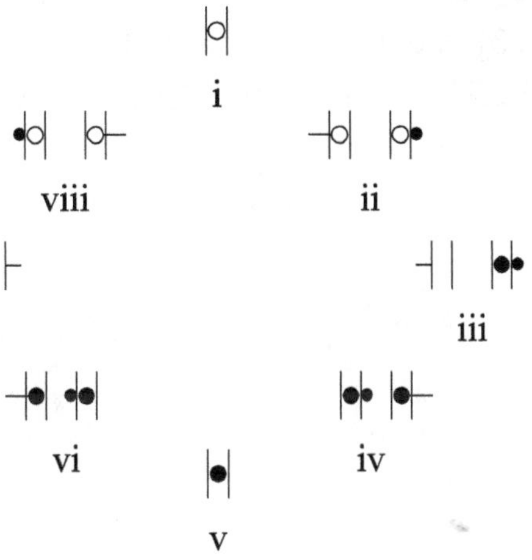

i

viii ii

vii iii

vi iv

1f v

2a 2b or 2c 2d 2e 2f 2g 2h

2i 2j 2k 2l 2m 2n 2o

3. Surfaces of the Arm

3.1. Ex. **3a** states the outer (elbow side) surface of the left arm; **3b**, the inner surface of the right arm; **3c**, the thumb edge side for the left arm; **3d**, little finger edge of the left arm; **3e**, the outer surface of the left upper arm; **3f**, the inner surface of the right upper arm; **3g**, the thumb edge of the left upper arm while **3h**, is the little finger edge; **3i**, the outer surface of the left lower arm, with **3j**, the inner surface of the right lower arm; **3k**, the thumb edge for the left lower arm, and **3l**, being the little finger edge for that part.

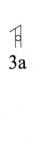

3a

3b

3c

3d

3e

3f

3g

3h

3i

3j

3k

3l

4. Joint Signs for the Arm

4.1. Where contact, touching, or grasping is involved, the joint itself is automatically understood. In **4a** the right hand grasps the left shoulder. By adding dots to a joint sign, the point just above or below that joint can be indicated: **4b** is the part just above the shoulder, closer to the neck, left and right side; **4c** is below the shoulder joint, the arm pit, left and right, illustrated in **4d**.

4.2. Ex. **4e** is the point just above the elbow joint, left and right; **4f** is the point just below the elbow, left and right; **4g** is the point just above the wrist, left and right; **4h** is the point just below the wrist joint, left and right. This last is in fact, the base of the hand.

5. Areas of the Arm Joints

5.1. The area around the shoulder joint is shown as **5a**, left and right; for the elbow, **5b**, and for the wrist, **5c**. Below the shoulder area, the arm pit, is indicated in **5d** or as in **5e**.

5.2. **Surfaces of the arms**. The interpretation of the front (the bony surface), **5f**, or the back (the inside) of the elbow area, **5g**, is comparable to the indication for the bony surface of the knee area, **5h**, and **5i,** the inner surface. Surfaces for elbow and wrist follow a similar logic, **5j**, **5k**, **5l** and **5m**.

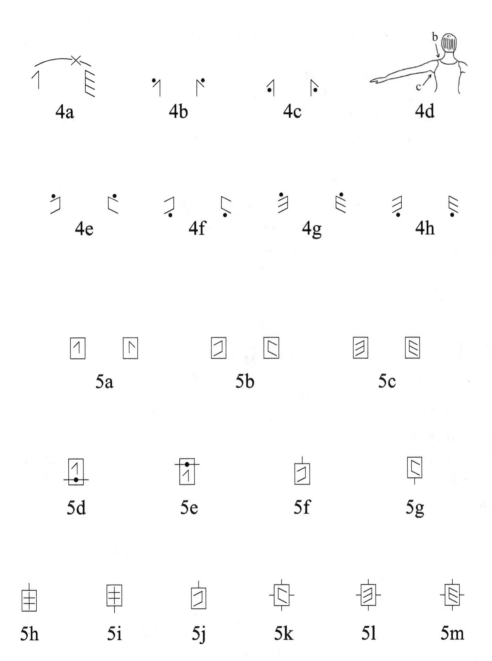

6. Movements of the Shoulder

6.1. Directional movements of the shoulder are well known: **6a** states raising the right shoulder, **6b** is lowering the shoulder; downward displacement is spatially smaller mainly involving the muscles. In **6c** the shoulder moves forward and then backward, **6d**.

6.2. The sideward movements of **6e** are more appropriately written as shifting movements as in **6f** and **6g**. These shifting movements are possible through the sliding action of the shoulder blade, the scapula, represented in **6h**. Thus, **6i** shows the right shoulder blade shifting to the right, then pulling into the left, a more limited action. Ex. **6j** shows an alternate drawing of the scapula.

7. Movements of the Shoulder Area

7.1. A raising of the single shoulder area, **7a**, involves movement in the right side of the rib cage; the greater the distance the more the rib cage is affected. Similarly, the actions of **7b** and **7c**, will be such augmented displacements. Diagonal displacements are stated in **7d** and **7e**. Note that the area of both shoulders, **7f**, the shoulder section, is the upper area of the chest and its actions are similar to actions of the chest (rib cage).

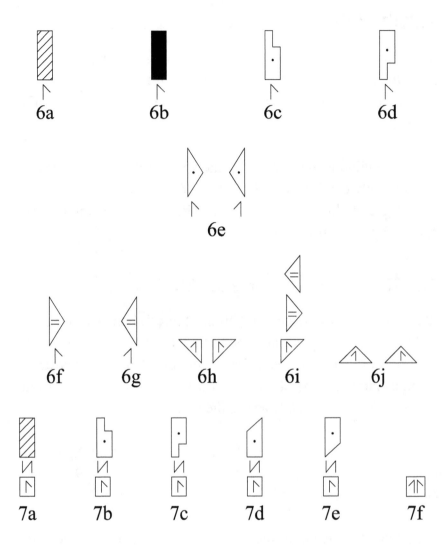

6a 6b 6c 6d

6e

6f 6g 6h 6i 6j

7a 7b 7c 7d 7e 7f

8. Limbs (Sections) of the Leg

8.1. The whole leg is indicated as the limb below the hip, **8a** indicates both legs, **8b** the left leg and **8c** the right leg, while **8d** indicates either leg. The indication of either side can be applied to the knee, **8e**, to the ankle, **8f**, and to the feet, **8g**.

8.2. The thigh is the limb above the knee, written as **8h** for both thighs, but usually condensed to **8i** for the left thigh and **8j** for the right. The lower leg is the limb above the ankle, **8k**, also more commonly written as **8l** for the left and **8m** for the right.

9. Surfaces of the Leg Limbs

9.1. Ex. **9a** states the ventral ('front', 'outer') bony surface of the left leg, while **9b** indicates the volar ('back', 'inner') surface. Ex. **9c** is the big toe edge and **9d** the little toe edge for the left leg. This can be written as **9e**, it being understood that the black circle always means the little toe edge even if placed on what visually seems the wrong side.

9.2. The surfaces for the left thigh are: **9f** the ventral; **9g** the volar; **9h** the big toe edge; **9i** the little toe edge. Similarly, examples   **9j** – **9m** indicate these surfaces for the left lower leg.

9.3. Intermediate points are as follows: **9n**, between the ventral and big toe edge of the left thigh; **9o**, between the volar and the little toe edge; **9p**, for the left lower leg, between the ventral surface and the big toe edge; **9q**, between the volar and little toe edge for the left lower leg.

8a   8b   8c   8d   or   8e   8f   8g

8h   8i   8j   8k   8l   8m

9a   9b   9c   9d   9e

9f   9g   9h   9i

9j   9k   9l   9m

9n   9o   9p   9q

10. Joint Signs for the Legs

10.1. When placed on the right or left side of the staff, **10a** indicates the hip. When written outside the staff this sign means both hips. By adding a dot, the point just above the hip joint can be indicated, **10b**, **10c**, left and right. A dot just below indicates the point just below the hip, **10d**, **10e**, left and right.

10.2. This same usage applies to the single hip signs of **10f** and **10g**. Note the correct drawing of this single hip sign, to distinguish it from a sideward flat pin (tack) **10f′** and **10g′**. The points just above the hip are **10h** and **10i**; **10j** and **10k** being the points below.

10.3. The use of the knee symbol, **10l**, **10m**, **10n**, follows the same logic, the points above the knee joint being **10o**, **10p**, **10q** and **10r**; and points below are **10s**, **10t**, **10u**, **10v**.

10.4. The signs for the ankle follow the same pattern: **10w**, **10x**, **10y** being the ankle signs and **10z**, **10aa**, **10ab** and **10ac** being the points above, with **10ad** and **10ae** being the points below.

11. Areas of the Leg Joints

11.1. The sign for an area, **11a**, can be applied to the various joints of the body, **11b** being the area of the hip and **11c** and **11d** the areas of the left or right hip, respectively.

11.2. Similarly, the area of the knee can be shown, **11e**, **11f** and **11g**. Areas of the ankle are shown in **11h**, **11i** and **11j**.

11.3. Surfaces of these areas are indicated by adding the appropriate pin, **11k** being the front surface for the left knee, **11l** the back, **11m** the big toe side, and **11n** the little toe edge.

The diagonal surfaces can also be shown, **11o** being the right front surface. Intermediate points are indicated by combining two of these indications, **11p** being the point between diagonal right and side.

+	⊹	⊹	⊹	⊹	⊣	⊣	⊢	⊢	⁼	⊩	⊣	⊢
10a	10b	10c	10d	10e	10f	10f'	10g	10g'	10h	10i	10j	10k

⊧	⊣	⊢	⊹	⊧	⊣	⊩	⊧	⊧	⊣	⊢
10l	10m	10n	10o	10p	10q	10r	10s	10t	10u	10v

⊧	⊣	⊢	⊧	⊧	⊣	⊩	⊣	⊢
10w	10x	10y	10z	10aa	10ab	10ac	10ad	10ae

☐	⊞	⊟	⊢	⊞	⊟	⊟	⊞	⊟	⊟
11a	11b	11c	11d	11e	11f	11g	11h	11i	11j

⊟	⊟	⊟	⊟	⊟	⊟
11k	11l	11m	11n	11o	11p

12. The Range of Foot-hooks

12.1. The foot-hook, derived from the ends of a horizontal contact bow, indicates not only the part of the foot contacting the floor for supports and gestures but also the angle of the foot in relation to the floor. Examples **12a** to **12m** show the basic range of foot-hooks.

12a	♪ or ℓ =		Toe nail
12b	◡ or ◟ =		Full toe tip (full pointe)
12c	♪ or ◟ =		Pad of toe
12d	♪ or ◟ =		Full ball, 3/4 toe, forced arch
12e	∠ or ◟ =		1/2 ball, foot at 45 degree angle
12f	♪ or ◟ =		1/4 ball
12g	– or – =		1/8 ball (heel only slightly raised)
12h	◁ or ▷ =		Whole foot
12i	◥ or ◤ =		1/4 heel, ball of foot slightly off the floor
12j	◥ or ◤ =		1/2 heel
12k	◥ or ◤ =		3/4 heel
12l	◥ or ◤ =		Full heel, foot at marked angle from the floor
12m	◡ or ◡ =		Unspecified contact

13. Timing in Use of Foot-hooks

Note: At the time when General Timing was widely in use, the centering of a foot hook on a direction symbol was understood to apply to the whole movement. It was Albrecht Knust who indicated Specific Timing by careful placement of these contact indications. In many notation situations there is a need to be very specific. Statement of Unit Timing or Specific Timing be given at the start of a movement score, although it may soon be evident when one starts reading.

13.1. When taking a step in any direction, the part of the foot making contact with the floor is shown by the appropriate foot-hook at the start of the step symbol. In **13a** the first arrow points to this moment of contact, the second arrow indicates the conclusion of the transference of weight. In **13b** the forward low step starts (and remains) on the ball of the foot. In **13c** the low step starts on the whole foot and then rises fluently to the ball of the foot. In **13d** the hold sign indicates that the whole foot contact remains until near the end.

13.2. In contrast, **13e** starts on the ball of the foot and lowers to the whole foot. Ex. **13f** shows a different timing for this action. In **13g** the whole foot contact occurs at the end. The closer placement of the whole foot hook at the end in **13h**, is considered easier to read.

13.3. For a starting position on full pointe, **13i**, the hooks have no time significance. A rise ending on pointe is stated in **13j**. This action might be achieved with a slight spring, bringing the feet closer together, **13k**, or **13l**. If the toes should remain on the same spot, i.e., just a rise, this can be stated by using caret signs, as in **13m**.

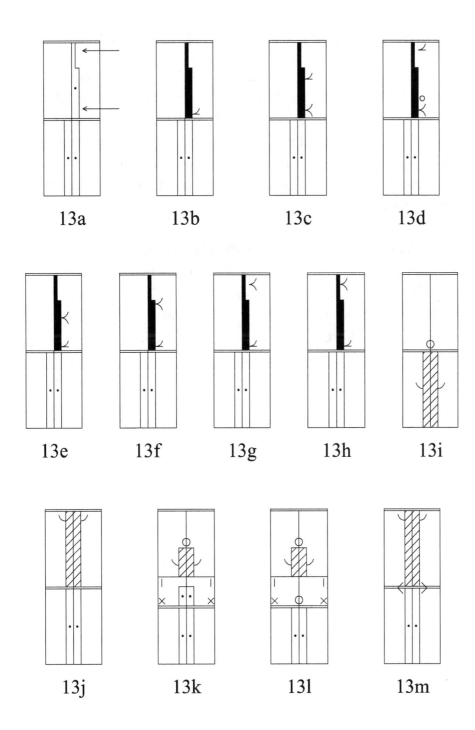

13a 13b 13c 13d

13e 13f 13g 13h 13i

13j 13k 13l 13m

14. Visuality of Placement of Hooks

14.1. The foot hook sign for the heel just off the floor is sometimes hard to see. In **14a** the small line placed close to the bar line is almost invisible, it is better placed as in **14b**. Use of a distance qualifier, as in **14c**, can produce a visual problem. Placing the hook at the start of the beat, as in **14c**, is correct, but the placement of **14d** is visually easier to read. As the direction symbol and the 'x' qualifier are understood to be a unit, this latter placement is theoretically correct.

In **14e** the hooks indicating continuous sliding are placed on the main body of the direction symbol. This is correct in that during the final centering of the weight over the new support, no further sliding occurs. If indication of sliding to the end of the step is desired, the placement of the second whole foot hook is usually indicated as **14f**. However, the closer placement on the indicator, as in **14g**, can be easier to read.

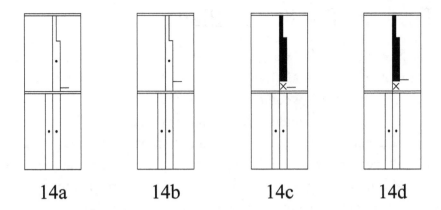

14a   14b   14c   14d

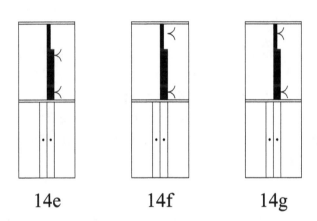

14e   14f   14g

15. Timing of a Step in Place

15.1. Starting with the weight on the left foot, the swift step in place on the right foot, **15a**, will doubtless be performed without thinking, the right leg closes in and takes weight. However, if the step in place is much slower, **15b**, the right foot should touch in place at the start of the symbol, on count 1, indicated in **15c**, the rest of the duration being the gradual taking over of the full weight onto the right leg. If the right leg starts out to the side, as in **15d**, the right leg rapidly moves in to place, to begin the transference of weight on count 1. In **15e** this performance is spelled out, the transference of weight starting on count 1 on the low ball of the foot and ending on the whole foot at the end of count 3 as the weight is fully transferred.

15.2. In **15f** the moving into place is shown with sliding, first on the low ball of the foot then on the whole foot. In contrast, in **15g** the heel lowers at once to start whole foot sliding into place. In these examples the movement into place takes 3 counts, the weight will be centered on the right leg only at the end of count 3. From a lifted left support, **15h** indicates closing into feet together with the knees bent.

16. Resultant Touch, Passive Leg

16.1. After a standard-length forward step, **16a**, the resultant passive touch on the ball of the other foot, as indicated at the end, will probably have the left knee slightly bent. In the case of a much longer step, **16b**, the left leg will probably be stretched; this can be specifically stated in **16c**.

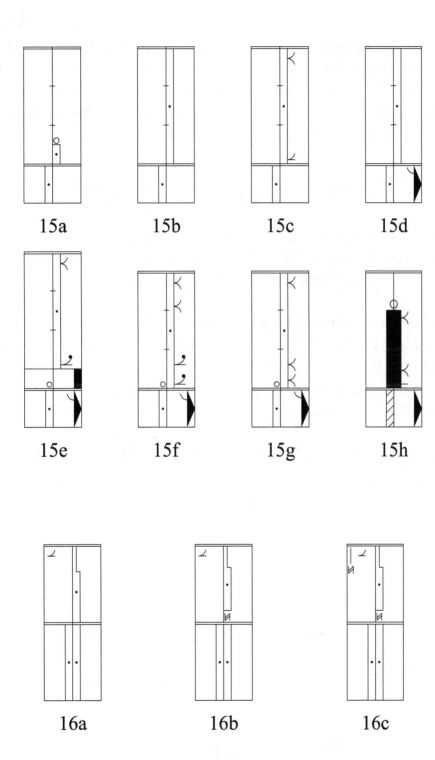

15a   15b   15c   15d

15e   15f   15g   15h

16a   16b   16c

16.2. The timing of the leg flexion for **16a** can be indicated, as in **16d** or in **16e** where the flexion starts sooner. Ex. **16f** specifically focuses on the rolling action for the left leg from the whole foot to ending with toe contact. (For Heel and Toe Drops see *Labanotation* (2005, 190); for Partial Weight for Steps, Leg Gestures see ibid. (69-70, 193, 401-402)

17. Exact Tip of Toes

17.1. The general use of the toe hook does not usually mean the tip of the toes, as can be seen in **17a** and **17b**, the latter being illustrated in **17c**. It should, more correctly be written as **17d**, the pad of the toes.

17.2. The transition through the foot, from the ball to the whole foot occurs on **17e**; **17f** features the passing use of high level as the transference of weight moves forward with an overcurve and ends in middle level. An overcurve step, **17g,** spells this use of the foot more specifically. Used in the 1840s, this step was called a *pas élevé*.

17.3. In contrast to **17f, 17h** shows a separated change of level producing an angular drop to middle level in contrast to the overcurve of **17f**.

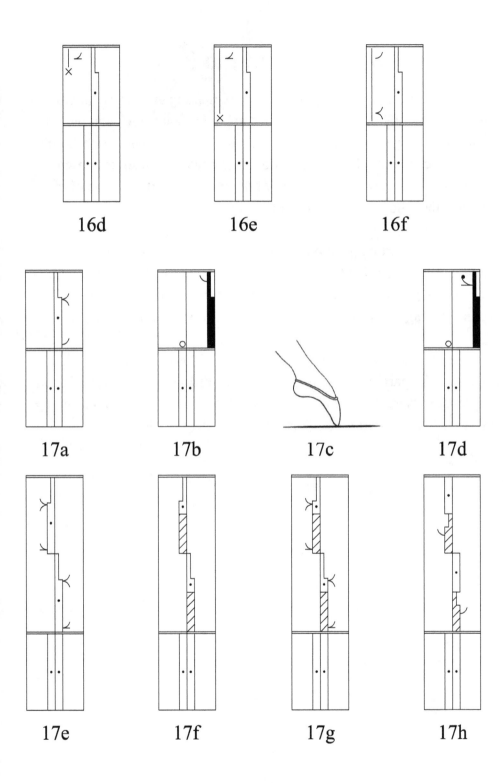

16d 16e 16f

17a 17b 17c 17d

17e 17f 17g 17h

18. Hooks for the Top of the Foot

18.1. With contemporary choreography making greater use of contact or support on the top of the foot, the need arose for hook signs that would relate to these usages. From the idea of a white circle attached to the hook expressing the idea of 'above', the following hooks have been proposed: **18a**, the top of the toes; **18b**, the front of the instep; **18c** the middle of the instep; **18d** the whole of the instep.

18.2. The starting position of **18e** is often used in ballet choreography. If the supporting leg is bent, the right toe contact is more likely to be **18f**. A further lowering of the support brings the right foot contact more onto part of the instep, **18g**. In **18h** the whole of the instep is touching the floor.

18.3. The following examples make use of these signs: **18i** is a low curtsey; in **18j** a partial weight is taken on the left foot (toe); in **18k,** from a high extension there is a slight spring into a low drop; in **18l,** from a swift ¼ turn there is a low drop forward into a kneel on the right leg.

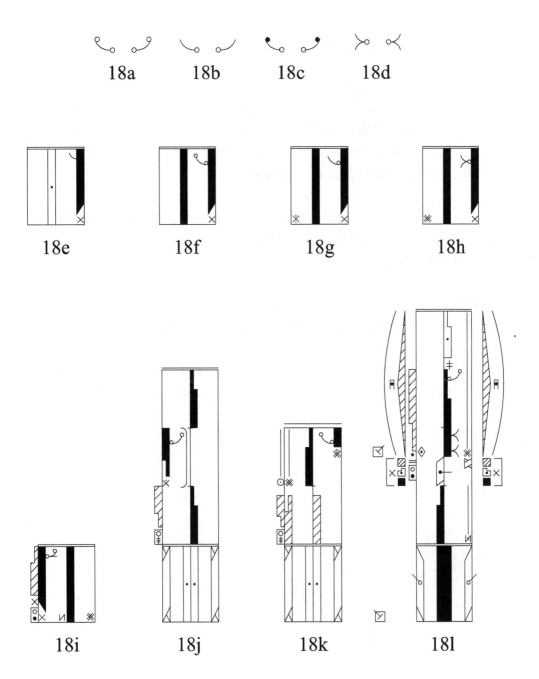

18a 18b 18c 18d

18e 18f 18g 18h

18i 18j 18k 18l

19. Areas of the Foot

19.1. The area of the foot, **19a**, is used when focus is on the forward part of the foot, when focus is on the back area **19b** is used. The tip of the toes is indicated by **19c**, with **19d** being the tip of the heel. Ex. **19e** is a general indication for the sole of the foot with **19f** being the general indication for the instep, the top surface.

19.2. The big toe edge is shown as **19g** for the left foot and **19h** for the right foot. Use of a black dot indicates the little toe edge, **19i** for the left foot and **19j** for the right.

19.3. When right or left specification is needed the foot sign is added, as in **19k** and **19l** for the sole and instep, respectively; left and right big toe edges are indicated in **19m** and **19n**. For the little toe edge, use of the black dot in **19o** and **19p** is understood automatically to mean the little toe edge, even though visually the dot is on the wrong side of the foot area symbol.

⊓	⊔		
19a	19b		

19c	19d	19e	19f

19g	19h	19i	19j

19k	19l	19m	19n

19o	19p

20. Sections of the Foot

20.1. The area of the foot is divided into three sections, **20a**, illustrated in **20b**. When focus is on the front of the foot **20c** is used, with **20d** focusing on the back. Ex **20e** is the underside, the sole surface of the toe area, with **20f** being the top surface of that area. Ex. **20g** is the center area of the sole of the foot with **20h** being the center area of the instep. The sole under the heel is indicated in **20i**; or it can be expressed as **20j**. Similarly, **20k** or **20l** indicate the higher area of the instep.

20.2. More specific areas are shown with small strokes. For example, for the right foot, **20m** indicates the big toe edge of the toe area of the foot, while the black dot of **20n** states the little toe edge of that area. The diagonal area at front left is shown in **20o**, and the front right diagonal area in **20p**. Placement on the staff indicates the right or left foot. When the need arises to specify which foot, then the foot indication is added, as in **20q** or **20r**.

20.3. The same diagonal area of the sole of the toe area can be shown as **20s** or by using the combined form of **20t**. Similarly, the top surface of that area can be indicated by **20u** or the combined symbol of **20v**. When needed other specific areas can be indicated through the appropriate use of these basic indications.

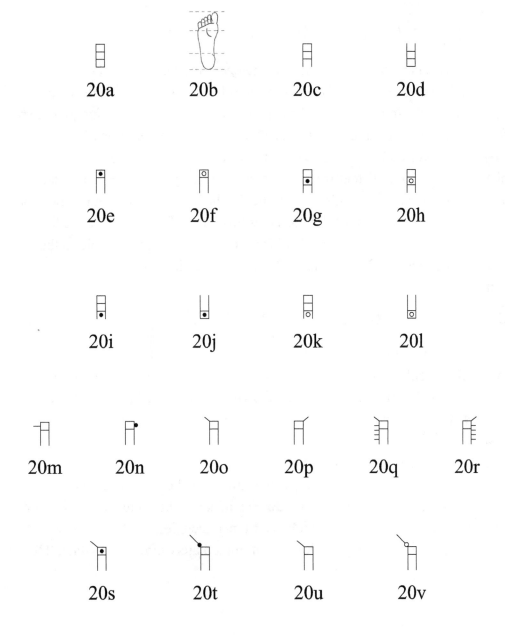

20a   20b   20c   20d

20e   20f   20g   20h

20i   20j   20k   20l

20m   20n   20o   20p   20q   20r

20s   20t   20u   20v

21. Specific Parts for Tap Dance

21.1. There are specific needs when notating tap dance. The metal plate at the front of the tap shoe is used in different ways. The following hooks are all for the left foot. The center of the plate, **21a**, which equals **21b** for part of the foot, can be written as **21c**. The back center edge of the plate, **21d**, equals **21e** and written as **21f**. The front center of the tap (as distinguished from the toe tip), **21g**, equals the foot area of **21h** and notated as **21i**. The outside edge of the tap plate for the left foot, **21j**, equals the foot area of **21k**, and the sign of **21l** indicates this lateral focus. Similarly, for the inside edge of the tap plate, **21m** for the left foot, is comparable to the foot area of **21n** and focus on the side is expressed in **21o**.

22. Duration of a Tap Contact

22.1. A single foot contact sign on a leg gesture shows a brief, momentary contact with the floor, **22a**. A brief sliding (brushing) action is shown by two of the same hooks, as shown in **22b** where there is a brief brush as the leg moves forward.

22.2. The brief sliding action produces a more curved pattern of motion, **22c**, while a single touch, which should make a single sound, suggests the angular deflection of **22d**. To make a single tap sound, the foot and ankle need to articulate, which is a trained technique. The single sound is clearly stated by putting a release sign immediately after the contact, **22e**.

21a   21b   21c   21d   21e   21f

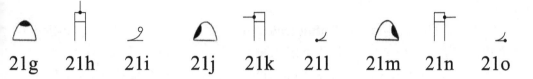

21g   21h   21i   21j   21k   21l   21m   21n   21o

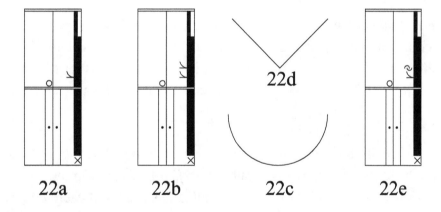

22a   22b   22c   22e

23. The Toes

Details about the toes are not commonly needed in the general recording of movement, that is of dance and other activities. However, in therapy, focus may be on the toes as well as on the foot as a whole. There could be a need to record the activities of a person who, missing arms, has to rely on performing many actions with the toes instead of fingers.

23.1. The symbol of **23a** indicates the toes of both feet: **23b** specifies the toes of the left foot, while **23c** indicates toes of the right foot. A black dot placed at the end of the stroke indicates a specific toe: **23d**, is the left big toe; **23e**, the right big toe; **23f**, the left middle toe; **23g** for the right middle toe. The little toes are shown in **23h,** for the left, and **23i** for the right. The other toe indications follow suit.

23.2. In a similar fashion to the fingers (see *Hands, Fingers, Advanced Labanotation, issue 5*), the toe knuckles can be indicated: **23j**, the base joint of the left big toe; **23k**, the mid joint of the left big toe; **23l**, the base joint of the left second toe; **23m**, the second joint of this toe, **23n** being the third joint.

23.3. The limb of each toe can be indicated: **23o** is the limb of the left big toe, with **23p** stating the upper (outer bony) surface and **23q** the inner (fleshy) surface. In a similar manner the limb and surfaces of each toe segment can be indicated, for example, **23r** shows the 'big toe' edge of the base segment of the left little toe, illustrated in **23s**, and 23t represents the 'little toe' edge of the base segment of the left little toe.

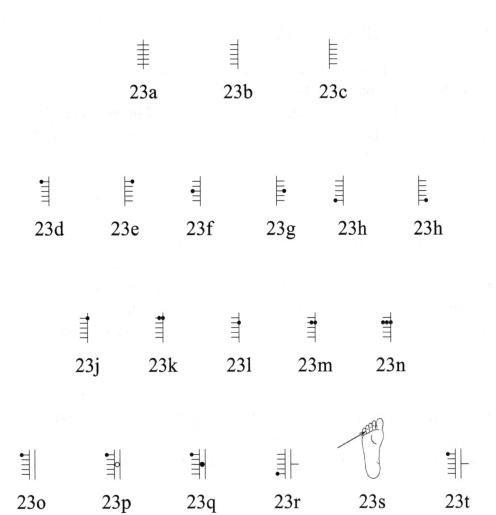

23a   23b   23c

23d   23e   23f   23g   23h   23h

23j   23k   23l   23m   23n

23o   23p   23q   23r   23s   23t

24. Torso Surface Signs

24.1. A small stroke attached to a body area sign indicates the center of the surface of that part. Ex. **24a** indicates the surfaces of the chest, the front, the diagonal right surface, the right side, etc. Ex. **24b** and **24c** indicate similar surfaces for the waist area and for the pelvis, respectively. Ex. **24d** indicates the front of the whole torso used for lying prone. For lying on the side, **24e** is used, and **24f** indicates lying on the back, lying supine. Lying on the diagonal surfaces is less usual because of the problem of balance.

24.2. **Intermediate Parts** for these surfaces are indicated through small higher or lower pins, e.g. a forward high or a forward low pin placed on the edge of the area sign. Ex. **24g** indicates the upper part of the breastbone, while **24h** states below the center of that area (the diaphragm). These pins can be applied to the waist area, **24i** and **24j**; and also to the pelvic area, **24k** and **24l**.

24.3. These higher and lower signs can also be applied to other surfaces of the chest: the diagonal right forward surface is shown in **24m**; to the side of the chest, **24n**; the diagonal right back surface, **24o**, and so on. Such details for each side can also be applied to the waist area, and to the pelvic area.

24.4. Intermediate surfaces can be shown by attaching two pins to the same surface symbol, as in **24p**. Such indications can be applied also to the waist and pelvis areas. Ex. **24q** states a surface between the right forward diagonal and the forward high surface of the pelvis. Indication of level is also given in **24r**; all such indications are possible for the chest, waist, and pelvic areas.

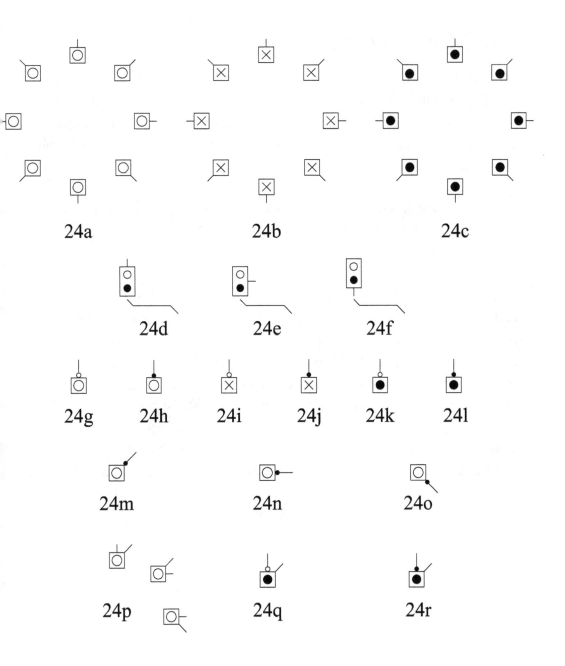

24a

24b

24c

24d

24e

24f

24g

24h

24i

24j

24k

24l

24m

24n

24o

24p

24q

24r

25. Moveable Parts

25.1. Moveable parts of the body areas are those parts that have the ability to expand and contract. This applies particularly to the chest, the rib cage. Such moveable parts are indicated by the appropriate displacement of the center of the area sign, as in **25a** and **25b** that show displacement in the chest and waist respectively.

25.2. The movements of the waist area are limited; however, through the flexibility of the spine, the back of the waist, **25c**, can be displaced (bulged out) backward.

25.3. The pelvis is more limited, the most moveable part is the abdomen, **25d**, which can contract and expand. The center back of the pelvis, **25e**, though limited in spatial displacement, can press backward, for example. The diagonal back areas of the pelvis, **25f**, the right and left buttocks, are capable of degrees of contracting. In such cases the action is more of a muscular contraction rather than a spatial displacement.

25. 4. **Actions for the Moveable Parts**. Aided by the action of breathing, the front of the chest can expand, **25g**, and also contract, **25h**. Ex. **25i** indicates the belly expanding three-dimensionally, while **25j** states the belly contracting three-dimensionally.

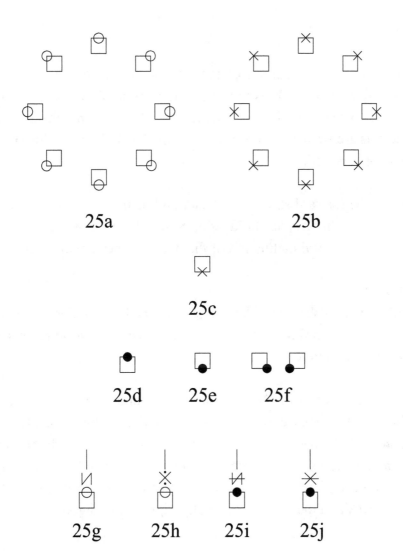

25a

25b

25c

25d 25e 25f

25g 25h 25i 25j

26. The Neck

26.1. Ex. **26a** is the sign for the neck, the limb below the head. The head inclining forward, **26b**, is in fact an inclination of the neck, **26c**, the head passively accompanying, i.e., being carried along. In Labanotation all such head tilts are written as movements of the head; the inclusion of the neck being understood.

26.2. The forward shift of the head, **26d**, is in fact a neck movement in which the head has a space hold, **26e**. Similarly, a sideward tilt of the head, **26f**, is a sideward inclination of the neck, the head being carried along, **26g**.

26.3. Ex. **26h** shows a sideward shift of the head, which can also be expressed as a sideward inclination of the neck while the head retains its spatial vertical direction.

26.4. **Surfaces of the Neck.** For contacts and other specific needs, the surfaces of the neck can be indicated: **26j** indicates the throat, the front (inner) side; **26k** the back (outer) side of the neck; **26l** shows the right side, while **26m** is the left side. An intermediate part is shown by combining the two appropriate surfaces, as in **26n** which indicates the area between the back of the neck and the right side, i.e., the right back diagonal part.

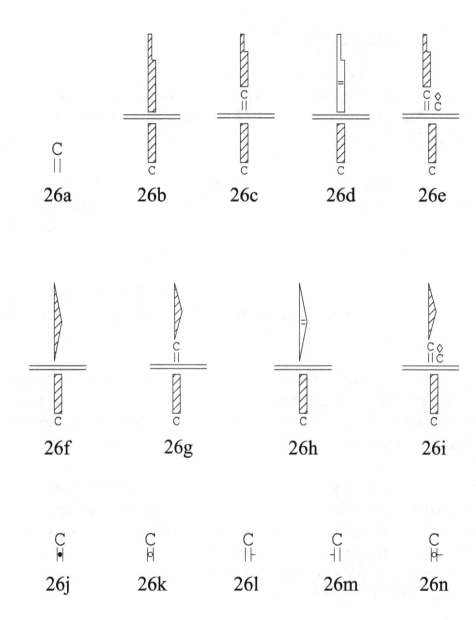

27. Signs for the Spine

27.1. The following specific set of signs are now used for the spine:
27a is the cervical spine (the neck); **27b** is the thoracic spine ('limb' of the chest); **27c** is the lumbar spine ('limb' of the waist); and **27d** is the sacral spine ('limb' of the pelvis).

27.2. Note that the vertical lines are narrower than the section symbol so as to distinguish the thoracic and sacral spine from an indication of a limb. Ex. **27e** indicates the outer or bony top surface of a limb while **27f** is the under or inner surface.

27.3. Placing the head symbol within the 'spine limb' symbol, **27g**, instead of after it as in, **27h**, distinguishes the cervical spine from the neck as a body part.

27.4. To identify the spine as a whole, or various spinal sections, the 'limb' symbol is enclosed between the signs for the identifying sections: **27i** is the whole spine; **27j** the cervical and thoracic spine; **27k** is the cervical through lumbar spine and **27l** the lumbar and sacral spine.

27.5. Individual vertebrae are identified by their location in a spinal section, numbered from the skull downward: cervical - 1st through 7th; thoracic - 1st through 12th; lumbar - 1st through 5th; sacral - 1st through 5th. The appropriate number is placed next to the spinal indication: **27m** indicates the 7th cervical; **27n** is the 2nd thoracic; **27o** indicates the 12th thoracic and **27p** the 5th lumbar.

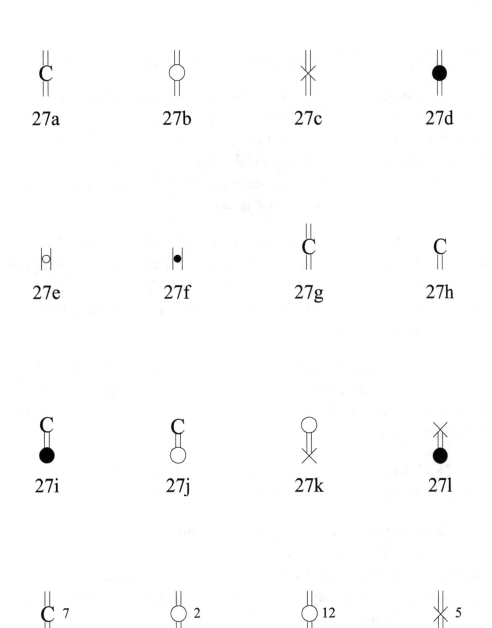

27a 27b 27c 27d

27e 27f 27g 27h

27i 27j 27k 27l

27m 27n 27o 27p

28. Pictorial Signs for the Head

28.1. Note that many of the following signs were presented in *Labanotation* (1970) but not included in the 2005 edition. Simple pictorial signs, developed in New York, have been used in scores: **28a** for the nose; **28b** represents the mouth; **28c** the tongue; **28d** the ears; **28e** the eyes; **28f** the right eye and **28g** the left eye, while **28h** represents the forehead and **28i** the jaw. The sign for the whole face is **28j**.

28.2. **The Nose**. The following are the symbols more recently developed to indicate specific parts of the nose. **28k** specifies the bridge of the nose with **28l** being under the end of the nose. The tip of the nose is shown in **28m**. Inside the nose is **28n**, with **28o** specifying the right nostril and **28p** the left nostril.

28.3. **The Mouth**. Specific signs for the mouth are as follows: **28q** is the lower lip with **28r** the upper lip. By adding the "x" sign, the inside of the mouth is indicated, **28s** being the teeth. The lower teeth are shown by **28t**, **28u** being the upper teeth.

28.4. **The Eyes**. More specific signs for the eyes: **28v** is the left eye area; **28w** the right eye area, stated by the use of the area sign.

28.5. **The Hair**. Use of the wide sign within the head symbol indicates parts on the outside of the head. Different possibilities are shown as: **28x** indicates the beard; **28y** the moustache; **28z** side whiskers; **28aa** the eyebrows; **28ab** the right eyebrow. Hair at the upper back of the head could be a ponytail, **28ac**.

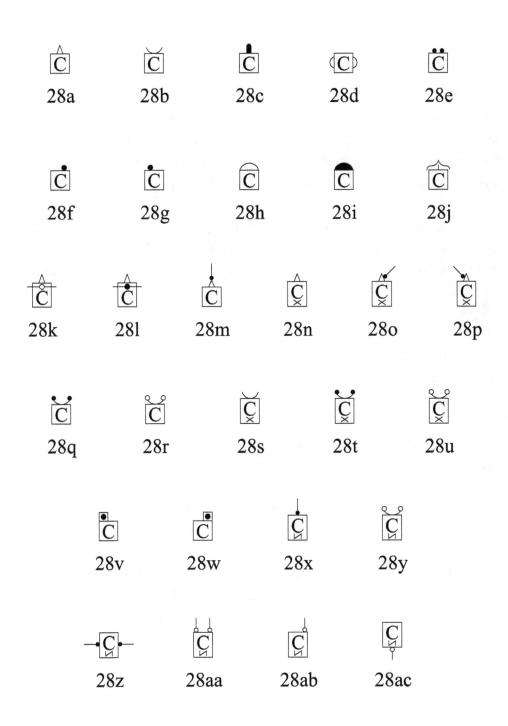

28a 28b 28c 28d 28e

28f 28g 28h 28i 28j

28k 28l 28m 28n 28o 28p

28q 28r 28s 28t 28u

28v 28w 28x 28y

28z 28aa 28ab 28ac

29. Signs Based on Symbol C

29.1. The following signs, based on the C symbol for the head, were established by Knust and provide an alternate choice of signs (see Knust 1979, vol. 1, 102, vol. 2, 54, Ex. 344a-n' for a fuller account): **29a**, top of the head (the crown); **29b** the forehead; **29c** the nose; **29d**, the chin; **29e** the throat; **29f** the right ear; **29g** the left cheek; **29h** the right temple, and so on.

29.2. Knust established the addition of the 'x' sign inside the 'C' sign to mean parts 'inside' the head, such as tongue and teeth, and use of the wide sign for parts outside, i.e., hair, beard, eyebrows, etc. This usage has also been applied to the pictorial signs.

29.3. **The Nose**. Detailed parts based on the C symbol for the head are as follows: **29i** the bridge of the nose; **29j** under the nose; **29k** tip of the nose; **29l** is inside the nose; **29m** indicates the right nostril, with **29n** the left nostril.

29.4. **The Mouth**. Based on Knust's ideas, the following have been developed: the general sign for the mouth is **29o**; **29p** indicates the lower lip with **29q** being the upper lip. Inside the mouth is shown in **29r**, the teeth. The lower teeth are shown by **29s**, with **29t** being the upper teeth and **29u** representing the tongue.

29.5. **The Eyes**. The right eye area is shown by **29v**, with **29w** being the left eye area; **29x** indicates both areas. The eyeball is shown by encircling the sign, **29y** being the left eyeball and **29z** the right.

29.6. **The Hair**. Addition of the wide sign inside the 'C' indicates outside the head, thus **29aa** indicates a beard with **29ab** being a moustache and **29ac** side whiskers. The eyebrows are indicated by **29ad**, **29ae** being the left eyebrow. Hair at the upper back of the head, **29af**, could be a ponytail.

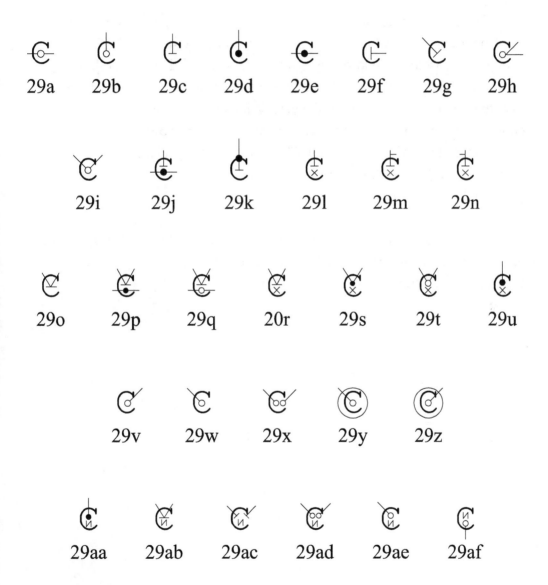

30. Use of the Parts of the Head

30.1. Wrinkling the nose, an upward contracting movement, is given in **30a**, while **30b** indicates flaring the nostrils. Listening with the right ear is expressed in **30c**.

30.2. Eyes indications with direction symbols mean movements of the eyes themselves, but when narrowing or widening are indicated it is the eyelid and muscles around the eyes that are involved. Thus, in **30d**, the eyes are looking side to side, as in Bharata Natyam. A wink with the right eye, is **30e**; then, **30f** is a blink with both eyes. Wide eyed is shown by **30g**. In contrast, **30h** means looking far into the distance, while **30i** indicates a very close focus. Frowning is shown in **30j** with **30k** being raised eyebrows (the lifted forehead). "Oh! how awful" or "I think I have a fever" could be when grasping the forehead, **30l**.

30.3. Possible actions of the whole face are as follow: **30m** squeezing the whole face, as in repulsion; **30n** a relaxed face; **30o** the whole face sagging; **30p** a bright, hopeful expression.

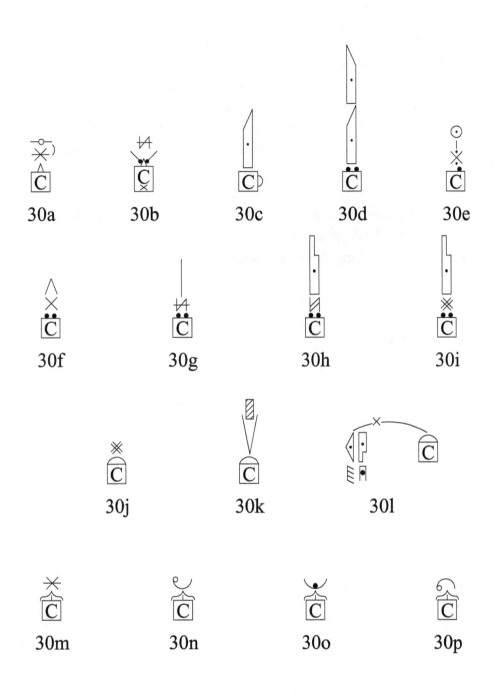

30a 30b 30c 30d 30e

30f 30g 30h 30i

30j 30k 30l

30m 30n 30o 30p

30.4. Placing the red dot, the 'Bindi' in Hindu culture, on the forehead with the fourth finger is shown in **30q**. Placing a contact lens in the right eye with the right index finger is stated in **30r**, while **30s** indicates thumbing the nose. Smoking a cigarette is expressed in **30t**, while **30u** indicates listening, cupping the right hand behind the right ear. In **30v** the tongue is flat as it extends. The right index finger is in the right nostril in **30w**.

30.5. Ex. **30x** states grasping the beard while **30y** indicates the thumb inside the mouth. "I am up to here" is expressed in **30z**, the hand being under the chin. Scratching the head is shown in **30aa**, while **30ab** indicates blowing a kiss.

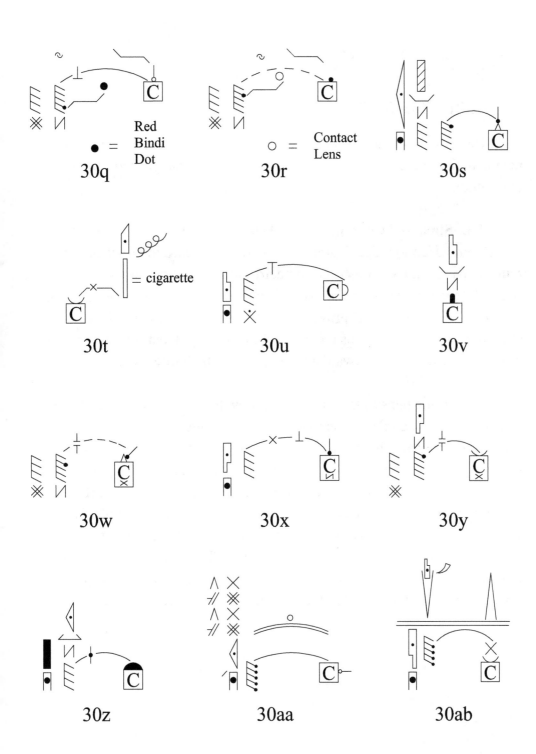

● = Red Bindi Dot

30q

○ = Contact Lens

30r

30s

= cigarette

30t

30u

30v

30w

30x

30y

30z

30aa

30ab

Chapter 2. Rotations

1. Arm Rotations

Because of the flexibility of the arm and the differences in individual people in their range of flexibility, Labanotation has established certain conventions.

1.1. **Standard Carriage of the Arms**. In order to provide a zero point from which to judge degrees of inward or outward rotations of the arms, Labanotation established a standard state of rotation for the arms; a 'parallel' carriage in which the inside surfaces of the elbow and wrist are in line, **1a**. This standard has proved to be very practical. Ex. **1b** shows the alignment for when the arms are down; **1c** is the alignment for the forward direction; **1d** for arms sideward and **1e** the place high direction.

1.2. While the surfaces for limbs follow the usage established for the hand, i.e., a black circle for the inner surface, a white circle for the outer surface, a pin for the thumb edge and a black dot for the little finger edge, for areas around a joint, it is more practical to have the usage of pins comparable to that established for the knee: **1f** is the front (inner surface) of the right elbow; **1g** the back of the elbow (the point); **1h** the thumb edge and **1i** the little finger edge. Thus, for the position of **1b**, **1j** indicates the standard alignment for the inner surface of the elbow area, **1k**, the facing direction for the inner surfaces of the wrist, and **1l** the facing of the palm. This alignment could be stated for each individual direction.

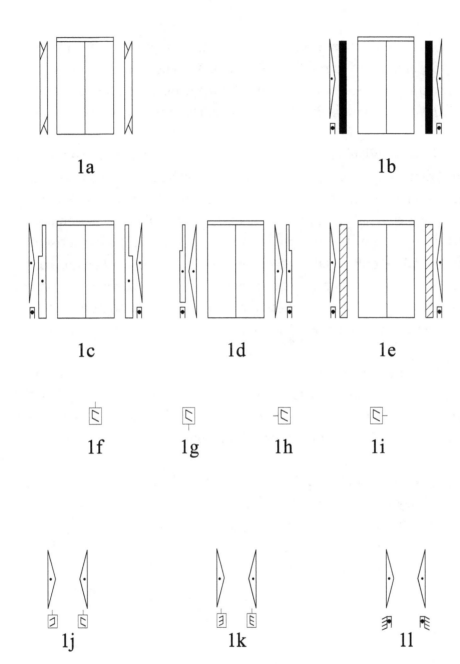

1a

1b

1c

1d

1e

1f

1g

1h

1i

1j

1k

1l

1.3. The above standard facings for palm and front of the elbow require the slight inward rotation of the elbow, as used in ballet; this is not the relaxed, natural state in which the elbow facing for most people will be as in **1m** when the arm is down; as **1n** when the arm is forward.

1.4. In establishing the standard convention for palm facing for each cardinal direction, we do not notate the subtle arm rotations that take place as the arm moves between the cardinal directions. When the arms move from place low to side middle, a gradual, subtle ¼ outward rotation occurs so that the palm ends facing forward, **1o**. From there, as the arms rise up, a subtle inward ¼ rotation takes place, the palm facing inward again, **1p**. Although we are usually aware of the palm facing directions, wrist facing would often be a better description to pin down the rotational state of the lower arm because the palm could, of course, be facing in another direction.

1.5. For many people, this standard alignment convention within the arm is not natural, thus there is the need to state a 'natural' carriage for the individual, **1q**. Here the 'back-to-normal' sign indicates the natural state for each individual. (See Section 7 for natural degree of leg rotation.)

1.6. **Direction of Arm Rotation, Twist**. When an arm is overhead or when the body is in an unusual configuration, it may not be easy to determine which is a rotation to the right and which to the left.   The following instruction can be helpful: outward rotation is toward the little finger and inward toward the thumb.

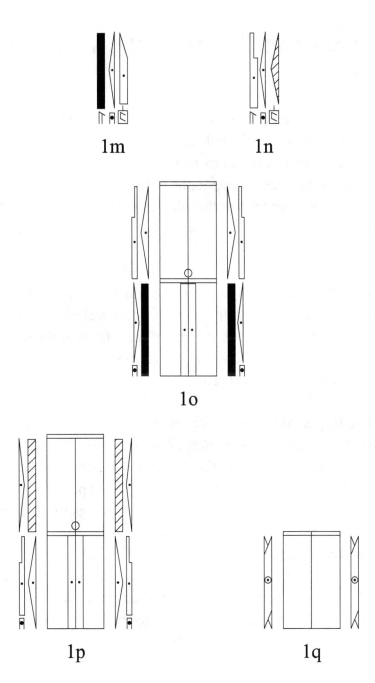

1m   1n

1o

1p   1q

2. Rotations and Twists for the Whole Arm and its Parts

2.1. **The Whole Arm**. In performing **2a**, normally the whole arm twists; there is no need to add the hold sign within the turn sign, as in **2b**, which is the specific indication for twist, i.e., the base is held. In this arm twist, the extremity, the hand, achieves the stated amount of 'turning', although the upper arm rotates less than the lower arm. The shoulder should not be affected. In the case of an exaggerated amount, **2c**, a twist in the hand itself will result (see: 2.5).

2.2. To indicate a rotation of the whole arm in one piece, the addition of the equal sign within the symbol is needed, **2d**. No change in alignment takes place. When the arm is bent, the axis of the rotation is the line between shoulder and hand. The range of such rotation is limited unless some shoulder participation takes place.

2.3. **The Upper Arm**. Physically the upper arm can only rotate, no twist is possible. An upper arm rotation carries the lower arm with it, **2e**. If the elbow is bent, there will be a noticeable change in spatial placement for the lower arm, **2f**. In this example, the lower arm ends up. Whatever the twisted state of the lower arm, it is not changed by an upper arm rotation.

2.4. **The Lower Arm**. The lower arm is physically capable only of twisting, **2g**, which indicates the wrist. The use of the limb sign for the lower arm, **2h**, is more specific, although **2g** is the commonly used indication. The upper arm should not be affected by a lower arm rotation.

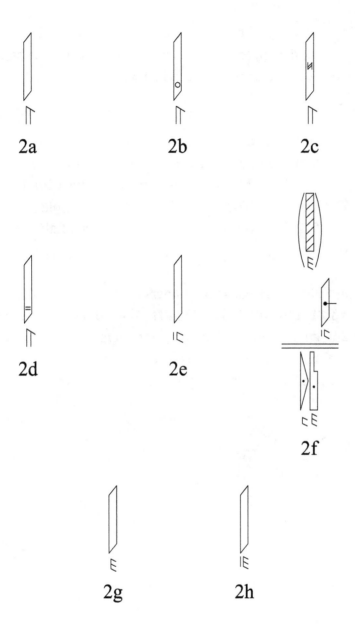

2a

2b

2c

2d

2e

2f

2g

2h

The hand is 'carried along', i.e., is passive, not activated. If the degree of twist is exaggerated, the upper arm will begin to be affected. A statement specifically to exclude the upper arm can be made, **2i**, or it can be shown to be included, **2j**.

2.5. **The Hand**. The hand can only be turned through the flexibility of the lower arm; however, if the focus is on the action of the hand, it needs to be so stated. In **2k** the right hand turns outward. If the degree is exaggerated, **2l**, then some twist within the hand will take place. (See *Labanotation* 2005, 257, also *Hands, Fingers,* Advanced Labanotation, issue 5, 44-45.)

2.6. **The Fingers**. Because the fingers themselves cannot rotate, Knust (1979, vol. 1, 116, vol. 2, Ex. 372a-f), adopted the convention that the indication of **2m**, an outward rotation for the fingers of the left hand be interpreted as a finger fan, illustrated as in **2n**. Therefore, the inward rotation of **2o**, would be a reverse finger fan, is illustrated in **2p**.

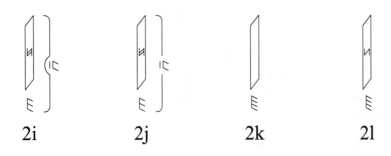

2i   2j   2k   2l

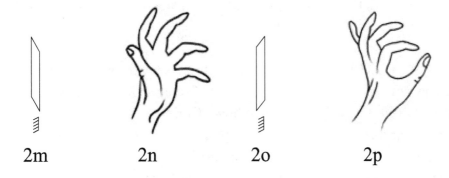

2m   2n   2o   2p

3. Rotations Within the Arm

3.1. **Elbow Rotations**. The center of the arm, the elbow, can rotate without involving the extremities, i.e., the shoulder and hand. The axis of such rotation is the line between the shoulder and hand (see *Labanotation* 2005, 256). To experience this, it is helpful to anchor the hand through touching or grasping a static object, such as a table.

3.2. Note that in describing direction, the sign in **3a** represents the upper arm; in **3b** the upper arm moves to side middle. For rotations, it is the elbow area that is active. With the arm to the side, the palm facing to the same side, **3c** indicates that the elbow rotates inward and then outward.

3.3. With the arm bent, as in **3d**, the spatial displacement caused by such elbow rotations is more evident.

3.4. **Wrist Rotations**. When the wrist is bent, a similar form of rotation can occur at the wrist. The axis of rotation is the line between the extremity (the fingertips) and the elbow. Compare **3e** in which the twist of the lower arm causes the hand to be spatially displaced, to the very different action of **3f**. Here, while in the same position but with the hand contacting the table, the wrist rotates inward and outward, the fingertips retain contact with the table. This movement could occur when one wants to look at a watch worn on that wrist.

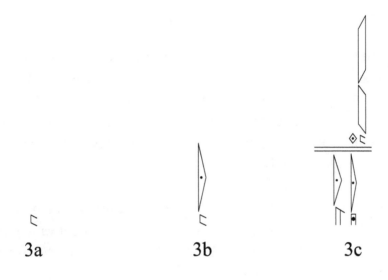

3a 3b 3c

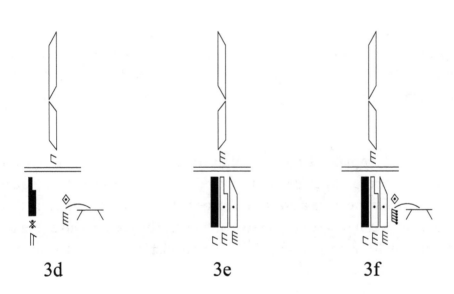

3d 3e 3f

4. Degree of Arm Rotation, Twist

4.1. **Using Turn Signs**. The amount of rotation can be a little or a lot, a more general description. Here we are being more specific. A black pin within a turn sign indicates the degree, the amount of turn judged from the previous location. In **4a** the lower arm twists 1/4 outward (to the right), then 1/2 inward. No starting state of rotation/twist is given; one can assume that it is the unrotated, untwisted state.

4.2. In **4b** white pins are used. These give the destination of the twist in relation to the unrotated state. Thus, **4b** states twist 1/4 outward, then twist 1/4 inward beyond the unrotated state. With white pins, the starting rotational state need not be known.

4.3. **Indication of Arrival State: Palm, Thumb Edge Facing**. Knust, our senior notator, avoided use of turn symbols for the arms because of the uncertainty in establishing the resulting degree; he preferred to state the palm facing direction. Thus, **4b** can be written as **4c**. Palm facing is the commonly used description. Of course, the many facing directions are only possible through the flexibility in twisting/rotating of the lower and upper arm.

4.4. **Appropriate Choice of Description**. In Labanotation, twists or rotations are written when that is the intention of the movement, the nature, the sense. Palm facing is a practical device but note that the direction that the palm faces can be very expressive. It may not be just a passive result. The palm can be 'alert', 'alive', giving a particular meaning to the direction that it faces.

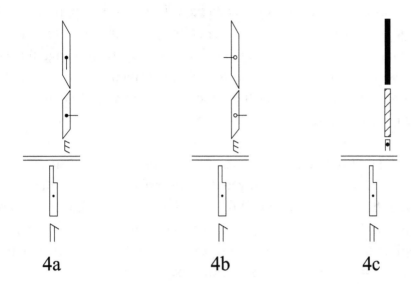

4a   4b   4c

4.5. **Thumb Edge Facing**. When palm facing is not appropriate, the thumb edge of the hand is often used, it not being 'weighted' with any expressive meaning. In the starting position of **4d**, the thumb edge for the right hand is shown in its standard state, i.e., up. It then 'faces' side right and then side left. This produces the same movement as **4b** and **4c,** i.e., outward and then inward twist.

4.6. **A Double Statement Needed**. If the established standard rotational state for the arm is followed, then the position of **4e** is the equivalent of the wrist being folded backward 90°, **4f**. But the reader may try other possibilities. If it is the gesture of a policeman stopping traffic, then **4g** will make that clear. Or the inward twist of the lower arm can be shown, **4h**. In **4i** the same gesture is shown by the direction of the fingertips. In the indication of **4j**, the thumb edge pointing down means the hand is directed to the left, the same as **4k**. The hand pointing to the right is the result of **4l**.

4.7. **Indication of Wrist Facing**. Also available, and often very practical, is the sign for the front (inner side) of the wrist area, **4m**. The policeman arm position of **4g** can be stated as **4n**.

4.8. **Indication of Elbow Facing**. Another way of indicating the rotational state for the arm is by stating where the point of the elbow is facing. The sign for the tip of the elbow, i.e., the back surface of the elbow, is **4o**. A 'dropped' elbow when the arm is held forward can be shown, as in **4p**. The natural carriage of the arm varies in different dance cultures. In classical ballet, it is standard for the elbow to be lifted (an inward rotation in the center of the arm), as in **4q**, or **4r** in which elbow facing is stated.

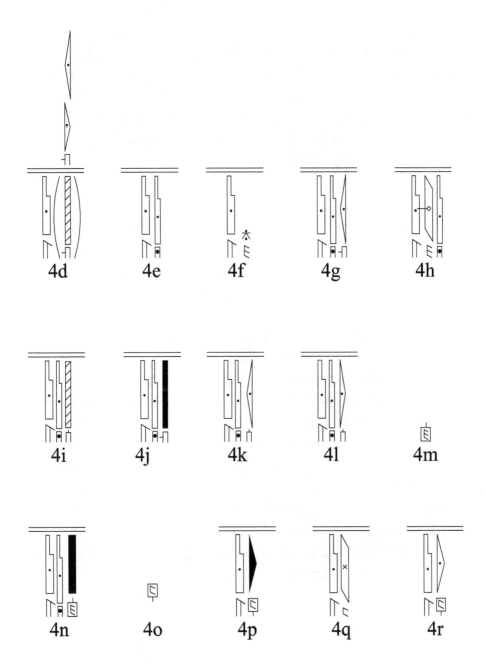

4d   4e   4f   4g   4h

4i   4j   4k   4l   4m

4n   4o   4p   4q   4r

4.9. **Consistent directions for Palm Facing, Thumb Edge Facing**.
In choosing which description to use, it is helpful to be aware of certain
constants. In the sagittal arm circling of **4s**, the palm facing to the left is
constant. Here the space hold (retention in space) for the palm is in
parenthesis just as a reminder; the thumb facing direction changes
constantly as the arm rises. If the arm starts with inward twist, the thumb
edge facing to the left, then that facing direction for the thumb becomes
constant, **4t**. In the horizontal circle of **4u**, the palm starts facing backward,
the thumb edge being up. Here, as the arm moves clockwise, the thumb
facing direction remains constant while palm facing changes all the time.
The reverse is true if the gesture starts with an inward twist of the lower
arm, **4v**, now palm facing down requires a retained space hold.

4.10. For the lateral arm circling of **4w**, there is an understood
automatic adjustment in arm rotation as the arm rises so that the palm faces
forward when side middle is reached; there will be continuous adjustment as
the arm moves to place high to have the palm facing to the left side again.
This is understood and need not be written (see *Labanotation* 2005, 111-
113). As a result of this constant rotational adjustment, neither the palm
facing nor thumb edge facing can be a constant. In **4x** the thumb edge
facing forward at the start is shown to have a retained space hold; as a
result, when the arm arrives place high, the palm is facing to the right side.
The arm finishes with a significant degree of inward twist. In each of the
above examples, continuation beyond the ending direction shown would
require limb rotation to complete the circling.

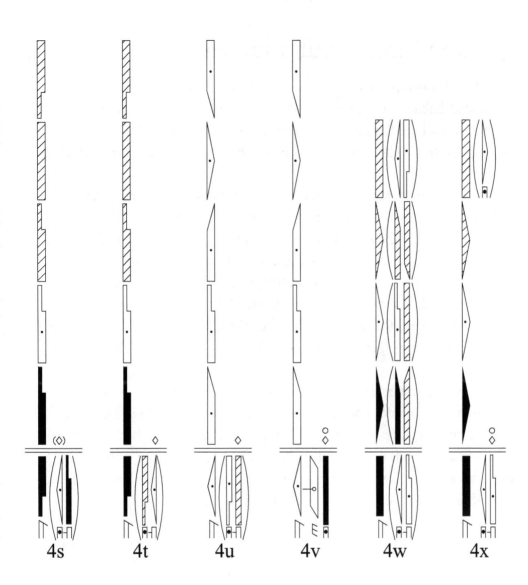

4s   4t   4u   4v   4w   4x

5. Hand Circles with Flexion

5.1. Hand circles are dealt with in detail in *Hands, Fingers* (Advanced Labanotation, issue 5, 46-51 and 134-135). Here we investigate circles that include flexion and the expressive effect when the action is led by the fingertips. The form of flexion that occurs is predominantly folding.

5.2. In **5a**, starting with the position of palm facing down, the hand folds and unfolds while describing a horizontal circular path led by the fingertips. This is shown in the Design Drawing description of **5a'**. Note that in performance the 'fingertips' is often mainly the middle finger. Ex. **5b** and **5c** indicate the fingertips circling, during which the hand folds and unfolds; the palm is shown passively to face backward and then return to facing down. Note that in these examples the main focus of the movement, the circling of the fingertips, is written closer to the center of the staff.

5.3. The 'inner' sagittal circling of the fingertips in **5d** brings the hand toward the center line of the body, **5d'** shows the Design Drawing description. It is physically possible to perform a small sagittal circling of the fingertips (hand) on the 'outer' side. The lateral circling of the fingertips in **5e** involves inward and then outward rotation as the hand folds and unfolds, **5e'** being the Design Drawing description.

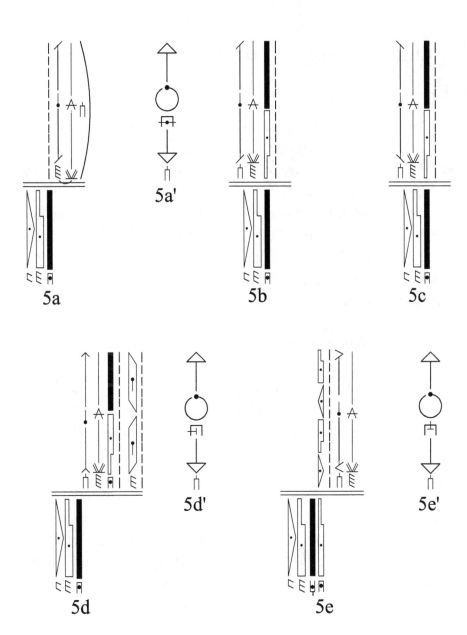

5a

5a'

5b

5c

5d

5d'

5e

5e'

6. Sequential Finger Folding with Hand Rotation

6.1. Hand rotation and finger folding may be led by the fingers moving in sequence, either starting with the thumb, **6a**, or by the little finger, **6b**. The action of the fingers moving one after the other is a form of canon, the sign for which is **6c**. Note the extension of the vertical line in the symbol for the left foot, **6d**, to distinguish this sign from the canon symbol. In **6e** the canon is led by the little finger, while in **6f**, the thumb is leading. The outward rotation and folding of the hand is led by the little finger, **6g**. This could be followed by **6h** in which the thumb leads the unfolding of the fingers during the inward hand rotation.

6.2. When the fingers move in canon without folding, each finger moves from the base joint (knuckle); **6i** represents the base joint for each finger. In **6j** the base knuckles of the fingers are shown to fold sequentially, led by the little finger. Here the fingers do not end flexed, but normally extended. This is followed by **6k** in which the base joints unfold led by the thumb.

6.3. Although the symbols of necessity take up a certain amount of space, an example such as **6j** may be performed very swiftly. The indication for very fast, i.e., very little time, can be added alongside to give this information. The symbol for Time is **6l**, from this **6m** was derived to mean Speed, thus **6n** means very fast, much speed. In **6o** this indication is applied to **6j**.

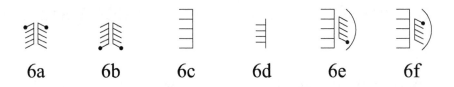

6a 6b 6c 6d 6e 6f

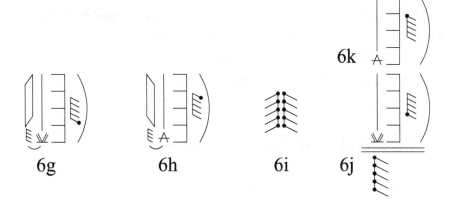

6g 6h 6i 6j 6k

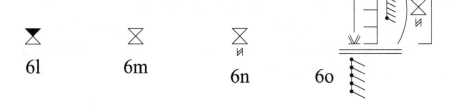

6l 6m 6n 6o

7. The Legs: Rotational State, Understood State

7.1. When nothing is stated, there is no automatically understood rotational state for the legs. Interpretation is open to each individual, **7a**. However, for a classical ballet score, it can be understood that much outward rotation is to be used, **7b**, while **7c** shows more or less of a 1/8 turn out. In modern and contemporary dance, some outward rotation is usual. In some traditional dances the understood rotation is parallel, pointing forward, **7d**. Inward leg rotation is less common, occurring in comic dances or for a buffoon where changes in leg rotation add to the expression and need to be stated.

7.2. Once a rotational state for a leg (or both legs) is stated in a Labanotation score it is 'strong', i.e., remains in effect, until cancelled by statement of another rotational state, **7e**.

7.3. **Rotational Statement in a Glossary**. Statements in a Glossary at the start of a dance score should be applied to the whole score. Such statements have the advantage of keeping the score free of extra symbols. However, a reader may pick up a score in the middle and not have time to check the glossary. More practical in this respect is to state the desired rotation when it is needed, as in **7e**, the information is right there, and one can pick up a score at any point and make sense of it.

7.4. **Normal for the Individual Person**. Each individual person has a different natural rotational for the legs. This personal 'normal' can be stated as in **7f**, thus, providing the required freedom.

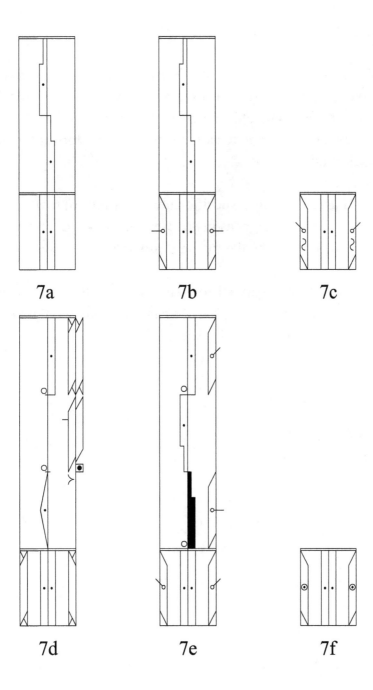

7a   7b   7c

7d   7e   7f

8. Specific Statement of Parallel Feet

8.1. The notion of parallel legs is usually understood as being with the feet pointing forward, specifically stated in **8a**. However, the feet can be parallel while pointing into a diagonal direction, as in **8b**. Although this is true, it is common practice to assume the feet point forward in the basic parallel indication.

8.2. Thus, cancelling a specific outward or inward rotation is usually indicated by the parallel sign, as in **8c**. Here the outward rotation used for the lunge is cancelled when the foot returns to place.

8.3. This return to parallel could be written as **8d** as the sense is one of inward rotation. Or it can be stated as an inward rotation to the destination of the foot pointing forward, **8e**.

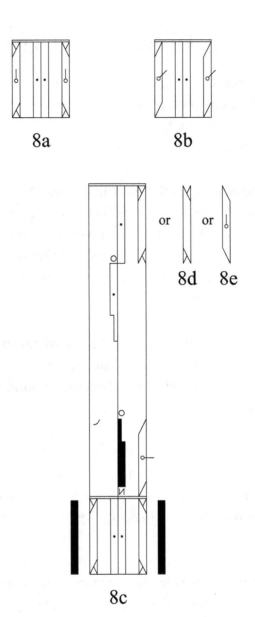

8a   8b

8d   8e

8c

9. Non-swivel Turns, "Blind Turns"

9.1. A turn sign in the support column is understood to involve a swivel of the foot on the floor, count 1 in **9a**. On count 2, the space hold for the leg causes a non-swivel turn, the body turns above the foot, causing an outward twist in the leg.

9.2. A preparatory leg rotation with the step, **9b**, allows the body as a whole to turn through a passive untwisting of the leg, returning it to the previous parallel state. On count 2, the inward rotation on the sideward step allows the next non-swivel turn (also called a 'blind turn') to return the leg to the parallel state. Use of blind turns occurs typically in ballroom dance as well as in T'ai Chi Ch'üan.

9.3. The full turn in **9c** starts as a blind turn but soon becomes a swivel turn indicated by the angular release sign which cancels the space hold. In contrast, in **9d** the swivel turn becomes a blind turn at the end before the step forward.

9.4. In **9e** the hopping turns in the air which involve a mixture of turning in the air and partial blind turns, is written simply by placing the turn sign outside the staff. In **9f**, the turning action is written in the staff. When spelling out what actually happens, **9g**, the desired fluency in turning is visually lost.

9.5. The slow 'promenade' turn in arabesque in ballet is given in **9h**; it is basically a blind turn but with the heel lifted frequently to allow the leg to untwist. In a double pirouette on *pointe*, **9i**, slow motion photography revealed that the ballerina actually performs 1/4 blind turn before rising to *pointe*.

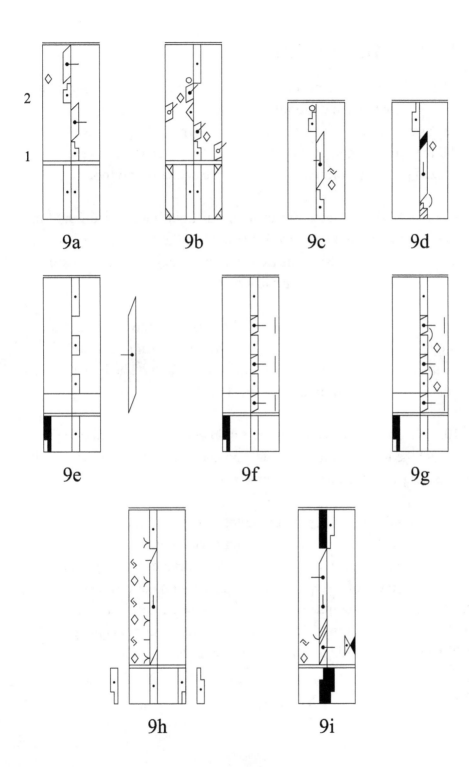

10. Rotations Within the Leg

10.1. Comparable to arm rotations, a rotary action can occur in the center of the leg when the extremity is fixed, as when standing. It is described as a rotation of the knee. **10a**. The degree of rotation is slight when the legs are straight. This action is used as a corrective exercise for knock-kneed people to align the knee over the center of the foot.

10.2. In Balinese dance, for example, a slight inward rotation of the knee causes the knees to be facing forward when the feet are slightly apart and slightly turned out, **10b**. This twist within the leg can be expressed as the degree of outward rotation for the lower leg.

10.3. **Lower leg Twist**. When the knee is held, the lower leg can twist through flexibility in the knee joint, **10c**. This example shows a person sitting, right knee forward and foot on the floor. The lower leg twist occurs through contact (sliding) on the 1/4 heel.

10.4. In **10d** the legs are together and bent; the knees (thighs) are parallel, and the lower leg turned out. The knees then rotate outward and inward, ending with the knees touching.

10.5. If the legs are bent with the feet apart, a greater degree of rotation can occur, **10e**. Here the direction of the thigh can be significantly changed, producing awareness of thigh direction rather than leg rotation. This action is typical of a step used in the Charleston dance in the 1920s; in **10e** the hand and knee contacts change. Although a rotary action is taking place, the performer is usually more aware of the directional change of the thigh (the knee). Thus direction symbols are used.

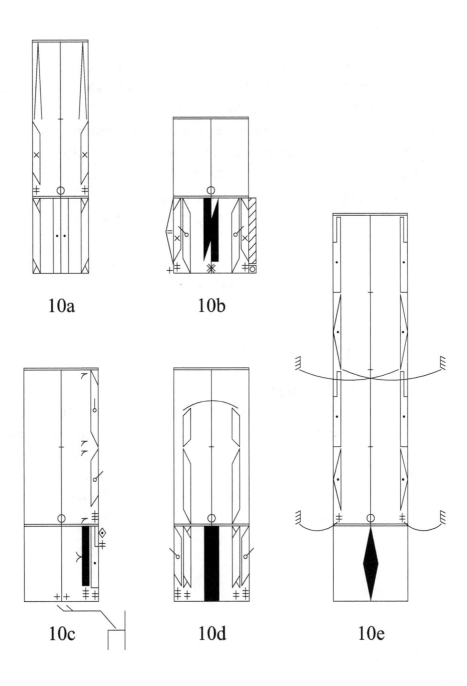

10a   10b

10c   10d   10e

11. Rotations of the Feet

11.1. In normal standing, the outward rotation of the feet, **11a**, places the weight onto the outer (little toe) edge of the foot, **11b**. As a result, the arch of the foot is raised off the floor. Inward rotation, **11c**, causes the weight to be on the inner 'edge' of the foot, **11d**, the outer edge being lifted from the floor, **11e**. Note that when these edge signs are placed within the staff they are understood to refer to the foot. Rotation of the whole unit can be shown by adding the equal sign within the turn sign, **11f**. This is usually understood and needs only to be stated if there is any doubt.

11.2. Rotations of the foot can occur during leg gestures, **11g**, but care has to be taken that it is a rotation of the foot as a whole.

12. Twists Within the foot

12.1. When a leg is gesturing, an inward or outward twist can occur in the foot, **12a**. The hold sign within the turn symbol indicates that the extremity turns more than the base, thus producing a twist, **12b**. Such actions occur in Cambodian as well as Balinese dance. Often the toes are spread when outward twist is used, **12c**, which indicates lateral spreading of the toes. Less usual is spreading the toes combined with inward foot twist, **12d**.

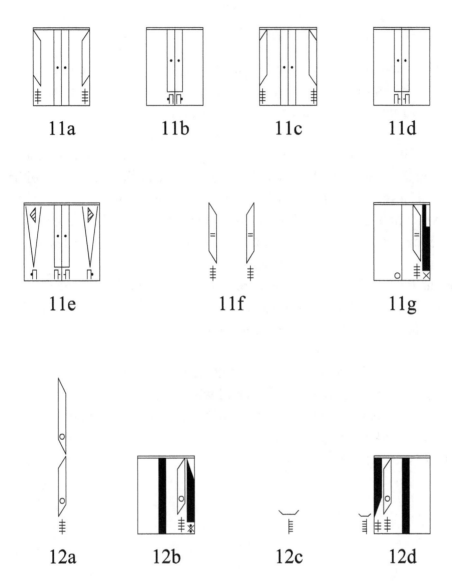

11a 11b 11c 11d

11e 11f 11g

12a 12b 12c 12d

13. Torso Rotations

These have been covered in some detail in the 2005 edition of *Labanotation*. Here we present a few examples not previously discussed, followed by rotations for the individual parts of the torso.

13.1. While lying on the ground, horizontal torso wheeling around the vertical axis can take place whether lying on the back, the front or either side. Ex. **13a** shows a full horizontal circle while lying on the back, probably facilitated by use of hands and/or feet. The axis (focal point) for the wheeling is understood to be in the center, the waist, **13b**. In **13c** the sign for the knees, centered in the circling sign, states that the circling is around the knees. This information could also be stated outside the staff to the right, as in **13d**. Ex. **13e** shows circling around the shoulders. Circular path signs have an understood reference to the Standard Cross of Axes.

13.2. Ex. **13f** shows lying on the left side of the torso and wheeling clockwise around the pelvis, the degree of wheeling is not given. In **13g** this same action is written but as a forward somersault path judged from the Body Cross of Axes. The statement of **13g** could be placed outside the staff when there are body actions, for example, leg movements occurring at the same time.

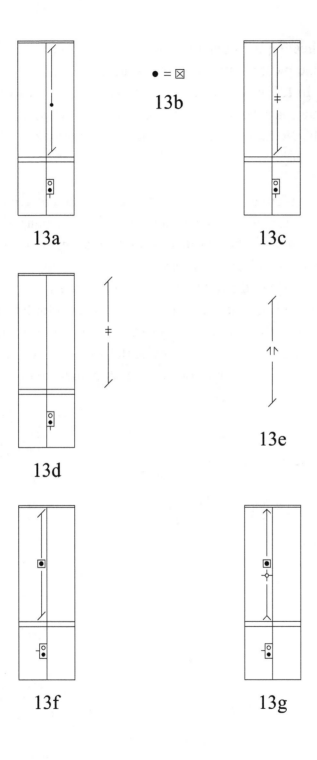

13a

• = ⊠

13b

13c

13d

13e

13f

13g

13.3. **Wheeling in Segments**. While lying on the side, **13h**, the body wheels 1/4 in one-piece whatever body part as the axis might be used, here none is stated. In **13i** the legs change direction, moving to forward middle. They then have a space hold while the torso moves backward, the result is the same at **13h**. No turn sign has been indicated but there is a 1/4 change of Front.

13.4. **Secret Turn.** The Secret Turn, contributed by Knust, is a mental decision to establish a new Front, even though no turn sign has been indicated. The new Front has resulted from the placement of the limbs. It is written in the support column at the end of the movement. In **13i** the secret turn indicates 1/4 turn to the right. A secret turn is often only 1/8th turn and never more than 3/8th, thus it is easy to see if the change of Front is to the right or the left. Ex. **13j** shows the range of secret turns. A typical example is **13k**, from sitting, you rise to your knees; the secret turn results from the placement of the lower legs since one rolls over onto them to rise to the knees.

Wheeling in Segments

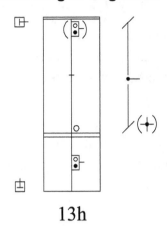

13h

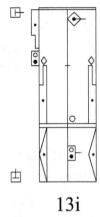

13i

Secret Turns

13j

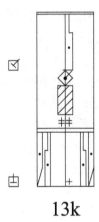

13k

14. Chest Rotations

14.1. In **14a**, the chest rotates around its vertical axis. It is usual for such rotations to be twists. However, a rotation in one piece is possible for long-waisted performers, and can be specified, as in **14b**. Ex. **14c** specifically states a twisting action.

14.2. By stating the axis for the rotation, as in **14d** where the left shoulder is the axis, a different result will be achieved: the right side of the chest is displaced forward.

14.3. **Lateral Rotations**. The image and idea of lateral rotations can occur around the sagittal axis centered in the chest, **14e**. Such rotations, **14f**, are possible through the flexibility of the rib cage in flexing and extending. These actions are familiar in certain African dances.

14.4. A different form of flexibility makes the concept of sagittal rotations of the chest possible. In **14g** the axis of the rotations is the central lateral line in the chest, clarified in **14h**. For the forward rotation, the upper part, the shoulder area, displaces forward, the lower ribs displace backward; the reverse is true for the backward rotation, as in **14i**. It is important, however, to realize that the chest should be rotating as a unit, **14j,** an action that long-waisted people can achieve with ease.

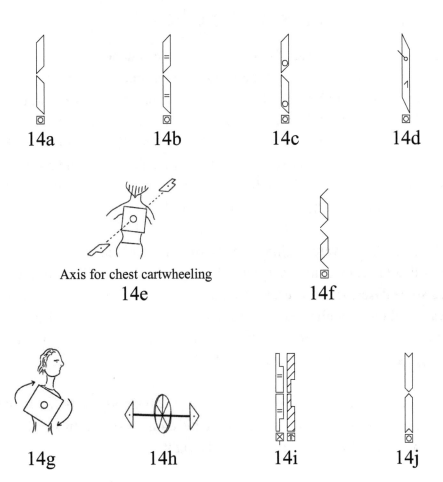

14a   14b   14c   14d

Axis for chest cartwheeling
14e   14f

14g   14h   14i   14j

15. Circular Paths of the Chest

15.1. Chest movements found in some African dances include circular paths for the chest area. The horizontal circling of **15a** is shown to start from a forward shift of the chest. As there is no change of Front, the number '1', is used, or '1/1' when that might be clearer. The spatial retention sign indicates that the chest remains upright. This action could be thought of as **15b**, a sequence of shifting forward, sideward to the right, backward and then to the left side before returning to being shifted forward. What is missing is the sense of a fluent circular displacement.

15.2. In the forward sagittal circling of **15c** the space hold sign indicates that the chest remains upright during the circling. This circling might also be described as **15d** in which the chest is shifted forward, down, backward and up through flexion and extension in the waist area. The indication of **15a** and **15c** provide the fluid intention of the movement, its continuity as well as spatial displacement.

15.3. Lateral circling is shown in **15e**; again, the body section remains upright. No indication is given as to where the circling starts. In **15f** the movement starts to the left and circles to the right.

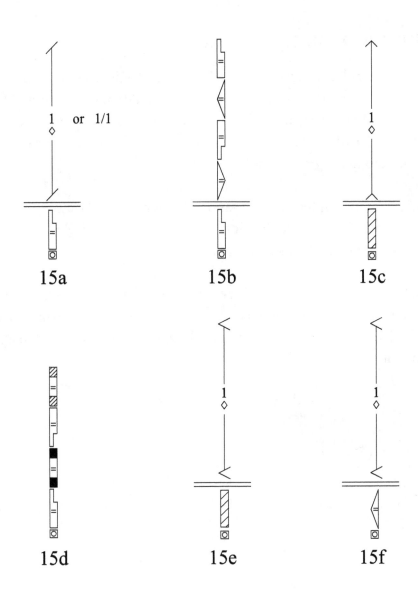

1   or   1/1

15a

15b

15c

15d

15e

15f

16. Pelvic Rotations, Axes

16.1. The pelvis can rotate around its vertical axis, **16a**, its lateral axis, **16b**, and its sagittal axis, **16c**. The pelvis should move as a unit with no emphasis on one hip or the other. For **16b** the axis runs through the center of the sides of the pelvis. For each of these rotations there is a physical limit to the degree possible.

16.2. The axis of the pelvic rotation of **16a** may be placed on one side or the other; in **16d** it is around the left hip. This brings the right side of the pelvis forward while the left side is not being displaced.

16.3. The sagittal rotation of **16e** indicates the hips as the axis of the rotation, thus causing the waist to be displaced backward as the pelvis slants backward. This could also be stated as the base of the pelvis being the axis of the rotation, **16f.**

16a

16b

16c

16d

16e

16f

17. Single Hip Action

17.1. While the hip is an integral part of the pelvis and cannot move independently, the focus of the action may be on the hip. Standing on both feet in middle level, **17a**, the raising of the right hip will cause the right foot passively to change to contact on the ball of the foot. Lowering the hip, **17b**, causes the right leg to bend slightly. The actions of **17a** and **17b** cause the pelvis to move in small degrees of lateral rotation. However, the attention of performer and audience is on the hip actions.

17.2. Displacement forward of a hip, **17c**, will cause the pelvis to rotate slightly counterclockwise, illustrated in **17d**. A hip displacement backward, **17e**, causes slight clockwise pelvic rotation, **17f**. In these examples, the dotted vertical line indicates that the rotation is a passive, resultant movement.

17.3. A sideward hip displacement, **17g**, involves a sideward shift of the pelvis, **17h**. The difference in intention is significant. In **17g** the energy, the focus, is on the single hip action, whereas in **17h** the awareness is of the whole pelvis being evenly displaced.

17.4. Steps in which the hip actively takes part produces a particular style of walking. In **17i** the hip is forward as the right leg steps forward, then the same for the left. Ex. **17j** shows a sideward displacement on each forward step, a contrasting style of walk to **17i**.

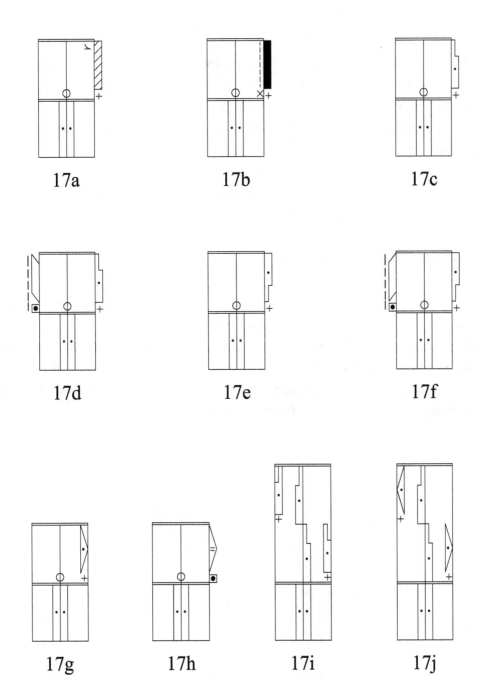

17a   17b   17c

17d   17e   17f

17g   17h   17i   17j

17.5. **Hips Swaying Sideways**. The lateral swaying of the hips in Hawaiian dance is often thought to be performed as in **17k**. According to Nona Kapua Beamer, specialist in Hawaiian culture, the hip movement is the result of weight placement on the high arch at the start of the step, **17l**, thus causing the hip to rise. This occurs on each step. Note the passive indication of the hip rising next to each step.

17.6. Leg gestures can be initiated from the hip. In **17m** the forward leg gesture is initiated from the hip. Note that the bow indicating the leading action ends before the gesture is completed, thus the leg ends as a normal forward gesture. In **17n** a similar action happens to the side.

17.7. A quite different movement is that of stretching the front of the hip area, the groin; this may happen with both hips at the same time. Such stretching is not a forward shift of the pelvis, it is purely muscular. Ex. **17o** is the symbol for the front of the hip area; in **17p** the front of the right hip area is shown to stretch. A contraction of the front of both hip areas, **17q**, will produce a slight backward displacement of the lower pelvis.

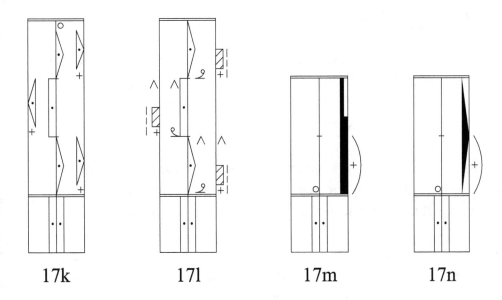

17k 17l 17m 17n

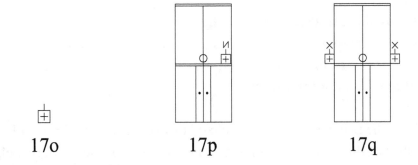

17o 17p 17q

18. Pelvic Circling

18.1. Circular paths can be performed by the pelvis. In **18a** the pelvis is shifted forward thus indicating the starting point of the horizontal circular path it then describes. The sideward shift in **18b** indicates the horizontal circling starts at the right side.

18.2. Such circling is augmented by including rotations. In **18c** a rotation to the right during the start of the circling is then cancelled before the second half of the circle is augmented by rotation to the left.

18.3. In all these circling movements the pelvis remains upright. If the pelvis is tilted, as at the start of **18d** in which from the waist down the pelvis is forward low, a horizontal circling of the lower part of the pelvis can take place.

19. Pelvic Circles, Lateral, Sagittal

19.1. In the lateral circle of **19a**, the start is comparable to a sideward shift of the pelvis (shown in parenthesis). To facilitate this circling, it helps to change the level of the supports, starting with bent knees and rising onto half toe at the height of the circling.

19.2. The backward sagittal circle of **19b** starts with a comparable forward shift of the pelvis. Again, the change in level of the supports helps to augment the circling action. In **19c** the high starting position suggest a backward pelvic shift to begin the circling.

19.3. The circling of **19b** can be augmented by the addition of pelvic rotations, **19d**. At the start the pelvis rotates sagittally backward, at the height of the circle this rotation is cancelled. Forward rotation then occurs to be cancelled as the circling concludes. Note this use of the 'away' sign for cancelling, often used when other cancellation indications seem less appropriate.

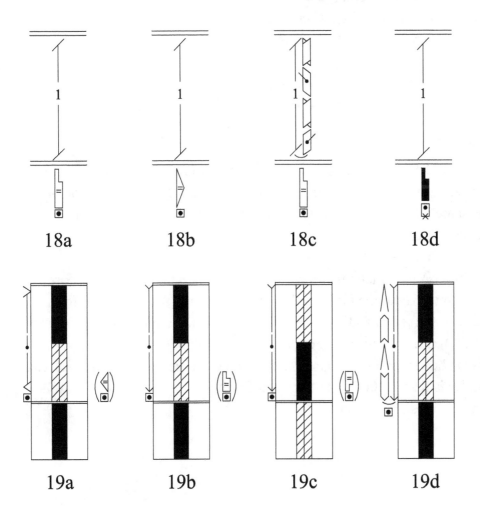

18a   18b   18c   18d

19a   19b   19c   19d

20. Rotations and Circular Paths for the Head

20.1. The series of movements tilting into different directions, as in **20a**, produces a circling of the head. With the focus on the circling, this is better expressed as **20b**. This movement can be augmented by rotating into the direction of the circling, **20c**. Note use of the 'away' sign to indicate cancellation of the rotation. Cancellation could also be indicated by the 'parallel', 'unrotated state' sign of **20d**.

20.2. In **20e** the same circling is combined by head rotations in the opposite direction, producing a sense of looking around, almost behind the body.

20.3. From a shifted starting position, as in **20f**, the head can describe a circular path while remaining upright. This circling can include rotations in the same direction, **20g**, or, less harmonious, rotations in the opposite direction, **20h**.

20.4. A small lateral circling is shown in **20i**, the head lifts before shifting to the right, then lowers through contracting the neck, continues into a shift to the left and returns to the lifted centered position. The path sign of **20j** provides the sense of smooth continuity. The space hold sign states the head remains upright. An important difference between these two examples is that in **20i** the starting shift for the circling is given; in **20j** the circling could start anywhere.

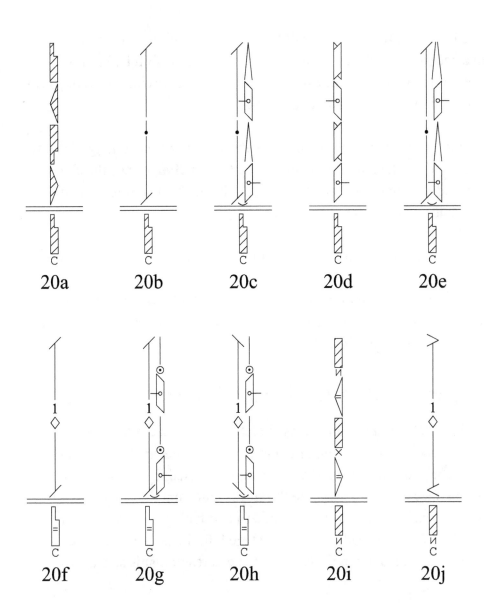

20a   20b   20c   20d   20e

20f   20g   20h   20i   20j

20.5. Ex. **20k** shows a small forward sagittal circle for the head. From a backward shift, it rises moving into a forward shift before lowering and returning to the start. In **20l** the forward sagittal circling, with the head remaining upright, could start at any point.

20.6. Lateral and sagittal head rotations have a limited range. With the head upright, lateral rotation to the right, as in **20m**, brings the chin to the left and the top of the head to the right, the neck remaining upright. The sagittal axis is the line through the nose.

20.7. In **20n** the forward sagittal rotation, the head, rotating on the atlas bone, stretches the back of the neck and brings the chin close to the chest; there should be no forward movement for the neck. In contrast, the backward sagittal rotation of **20o** has a greater range, the back of the neck contracts, but the neck remains upright.

21. Destination for Head Rotations

21.1. The destination, facing direction, for a head rotation in terms of the stage directions can be important in classical ballet and in other forms. The straight pins, taken from the Front signs are used inside the turn sign. In **21a** the face ends up looking to the stage right front diagonal. Ex. **21b** shows the facing to be between that of **21a** and facing stage right. Turning to the left in **21c**, the head ends facing stage left. In each of these the previous situation is not indicated; it is the end result that is stated.

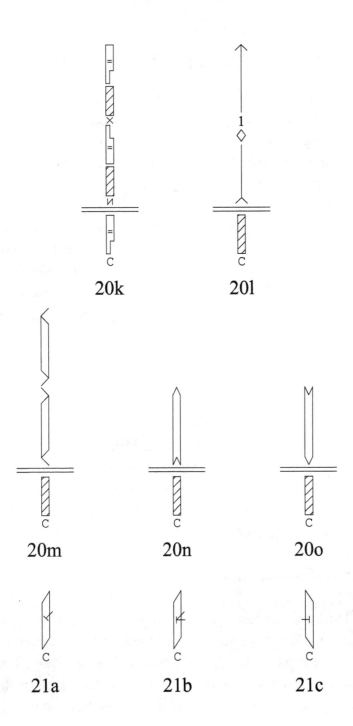

20k 20l

20m 20n 20o

21a 21b 21c

Chapter 3. Flexion and Extension

The actions of flexing and extending in the body have many everyday names. For example, bending, contracting, folding, narrowing, shortening, shrinking, closing in, all describe flexion. For extension we have stretching, elongating, separating, widening, unfolding, lengthening, expanding, or opening out. Specific analysis of the different forms of flexion and extension in the body are clearly covered in the existing textbooks. The difference between contracting and folding and between lengthening and unfolding for single joints and multi-jointed parts of the body have been covered. They are clearly illustrated in *Your Move* (Hutchinson Guest 2007, 154–164, and in more detail 377- 413). However, in this presentation certain information already in the textbooks will be repeated for ease of understanding in following the exposition.

1. Terminology

1.1. Knust presents "Quantity Signs" and uses the term "Space Measurement Signs" (vol. 1, 49–50, vol. 2, 110, examples 639a-b, g-h) for the signs of **1a**. When applied to steps, they indicate the distance (length) of the steps from the point of departure. In **1b** a very small sideward step is followed by a very long step forward. This is standard. In his Dictionary, Knust applies this same concept to the arms, the distance of the extremity from the base, i.e., near, very near or far, very far. For gestures the signs of **1a** are degrees of contracting and extending, elongating.

1.2. Direction for gestural movements of flexion and extension is determined by the line from the 'base' of the limb to its 'extremity'. Other terms used are 'the fixed end' and 'the free end' respectively. For the arm, the free end is the hand, the fixed end is the shoulder. Because the hand, as well as the fingers, may have a particular configuration out of alignment, direction is determined by the wrist. In **1c** the direction symbols indicate that the arm begins very flexed, it then moves into the diagonal with the hand up, stated here with direction symbols.

Note that an 'arm extremity' in relation to the center lines of the body may vary according to the arm configuration, (see chapter 6, p.198 in this book).

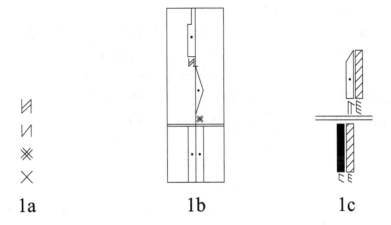

1a   1b   1c

2. Any Form of Flexion and Extension

While Labanotation is designed to be specific in describing movement, there can be a need to be very general, a need fulfilled by Motif Notation, which uses the basic symbols more freely. The presentation of 'any' indications seems worth including here.

2.1. The horizontal Ad Libitum (ad lib.) sign in **2a** indicates any form of flexion; **2b** states any form of extension. Because for the torso in particular, a contraction may be over any surface, **2c** indicates this 'any' idea.* In contrast, **2d** is the specific statement for contract 'over the front surface'; thus, **2e** indicates over the right front diagonal surface, with **2f** being over the right side, **2g** the right diagonal back side and **2h** over the back, and so on.

2.2. Because the placement of dots in the 6/6 scale indicates the degree of contraction, as in **2i**, freedom in degree is shown by the vertical placement of the ad lib. sign, **2j**.

2.3. Similar indications are used for folding: **2k** shows folding over the front (inner) surface; **2l** is folding over the right front diagonal, and **2m** over the right side and so on. Ex. **2n** states folding over any surface. The vertical dots in **2o** indicate folding three degrees, thus any degree of folding over the front surface is shown as **2p**, i.e., vertically.

2a	2b	2c	2d	2e	2f	2g	2h

2i	2j	2k	2l	2m	2n	2o	2p

3. Three-dimensional Flexion, Extension

3.1. Flexing, contracting three-dimensionally, is shown as **3a**, the horizontal line representing the third dimension; three-dimensional expansion is **3b**. These indications are particularly applicable to the hands and the chest (the rib cage), for the latter, one is aware of muscular contraction and expansion. Note that the contraction sign of **3c** combining with the lateral closing, **3d** and that for sagittal closing, **3e**, produce the composite sign for any form of flexion, **3f**. However, because this sign is unwieldy, the simple sign of **3a** is the standard sign for three-dimensional flexion. Similarly, **3g** representing lengthening, together with lateral spreading, **3h** and sagittal spreading, **3i**, produces the 'all possibilities' for extension in the sign of **3j**. Here again the simpler symbol of **3b** is the standard statement. Three-dimensional flexion, any degree, is **3k**, three-dimensional extension, any degree, is **3l**.

3a		3c		3d		3e		3f
✳	=	✕	+	△	+	▷	=	✳

3b		3g		3h		3i		3j
⊬	=	⼒	+	◡	+	⟨	=	⫯

3k	3l
✳	⊬

4. Neither Bent nor Stretched

4.1. In their natural state, the arms and legs are relaxed, neither bent nor stretched. The symbol for this is **4a**. It is useful when that state is required after flexion or extension indications. In **4b** it cancels the retained 'x' for the sideward step. The cancellation could be indicated as a return to normal, **4c**, or with the 'away' cancellation sign of **4d**. But the latter, as cancellation signs, do not have the direct movement statement that **4b** provides.

4.2. In **4e** an extended arm gesture returns to its starting situation and state while the other arm extends in a sideward gesture. Note that the 'neither bent nor stretched' sign is used here for the right arm to provide awareness; the ordinary place low symbol involves this same state without it being explicitly written.

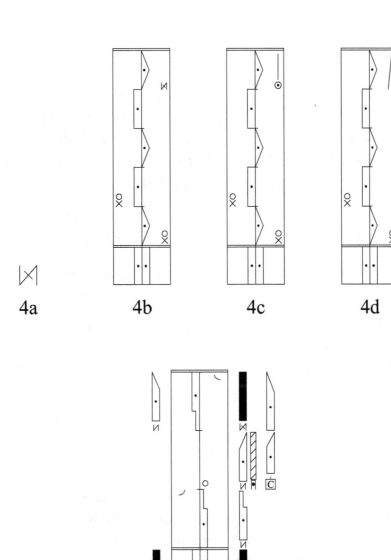

4a   4b   4c   4d

4e

5. Derivation of the Folding Symbols

5.1. The sign for folding is based on the long established 'x' for contraction. Dividing the sign in half, **5a** (folding affects only one joint, while contracting involves two) the sign became **5b**, with **5c** the greater degree. Backward folding is **5d**, over the right side is **5e**, and so on. From **5e** these signs acquired the nick-name of the 'K signs'.

--✗--	⩔	⩔	木	K	∧	△	⫢	A
5a	5b	5c	5d	5e	5f	5g	5h	5i

5.2. The sign for unfolding is based on the 'away' sign, **5f**. Placement of the base of the sign, as in **5g**, was avoided; it was moved up a little, **5h**. A sign looking like the letter 'A', **5i,** was avoided. Note that **5g** was later used to indicate angling for kneeling supports.

6. Focus on Actions of the Joints

6.1. In the early 1940s notators at the Dance Notation Bureau in New York were faced with writing the Graham modern dance technique. They found that the standard directional description for the parts of the limbs were not adequate in describing the floor exercise in a fourth position sit with the front leg 'on the walk' (the Graham term). We could not write the foot action that occurred when the torso twisted to the right. It was not a new direction for the lower leg nor a new direction for the foot. As described in **6a**, it was an articulation of the ankle joint: from having been contracted, it extended and then contracted again as the torso returned to the starting position. In the notation example given here, details of the torso movement are not given, the focus is on the actions of the ankle.

6.2. **Degrees of Contraction, Extension**: In the **6a** exercise, a 45° of contraction is needed. The 6/6 scale, **6b**, had been established by Laban; it provided angles of 30°, 60°, 90°, etc. Over time the need for 22½°, 45°, 67½°, etc. resulted in establishing the 8/8 scale.

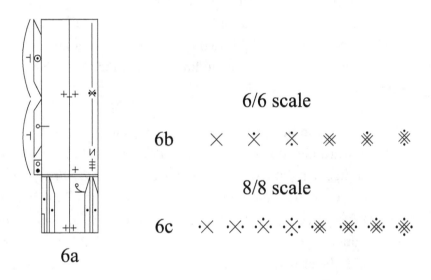

6/6 scale

8/8 scale

6a

7. Contraction, Extension for the Arms

7.1. Flexion of the Whole Arm. Both contraction and folding for the whole arm occur over the 'front' or 'inner' surface of the limb, with few exceptions. Specific contractions and folding for the arm as a whole are followed by exploration of the individual joints.

7.2. Extension of the Whole Arm. When the arm hangs down at the side of the body, the elbow, wrist and hand are relaxed, **7a**. When raising the arm forward this same condition for the arm remains. One degree of stretch, **7b**, brings the arm straight; two degrees produces a taut arm, **7c**. Any further lengthening involves including the shoulder, **7d**. Further lengthening involves the shoulder area, **7e**.

7.3. Contraction of the Whole Arm. Bringing the hand (the extremity) in toward the shoulder (the base), does not include a contraction in the hand, but in a sympathetic reaction, the hand and wrist may curve a little. In **7f**, where the arm starts forward middle with the elbow pointing to the side, the 90° contraction will produce the position of **7g**, illustrated in **7h**. The subsequent neither bent nor stretched returns the arm to its original alignment. In **7i**, the arm starts in the same direction but with the palm facing up and the elbow pointing down. The same degree of contraction results in the position of **7j**. Here the cancellation results in a stretched arm.

7.4. Contraction of the Elbow. If the description of **7f** is of the elbow contracting, **7k**, there is the same spatial result for the arm, **7l**, but focus is on the elbow action; the hand remains normally straight, it is not affected by the elbow action. Ex. **7m** is comparable with **7i**.

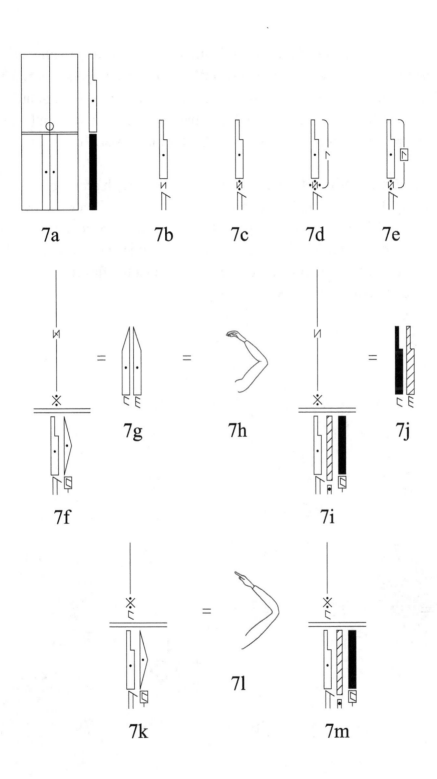

7a 7b 7c 7d 7e

7f 7g 7h 7i 7j

7k 7l 7m

7.5. **Contraction of the Wrist**. With the arm forward, resting on a table, palm down, the wrist contraction of **7n** brings the fingers in toward the elbow, illustrated in **7o**. Knust referred to this action as a 'wrist bulge' (1979, vol. 1, 28, vol. 2, 15, Ex. 151b). In the same arm situation but with the palm up, a wrist contraction over the back of the wrist, **7p**, produces **7q**.

7.6. **Contraction of the Hand and Fingers**. With arm forward, palm facing down, the hand contraction of **7r** brings the fingertips towards the wrist, **7s**. The base knuckles rise forming angular cupped hand, a hand position familiar in Graham technique. In **7t** the same action occurs with the arm to the side, palm up, **7u**. Contraction of just the fingers, **7v**, produces a claw-like hand, **7w**.

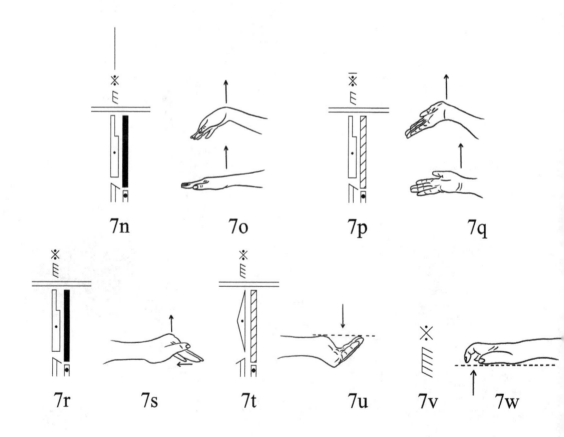

7n   7o   7p   7q

7r   7s   7t   7u   7v   7w

8. Contraction, Extension for the Leg

8.1. Extension of the Leg. In normal standing, **8a**, the legs are relaxed, i.e., neither bent nor stretched. Straight legs are indicated in **8b**. A further degree of stretching, **8c**, involves taut, muscular tension.

8.2. For a leg gesture, the leg should be raised neither bent nor stretched, **8d**. Such a state is mainly applicable to folk dances; trained forms of dance tend automatically to stretch the leg, **8e**. With two degrees of lengthening, **8f**, the whole leg will be taut. Earlier the double degree of lengthening meant pulling out from the hip, **8g**. Such usage exists now in the simpler statements used in Motif Notation. Inclusion of the hip is written as **8h**; if a greater degree of pelvic involvement is required, it is written as inclusion of the hip area, **8i**.

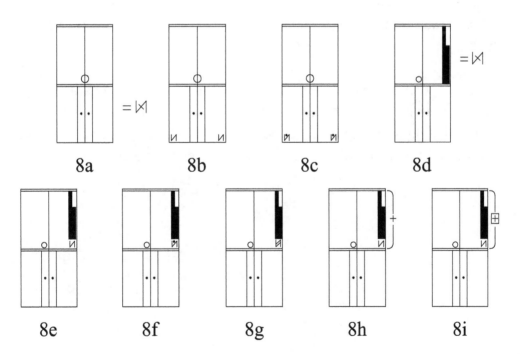

8a   8b   8c   8d

8e   8f   8g   8h   8i

8.3. **Contraction of the Leg**. A contraction of the whole leg brings the foot, the free end - or the heel [ankle] if the foot is in another direction - closer to the base, the hip. In **8j**, while sitting with the legs forward, **8k**, the legs contract 90°, **8l**; they then extend, thus returning to the starting position. Here the legs are parallel, if they were turned out the knees would point sideward. In **8m** the legs are sideward, shown in **8n**, the right leg contracts 90°, illustrated in **8o**.

8.4. **Contracting the Hip Joints**, means bringing the torso and the legs closer together. In **8p**, while lying on the back, legs forward horizontal, the contraction of the hips to 90° brings the torso and the legs towards each other, illustrated in **8q**. If this action were to happen while lying on the water, as in **8r**, the displacement would be as illustrated in **8s**. The hip extension that follows returns the limbs to their previous state. It is important to note that when a limb is resting on the floor or other flat surface, the surface governs the movement, thus it is different when the limb is free in space, as illustrated in **8s**.

8.5. **Contracting the Knee**. While sitting with legs forward middle, **8t**, contracting the knee 90°, illustrated in **8u**, is the same as contracting the legs in that position, but the focus here is on the action of the knees. In **8v**, the sign for neither bent nor stretched, **8w**, is used to cancel the bend in the knees.

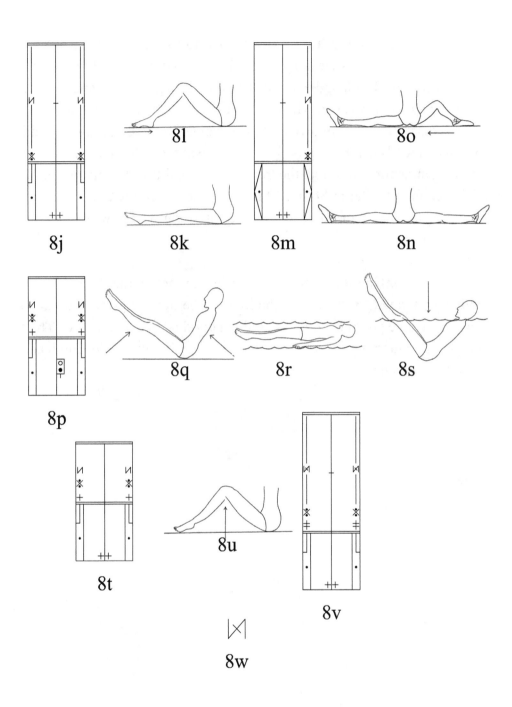

8j

8l

8k

8m

8o

8n

8p

8q

8r

8s

8t

8u

8v

8w

8.6. **Contracting the Ankle**. Ex. **8x**, illustrated in **8y** and **8z**, brings the toes closer to the knee, slightly raising the lower legs, the thigh direction is not affected. The lengthening that follows brings the foot and lower leg into line again. However, when sitting as in **8aa**, the floor dictates that the ankle contraction will involve a spatial change for the thigh, illustrated in **8ab** and **8ac**. When the leg is gesturing forward, off the floor, as in **8ad**, the ankle contraction will affect the thigh direction, illustrated in **8ae** and **8af**. This action is similar to **8t**, in that the toes, the extremity, are drawn on a straight line toward the knee. (Compare ankle contraction with ankle folding, 12d.)

8.7. **Contraction of the Foot**. With the foot on the floor, **8ag**, the foot contraction lifts the sole of the foot off the floor, illustrated in **8ah** and **8ai**; the degree possible depends on the individual foot flexibility. The range for contracting the toes, **8aj**, **8ak**, again depends on the length and flexibility of a person's toes.

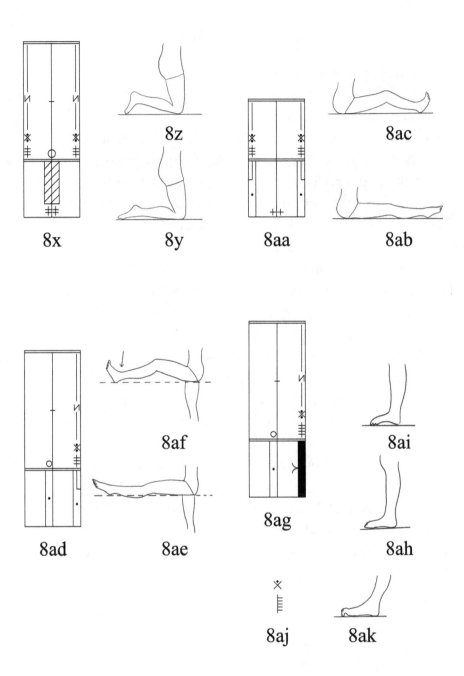

8x

8z

8y

8aa

8ac

8ab

8ad

8af

8ae

8ag

8ai

8ah

8aj

8ak

9. Torso Contracting, Extending

9.1. In contracting the torso, the free end, the shoulder line, approaches the fixed end the base, i.e., the hips, on a straight line, the spine becomes curved, the center part at the waist bulging backward. One degree of contraction, **9a**, is illustrated in **9b**, two degrees in **9c** and **9d**, with three degrees shown in **9e** and **9f**. The amount of contraction possible depends on the flexibility of the performer. In these examples it is understood the contraction is over the front surface of the torso. Contractions over other surfaces are possible. This is shown by use of the meeting lines representing the performer, thus **9g** specifically states contract over the front, with **9h-n** giving the range of surfaces – over the back, the side surfaces, and the four diagonal surfaces. Ex. **9o** illustrates sideward contraction to the right, and **9p** contraction over the back.

9.2. Note that the head is carried along naturally in these movements, however, use of an inclusion bow, **9q**, gives a specific indication of head involvement. The augmented unit of head to pelvis can be stated, **9r**, the contraction degree is then judged from the top of the head.

9.3. Contractions over the back diagonals were used by Nijinsky in his ballet *L'Après-midi d'un Faune* when the Faun is aggressively stalking the leading nymph (see Hutchinson Guest 1990). Interestingly, his analysis was to combine a diagonal forward tilt of the whole torso with a diagonally backward tilt of the chest, **9s**, the result being the contraction statement of **9t**.

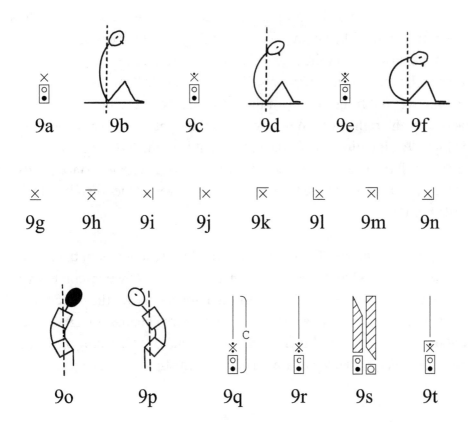

9a 9b 9c 9d 9e 9f

9g 9h 9i 9j 9k 9l 9m 9n

9o 9p 9q 9r 9s 9t

9.4. When the torso is upright, it contracts over the front surface. It is also the front surface when combined with tilting forward. In other directions it concaves over the surface of the direction of the tilt, i.e., the direction of the movement, unless otherwise indicated. Thus, **9u** involves contracting over the front surface of the torso and **9v** states the torso contracts over the right side. While lying on the right side, raising the torso to side high, **9w**, the direction of the movement is to the left, thus the contraction will be over the left side of the torso. A different surface needs to be specified, as in **9x** where the right side concaves as the torso lifts to right side high.

9. 5. **Extending the Torso**. In its normal upright position, the torso is naturally relaxed. One degree of lengthening, **9y**, lifts the vertebrae; two degrees gives a greater sense of rising through the spine, **9z**, illustrated in **9aa**. When this lengthening is combined with a torso contraction, **9ab**, the result, **9ac**, is of a 'scooping' feeling, the shape uses a little more space and requires more energy, facts that are difficult to illustrate in a drawing.

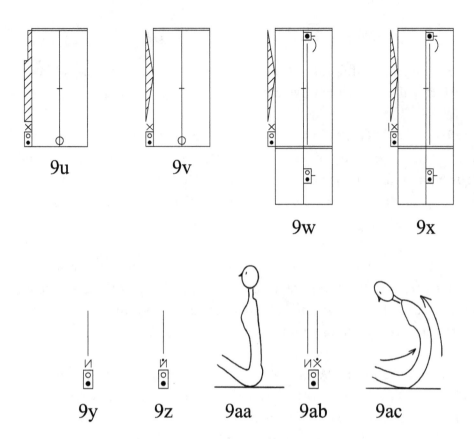

9u   9v

9w   9x

9y   9z   9aa   9ab   9ac

10. Degrees of Folding the Arm

Folding and unfolding actions are body related, they are not affected by the particular directional System of Reference being used.

10.1. Example **10a** indicates the 6/6 scale of folding, while **10b** gives the 8/8 scale. The need for degrees of unfolding has not been experienced. In **10c**, total unfolding occurs. The motion of unfolding in **10d** leaves the amount unstated; if needed, a destination of a degree of being folded can be indicated, as in **10e**.

10.2. As with contractions, folding of the arm is always toward the inner surface, with the exception of the wrist, which can fold backward and also sideward. Slight backward folding of the elbow occurs for people who have hyperextension in that joint.

10.3. **Folding the Whole Arm** begins as a rounding of the arm. In the 8/8 scale, two degrees, **10f**, is usually needed for the rounded arm in ballet in 2nd position, **10g**. This position has often been written with a contraction sign, **10h**. Technically this is incorrect for ballet, as contracting will cause the upper arm to move backward. In folding the whole arm, the base direction gradually changes; **10i** indicates a fully folded arm in the forward direction, hand and wrist curled in, **10j**.

10a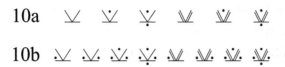

10b

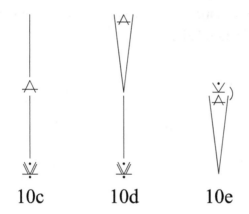

10c   10d   10e

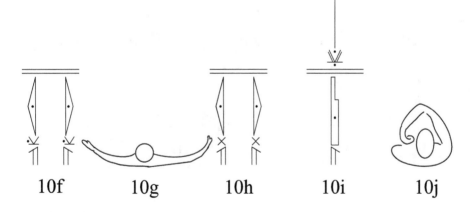

10f   10g   10h   10i   10j

10.4. **Folding the Elbow** 90°, as in **10k**, displaces the spatial situation of the lower arm. The resulting lower arm direction depends on the location of the upper arm and its state of rotation. This description focuses on the elbow action. In **10l** the same elbow folding occurs as in **10k**, but the left elbow fold produces the spatial result of **10m**. In **10n** the placement of the arm produces a different spatial result, **10o**. Folding the elbow backward, **10p**, produces a hyper- extended arm, **10q**.

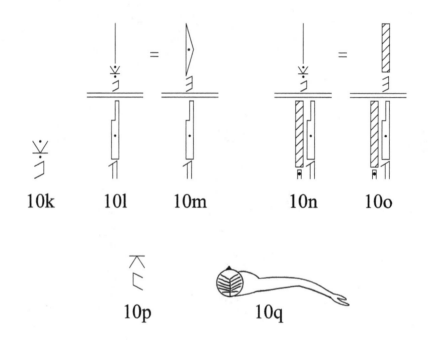

10k   10l   10m   10n   10o

10p   10q

10.5. **Folding the Wrist** 90° forward, **10r**, remains the same physical action wherever the arm is in space and whatever its rotational state; the same is true of folding the wrist backward, **10s**.

10.6. Sideward folding of the wrist is also possible, folding toward the little finger edge (ulna flexion), **10t**, illustrated in **10u**, has a greater range than toward the thumb edge (radius flexion), **10v** and **10w**. Ex. **10t** is much featured in the role of the Faun in Nijinsky's ballet *L'Après-midi d'un Faune,* as indicated in **10x**.

10.7. **Folding the Hand** forward brings the fingers in toward the palm. The greatest degree of folding, **10y**, produces a fist, **10z**. Backward folding, **10aa**, produces the backward curved hand familiar in Balinese dancing, **10ab**. Fingers folding are **10ac** and **10ad**. Detailed movements for the hand and fingers are given in *Hands, Fingers,* Advanced Labanotation, issue 5.

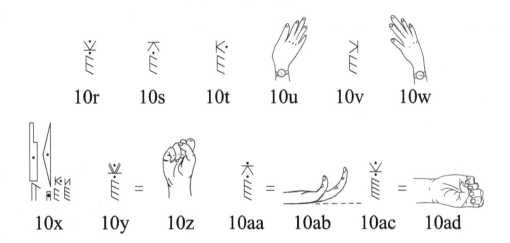

10r	10s	10t	10u	10v	10w

10x	10y	10z	10aa	10ab	10ac	10ad

11. Contracting/Unfolding/Folding/Lengthening

11.1. In **11a** the right arm starts forward middle, then contracts 90°; the unfolding that follows brings the arm into the forward diagonal direction. From there the arm again contracts 90° and again unfolds, bringing the arm to side middle; the resulting directions are shown here in parentheses. This result is because the line of direction in contracting is from the shoulder to the arm extremity; unfolding brings the lower arm in line with the upper arm. Ex. **11b** shows a similar example using folding and lengthening.

11.2. The above examples illustrate in clear degrees the possible mixing of contracting and elongating with folding and unfolding. Sigurd Leeder used this idea in his barre exercise, indicated in **11c**, in which the image is of repeatedly putting a sock on one's foot. Repeating the movement causes the leg slowly to rise because the line between the foot extremity and the knee changes slightly with each foot folding.

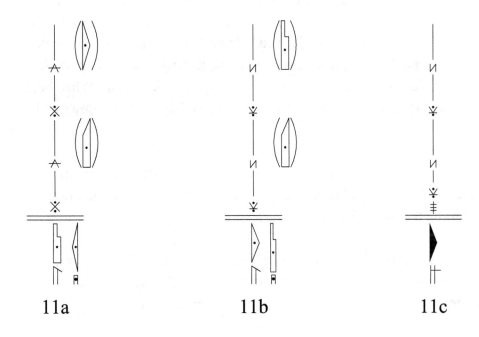

11a 11b 11c

12. Folding, Unfolding the Leg Joints

12.1. **Folding the Hip Joint**. The rotational state of the leg affects the result of hip folding. In **12a**, the legs are parallel, the forward hip fold brings the thigh forward to middle level, **12b**; if well turned out, as in ballet, **12c**, the thigh will end side middle, **12d**. When lying, as in **12e**, folding the hips will raise the legs, illustrated in **12f**. If the folding indication is written in the body column, **12g**, then the torso will hinge forward, **12h**. When both legs and torso fold, **12i**, the result is the position of **12j**; spatially described as **12k**.

12.2. Anatomically, **the knee** can only fold backward, toward its inner surface. Thus, from the standing position of **12l**, the knee folding to 90° will bring the lower leg to backward middle.

12.3. **Folding the Ankle** forward follows the logic of hip folding. In **12m** folding the ankle 90° brings the foot to place high, **12n**; unfolding brings the foot in natural alignment with the lower leg, **12o**.

12.4. **Folding the Toes, 12p**, in contrast to contracting them, is possible when the foot is off the floor, **12q**.

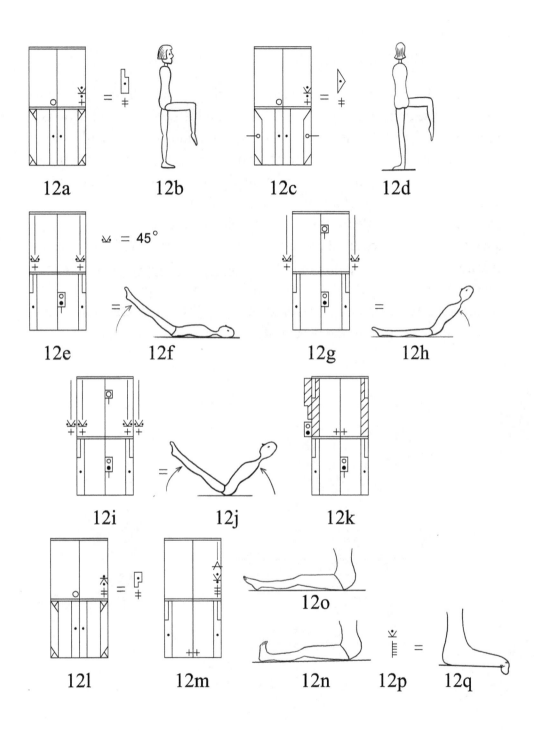

12a 12b 12c 12d

$\lambda\!\!\!\swarrow = 45°$

12e 12f 12g 12h

12i 12j 12k

12l 12m 12o

12n 12p 12q

13. Torso Folding and Unfolding

13.1. Folding the spine is usually described as a folding of the whole torso, the base being the pelvis and the free end the shoulder line. Unless otherwise indicated, the head is carried along. Folding can be in all directions but, as a result of the structure of the vertebrae, over the front is the most usual and comfortable. With the differences in body build and flexibility, the question of maximum degree of folding comes up. As a result of training and flexibility, contortionists achieve a remarkable degree, especially in the backward direction. A person with rare flexibility can fold forward to the point of having the head between the thighs. With that as the greatest degree possible, the 8/8 scale of folding for the torso could be established, illustrated in the drawings of **13a**. Obviously, few people can go beyond 4 degrees, but the possibility for more exists.

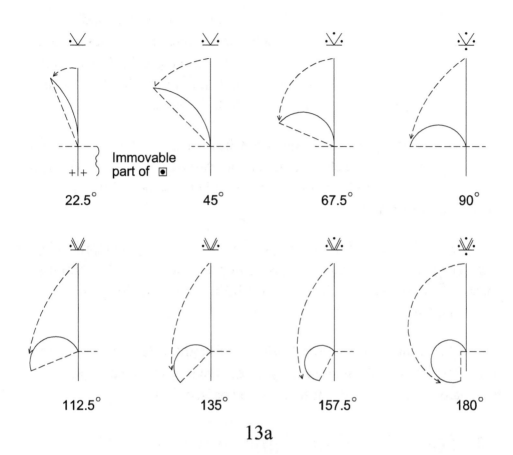

22.5°   45°   67.5°   90°

Immovable part of ◉

+|+

112.5°   135°   157.5°   180°

13a

13.2. While sitting on the floor, as the torso folds more and more forward, **13b**, the pull can be felt much lower, stretching the muscles at the back of the pelvis. A sideward fold of the torso to the right, **13c**, can reach deeply into the left hip joint without lifting that hip from the floor. This form of lower articulation is familiar in Graham technique.

13.3. **Folding the Rib Cage, the Chest**. The waist is the 'base' for chest folding. In **13d** the chest folds forward two degrees, illustrated in **13e**. The sideward tilt of **13f** is followed by a fold in the same direction, illustrated in **13g**, and in **13h**.

13.4. Folding actions can be performed with elongation, producing an arch. The chest arching backward, is a lifted, extended action. In **13i** the chest arches backward, at the same time lifting and 'separating' the vertebrae, **13j**.

13.5. **Folding the Upper Spine, the Shoulder Section**. This part folds from its base, the line (roughly) under the shoulder blades. In backward folding, **13k,** the head is carried passively, **13l**.

14. Torso Folding, Cancellations

14.1. The torso folding forward in **14a** is cancelled by unfolding, as is folding in other directions, **14b** for example. In **14c** folding is cancelled by a 'neither bent nor stretched' sign (the normal state for the 'limb'). In **14d** the back to normal sign clearly cancels the previous folding, bringing the torso upright again. When folding is followed by elongating, as in **14e**, the lengthening is along the line between the hips and the shoulders, thus, the result will be approximately forward high.

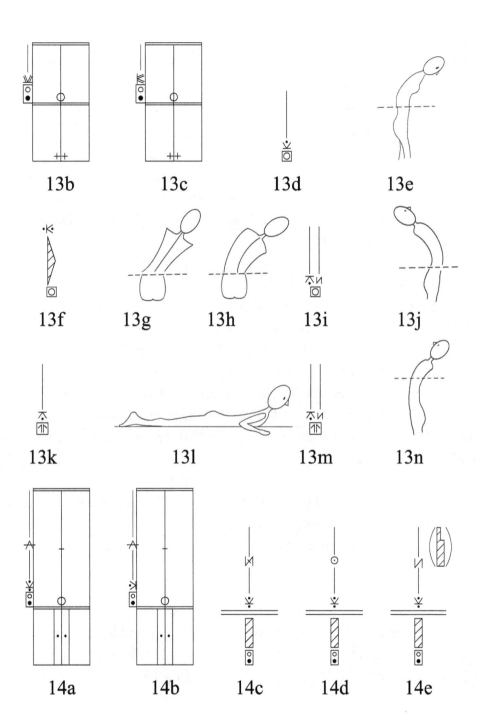

13b   13c   13d   13e

13f   13g   13h   13i   13j

13k   13l   13m   13n

14a   14b   14c   14d   14e

15. Lateral, Sagittal Opening, Closing

15.1. **Terminology**. In anatomical circles, a limb moving laterally
away from the body midline is called 'abduction'; moving to or across the
midline is called 'adduction'. Although we use these terms, other
established anatomical terms conflict with our usage. A limb moving
sagittally forward away from the midline is anatomically called 'flexion';
sagittally backward is called 'extension'. Instead we speak of sagittally
spreading and closing. The terms 'separating' and 'joining', 'opening' and
'closing' may also be used.

15.2. **The Need for This Movement Description**. Awareness of
movement of the limbs in relation to the torso, to the body center line,
called for a means of describing these body actions in those terms. These
actions have an understood Body Key. The symbol for lateral opening is
15a, lateral closing, **15b**; the signs for sagittal opening, **15c**, and sagittal
closing, **15d**. For the hands these actions are covered in detail with clear
illustrations in *Hands, Fingers*, Advanced Labanotation, issue 5, sections 14
and 18. Diagonal opening and closing, **15e**, **15f**, **15g** and **15h** are also
possible for the arms and legs.

15.3. **Degrees of Opening, Closing**. Ex. **15i** gives the six degrees of
lateral spreading; the six degrees of lateral closing are shown in **15j**; the
degrees for sagittal opening, **15k**, are followed by the degrees for sagittal
closing, **15l**.

15.4. Spreading and closing may be just one sided; to indicate this,
the appropriate end of the sign is thickened. Thus, **15m** indicates the right
side opening, with **15n** being the left side. The side which is closing in is
shown by **15o** and **15p**. This applies also to **15q** – **15t**.

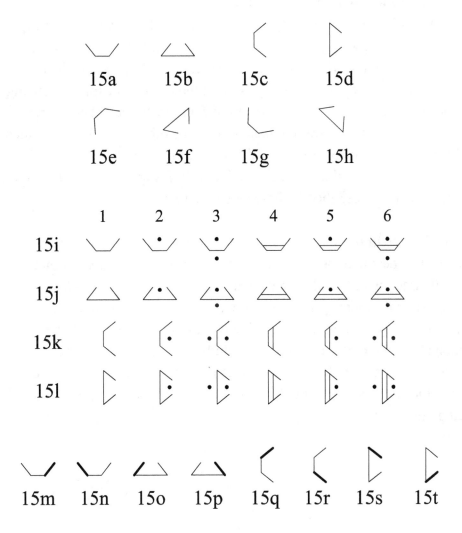

15. 6. **Limb Relationship to Body**. Spreading and closing often involve a relationship to the body, the center line. The movement concept may be of the arm moving away from the torso, creating space between the two, **15u**, illustrated in **15v**, a separation which is not expressed when direction symbols are used. Equally, joining the limb to the torso, reducing the space between them, can have a very different meaning when energy, pressure is included. Separating one leg from the other leg, **15w**, illustrated in **15x**, can provide an awareness of the distance between them, rather than arriving at side low or side middle. Similarly, limbs crossing the body, the center line, can be described in these closing terms.

15.7. **Destination of Spreading**. Note that all flexion and extension signs indicate destinations. Examples **15y** – **15ad**, give the approximate sideward directions for each of the six degrees of spreading. In **15ae** the right arm spreads laterally 90°. In all the above the action is shown at the start, followed by a duration line to give the timing. If there might be any question about the meaning of the duration line, it can be tied to the indication of the action, **15af**. This can also be expressed by stating the action at the end, and tying it to the duration line, **15ag**, a familiar usage in Kinetography Laban.

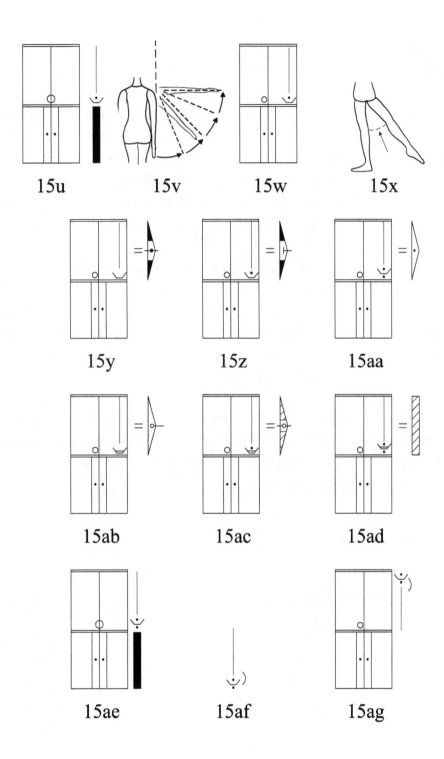

15u   15v   15w   15x

15y   15z   15aa

15ab   15ac   15ad

15ae   15af   15ag

15.8. **The Motion of Spreading**. In **15ah** the indication for the arm of much spreading is placed within a long 'V' increase sign indicating motion toward a separated state without indication of exactly how much. This is followed by the motion of closing: focus is on the motion itself; the performer is given freedom as to degree. In contrast, **15ai**, written in Motif Notation, indicates the right arm closing into the body a small amount, followed by opening laterally to the destination of 90°. Crossing the body, **15aj**, is automatically understood to be in front unless crossing behind is indicated, as in **15ak** where both arm and leg cross behind.

15.9. **Shoulders Widening, Narrowing**. Lateral widening and narrowing are particularly applicable to the shoulders through the actions of the shoulder blades, the scapulae. Right and left shoulder blades are shown in **15al**. In **15am**, with the right arm out to the side, the right shoulder pulls in laterally and then widens laterally. In **15an** this action is written specifically for the right shoulder blade.

15.10. In **15ao** the right shoulder blade opens laterally and then draws in, before returning to normal, here indicated by the back to normal sign. The neutral sign for this kind of action is the combination of the two signs, i.e., 'neither spread nor closed', **15ap**.

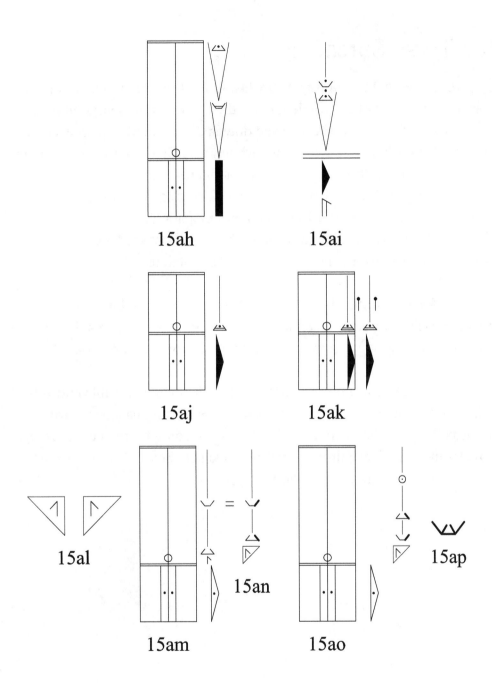

15ah

15ai

15aj

15ak

15al

15am

15an

15ao

15ap

16. Torso Spreading

16.1. **Lateral Spreading and Closing for the Torso**. Physically the most moveable part of the whole torso is the chest, but the sensation of widening the whole torso laterally and drawing it in can be experienced. In **16a** lateral spreading is shown for the whole torso. The addition of the arms opening sideward at the same time, **16b**, facilitates this lateral expansion. Lateral closing in, **16c**, is also aided by the closing of the arms, **16d**. One sided opening, to the right in **16e**, could be a preparation for a sideward shift, **16f**. One sided closing in, **16g**, might result from wanting to move away from someone on your right, a muscular reaction.

16.2. **Chest Lateral Spreading**. With the action of breathing, the chest can easily experience lateral spreading, **16h**. Sagittal spreading, **16i**, is also possible, although it may be mainly in the forward direction, **16j**.

16.3. **Pelvis Spreading**. For the pelvis the main moveable part is the abdomen, shown in **16k** to 'spread' forward. Spreading backward, **16l**, means pulling the abdomen inward. Lateral spreading for the pelvis, **16m**, provides more an image than a physical movement possibility, an image that may have some muscular result.

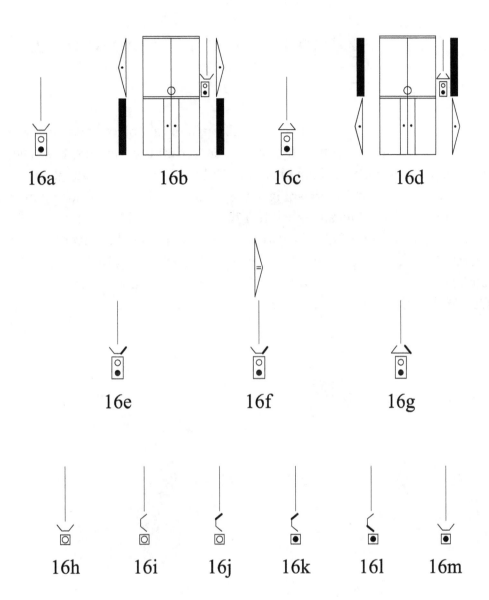

17. Grasping Through Lateral Spreading and Closing

17.1. Certain objects can be held through the action of opening laterally. A small glass is held by two fingers separating laterally, **17a**. The top of a pair of trousers is being held in **17b** by the hands through lateral expansion of the arms, no grasping action is indicated. Lateral closing may be the means of holding an object. In **17c** two fingers hold the edge of a paper cup. A cigarette is held between the index and middle finger through lateral closing, **17d**. A vase is being held by the wrists in **17e** through lateral closing of the arms. Note: these examples were not included in *Handling of Objects, Props,* Advanced Labanotation, issue 8.

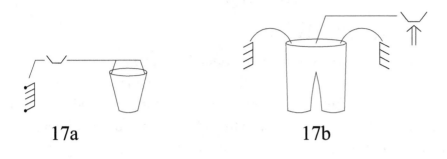

17a 17b

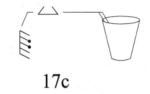

17c

17d 17e

Chapter 4. Vertical Bows
1. The Phrasing Bow

1.1. In music a series of notes are often linked by a horizontal phrasing bow to indicate the sense of the passage, what is one music 'idea' and what is another. These phrases may be fairly short or extending over a longer sequence of notes. The same is true of verbal sentences which have a beginning, a middle and an end, and convey a thought, a message or a feeling of some kind. As Peggy Hackney, a leading LMA practitioner writes: "Phrases are perceivable units of movement that are in some sense meaningful" (1998, 47).

1.2. **The Meaning of 'Phrasing'**. Phrasing is an indication of 'unity of thought'; where several movements belong together from the initiation to the end. The phrasing bow also can indicate the 'long line of the movement sequence'; it may indicate an incomplete 'sentence,' or one that, having a beginning, a middle and an end, is complete.

1.3. **Phrasing for a Circular Movement**. Circular movements are often written with four consecutive direction symbols; if there are no gaps between symbols, then there should be continuous motion. When such circling is continuous, it may be helpful to show how it should be phrased. With phrasing indicated, there may be a subtle breath pause at the end of each phrase so that the sense of beginning a 'new idea' is created. Ex. **1a** illustrates this idea, the sagittal half swing being a new idea. In **1b** the bow encloses consecutive displacement deviation pins, thus expressing a circular movement.

2. The Initiation Bow

2.1. The vertical bow of **2a** has a thickened beginning, derived from the accent sign of **2b**, to indicate a moment of energy which begins the movement phrase. However, phrases can begin without any overt emphasis.

3. Simultaneous Actions

3.1. A vertical bow is used to indicate that two actions, written one after the other, should in fact occur at the same time or that they have a certain amount of overlap, a smooth transition between the two. In **3a**, as the weight is transferred forward, a turning action takes place at the same time; the bow covers both symbols. In **3b** the leg gesture and ankle action occur at the same time. Because the addition of such bows may interfere with other movement indications, the bow has been reduced in size, **3c**, but a complete smooth overlap is still understood.

Phrasing Bow   **Initiation Bow**

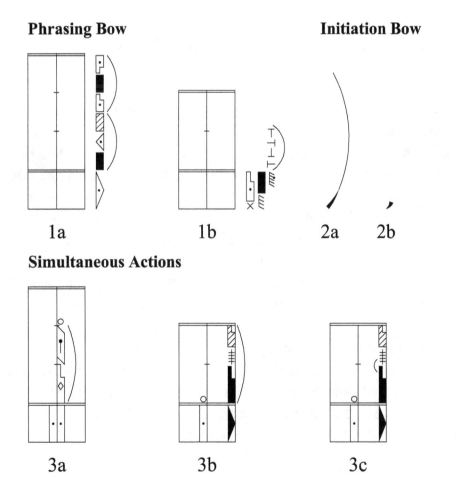

1a   1b   2a   2b

Simultaneous Actions

3a   3b   3c

3.2. **Overlap in Timing**. The specific timing of an overlap can be indicated, as in **3d**. Similarly, a step-turn can have the amount of overlap of the actions shown, as in **3e**. In **3f** there is very little overlap.

4. The 'Passing State' Bow

4.1. This name is given to the vertical bow when used to indicate additional features which lasts only for the duration of the movement next to which it is placed. These are: **4a** a deviation; **4b** the straight path shape of the gesture, and **4c**, a sequential movement. Each is completed by the end of the bow.

5. Deviation; Modification of a Path

5.1. Gestures with a slight curve are often more gracious, they add interest. Take the gesture where, starting with the hand at the shoulder, the arm extends forward horizontally, **5a**. Usually, this gesture follows a straight path. How charmingly the message is modified by a slight deviation upward, **5b**. Or the deviation may be downward, or to one side or the other. Also to be considered is the timing: does the deviation occur only at the start, as in **5c**; or only toward the end, as in **5d**? Each of these provides a different 'message'. More than one deviation can occur on a single path. What flourishes! Think of the cavalier doffing his hat to Milady, **5e**, with up and down curves. Some intricate paths of the arm extremity, the fingertips, the hand, are based on such deviations.

5.2. A gestural path that is naturally curved may be modified to follow a straight line from start to finish, **5f**, the dotted line in **5g** indicates the normal curved path. To accomplish a straight path, the limb will need to flex somewhat and then return to normal extension. This passing state of flexion is understood to occur and is not written.

Overlap in Timing

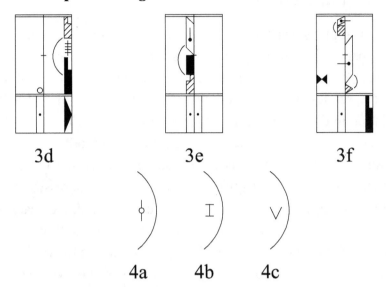

3d 3e 3f

4a 4b 4c

Deviation, Modification of a Path

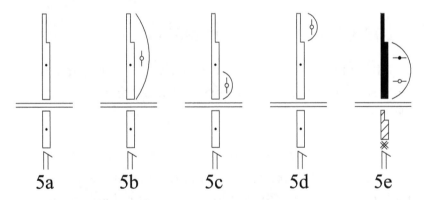

5a 5b 5c 5d 5e

A Straight Path

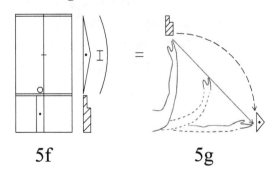

5f 5g

6. Sequential Movements

6.1. This topic is dealt with in detail in *Sequential Movements, Advanced Labanotation*, issue 4. Here we are concerned with the use of vertical bows. An outward sequential movement can be written with the V sign used as a pre-sign, **6a**, or placed within a vertical bow, **6b**. This latter allows variation in the timing of the succession which may be at the start of the gesture, as in **6c**, or toward the end of the movement, **6d**. Successions, 'ripples', can occur in the arm without its changing direction. To achieve this there needs to be a minor displacement which then progresses through the limb; it may be upward, downward, forward, backward, etc., each a very small spatial movement. A rotary action in the centre of the limb can make the movement more snake-like. In **6e** the ripple is a slight forward displacement. Overlapping ripples may takes place as in **6f** where one displacement flows into the next. Note that all these are 'Passing States'.

7. Inclusions: Active, Passive

While the topic of Inclusions, particularly of the body in arm gestures, was well covered in *Labanotation* (2005, 223-227), there is additional material to consider.

7.1. In the walking sequence of **7a**, the arms swing in the normal way. Note here the use of Unit Timing. Instead of just arms alone, a slight inclusion of the upper-body, **7b**, results in one side going forward as the other goes back, i.e., a slight rotation of the upper-body. The bow connecting the arm gesture to the body column, **7b**, indicates this. A solid line inclusion bow means that the inclusion is active, intentional, as in a march. By using a dotted bow, **7c**, a passive, resultant inclusion is indicated.

Sequential Movements

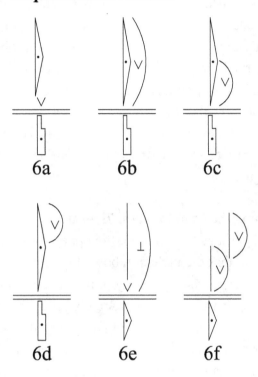

6a   6b   6c

6d   6e   6f

Inclusion

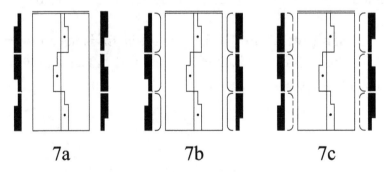

7a   7b   7c

7.2. Instead of an isolated arm movement from side high to side low, the upper body becomes sympathetic and is included, **7d**. An inclusion may occur only at the start of the arm movement, as in **7e**, or begin halfway through, **7f**. Body inclusions in arm gestures may involve a tilting or a turning action of the body, or both. In **7g** the directions of the arms produce a twisting action, but they cancel out any tilting, action that would have resulted if only one or other of the arms were moving alone. The addition of the wide sign to the inclusion for the left arm in **7h** results in a tilt and a slight twist to the right. Degree of inclusion can be indicated with measurement signs.

7.3. Inclining the head forward, **7i**, is an isolated movement. To express apology, perhaps humiliation, the upper body should be included, **7j**. It is understood that the inclusion bow at the left refers to the upper body in general. For a deeper apology, it may need to include even the rib cage, the chest. Inclusion of the chest area is given in **7k**. An interesting example of torso inclusion comes from Hungarian dance: **7l**, shows slapping the boot just above the ankle when the leg is forward middle and the torso included in the arm gesture. In these boot-slapping dances the body often needs to be included to facilitate reaching the boot. Note the Hungarian indication of a clap with an understood (but not written) hand symbol.

7.4. **Passive Inclusion**. The hand wave in **7m** is not an isolated hand gesture, the arm is passively included. The overhead hand circles in **7n** are augmented by the passive inclusion of the lower arm.

Inclusion continued

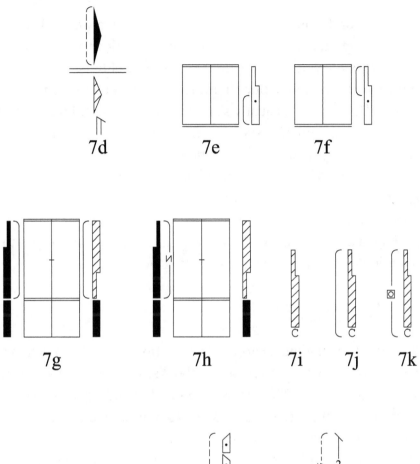

7d   7e   7f

7g   7h   7i   7j   7k

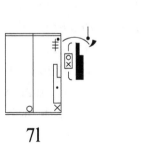

7l

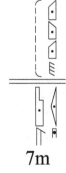

7m

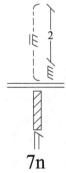

7n

8. Inclusions: Partial Weight

8.1. A clear distinction is usually made between a weight-bearing action, a full support, and a leg gesture touching the floor which is free of weight. There is no weight on the right leg in **8a**. In **8b** the inclusion bow connecting the gesture to the floor indicates partial weight-bearing, specifically 1/3. Weight is equally shared in **8c**, while in **8d** the support is shown to be 1/3 a gesture, 2/3 support. Ex. **8e** is a full transference of weight. In **8f** the leg slides out to the side with inward rotation, then diagonally with outward rotation, all the time including partial weight-bearing. An example of a brief partial weight-bearing step is **8g**, the weight shifts forward then quickly shifts backward. Ex. **8h** is similar but with less weight being taken. A momentary forward shift of the center of gravity, is spelled out in **8i**. This action is like a limping step.

9. Exclusions

9.1. While excluding a part of the body from a particular action has been covered very briefly in previous textbooks, some additional typical examples are given here. The exclusion bows, left and right, are **9a**. The head is excluded in the turn of the torso in **9b**; normally the head is carried along in torso movements. A similar action is for the face, to have a space hold while the torso turns, **9c**; this, however, has a different intention, a different expression. The head may also be excluded in a torso tilt, **9d**, remaining upright. A very similar result would come from **9e** where a space hold is given for the head. If written as **9f** the spatial retention for the face gives a different message. Excluding the hand in an arm movement is indicated in **9g**, the hand remains low. This action could be described by a retained wrist leading, **9h**, but there the emphasis, the intent of the movement, is quite different.

Partial Weight

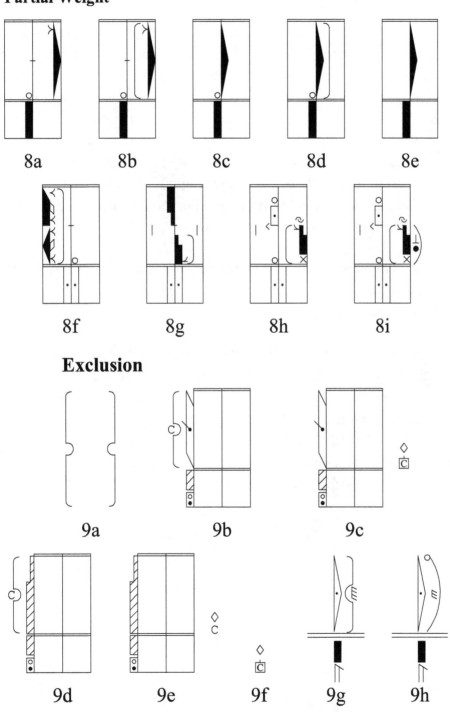

8a   8b   8c   8d   8e

8f   8g   8h   8i

Exclusion

9a   9b   9c

9d   9e   9f   9g   9h

10. Minor Angular Vertical Bows, Carets

10.1. The small round vertical bow is used to connect a previous location to an ending result. In **10a**, the result of the space hold for the arm and leg is stated at the end of the turn, the small round bow links it to the new destination. The small angular 'bow', known as a caret, **10b**, always indicates "the same". In **10c** the caret states that the right foot is 'the same', thus it is the left foot that steps out to produce the 2nd position. A caret is used to indicate the same part of the body, **10d**; it also links a circular path sign from one staff to the next, **10e**, indicating it is the same. When jumping from 1st position to 2nd, if the left foot should land where it was before, the caret, meaning 'the same', is used, as in **10f**.

10.2. **The Same Spot Caret**. The same spot carets are shown in **10g**. These symbols are derived from the spot hold (retention of a spot), shown in **10h**, and may be used to provide a stronger statement, as in **10i**.

10.3. **The 'Zed' Caret**, **10j**, links a leg gesture to a support. By linking the left leg gesture to the following step, as in **10k**, it provides the message that the purpose of the gesture is to lead into the step, i.e. not reaching the normal forward low direction. Similarly, the touching forward gesture of **10l** is linked to the following step with a 'zed caret'. In **10m** the 'same spot zed caret' indicates that the right foot should step on the spot directly below where the side gesture was.

Minor Angular Vertical Bows

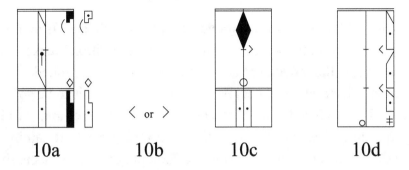

10a   10b   10c   10d

The Same Spot Caret

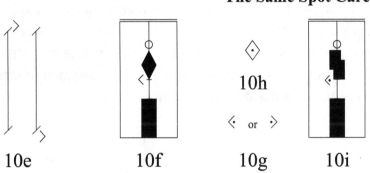

10e   10f   10g   10i

10h

The 'Zed' Caret

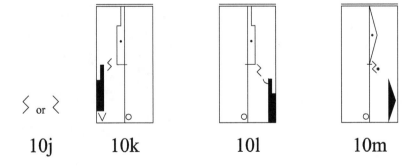

10j   10k   10l   10m

11. The Addition Bracket

11.1. With a series of fast movements for which there is no room to state a modification for each direction, an angular addition bracket, **11a**, can placed alongside the movement description to provide the added information. All movement enclosed within the bracket is to be so modified. Thus, where the bracket starts and ends is important. In **11b** the arm is constantly flexed until the final forward movement. Retaining the forward direction for the arms during the shoulder area rotations is shown in **11c**. In **11d** the fact that each movement should be a shifting action can be stated in the addition bracket. The constant cross of axes is to be applied to the arm gesture in **11e** during the torso twists. When Design Drawing is being used, the timing of the segments can be shown in an addition bracket. In **11f** the design is marked off into segments, the duration of these segments is given alongside in the addition bracket.

Addition Bracket

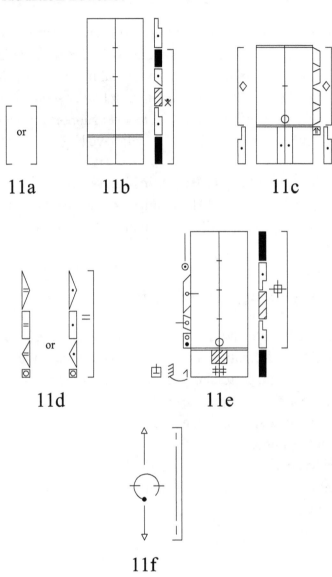

11a   11b   11c

11d   11e

11f

12. First and Second Endings, Beginnings

12.1. **First and Second Endings**. In a dance score, a section that is to be repeated may have a different ending on the repeat. This usage is familiar in music; the device we use, a vertical bracket at the left, is derived from music notation. In **12a**, the ending of a longer sequence is shown, the three high steps are replaced by a middle level support on the third repeat. The "Repeat alternating sides 3 times" will have begun at measure 7.

12.2. **First and Second Beginning**. Less frequent but also needed in dance, is the First and Second Beginning, which is handled in a similar way, as indicated in **12b**. Here a different amount of turn is needed on the repeats.

13. The Theme Bracket

13.1. In Charlotte Wile's book *Moving About* (2010), chapter XVII provides detailed information on the use of the Theme Bracket. To indicate the theme of a piece a particular angular vertical bracket is used, **13a**. In it is written those actions or qualities to be featured. The Motif Notation symbols in **13b** state that the sequence should include arm movements, some form of turning, some springing, strong accents and travelling. A similar idea has been expressed in Motif Notation by the statement of **13c**, the information being placed between horizontal double lines. No indication of timing is given in these examples.

1st and 2nd Ending

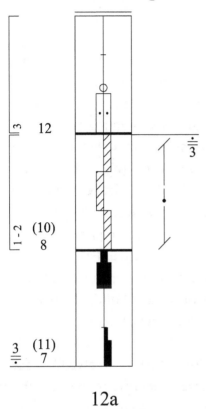

1st and 2nd Beginning

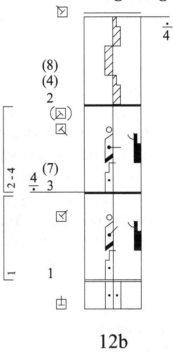

12a

12b

Theme Bracket

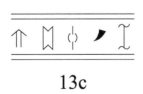

13a

13b

13c

Chapter 5. Initiations
1. Point of Interest

In exploring various movement ideas, dynamics and the point of
origin for a body movement, Sigurd Leeder introduced the idea of a **Point
of Interest** in the body. He gave the image of a shaft of light focused on,
say, the front of the left shoulder, or of a butterfly alighting on a spot.
Immediately your imagination causes a slight tension in that part of the
body, it becomes energized, producing an awareness of it. The result is
experienced by the performer and observed by the audience. Think of a
person whose face is relaxed except for the side of the mouth, perhaps they
had had a stroke, your eye is drawn to the frozen, tensed part. By giving
extra energy to a part of the body, it can become 'active' leading to
initiating a movement in space. This subsequent movement might be
designated, or it might be left totally free, flowing out of the body in an
unplanned way, thus allowing exploration, improvisation.

1.1. **The Point of Interest Indication**. What is involved? A focal
point, **1a**; an awareness, **1b**; a slight increase in energy, **1c**; perhaps the V
for out flowing of energy, **1d**, is appropriate; the use of an arrow to draw
attention to something, **1e**, is appropriate. By combining **1a** and **1e**, we
have the sign **1f**, which can be angled to point toward any particular body
part, **1g, 1h**.

1.2. **Initiation of a Movement**. In **1i**, the point of interest on the
right elbow is followed by a movement of some kind. In **1j** the energizing
of the left shoulder is followed by a sequential arm movement diagonally
up. In example **1k**, the energized left elbow then leads the upward
movement. This could also be written as **1l**.

How does this differ from where only the elbow leading is given? A part leading, **1m**, may be moving with no emphasis on the body part, no dynamic awareness.

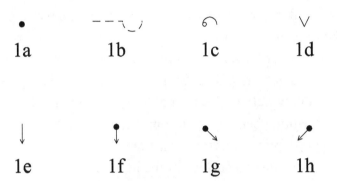

1a   1b   1c   1d

1e   1f   1g   1h

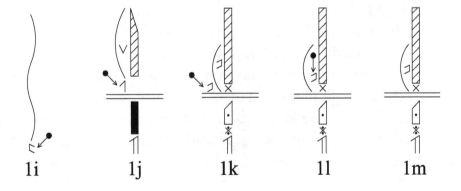

1i   1j   1k   1l   1m

2. Part Leading, Guiding

In some languages there is no difference between the words 'leading' and 'guiding'; in Labanotation there is a distinct difference. **Leading** means that a part goes ahead, illustrated in ex. **2a**. In the body it is often a joint that goes ahead, producing a 'bulging', as when the wrist leads into the direction of the movement. Part leading usually involves flexion of a joint or spatial displacement of a segment. **Guiding** can be compared to a person being next to a blind person and guiding them by using slight pressure on their shoulder or elbow, **2b**, or the man holding onto the guide dog's collar. A comparable situation occurs in ballroom dance when the man guides his partner through appropriate pressure of his hand on her back. In movement such guidance occurs when a surface of the limb presses into the direction of the movement, as when an inner or outer surface of the arm guides the change from up to down of the arm, no bulging occurs. Guidance often involves a rotation to place the limb surface or edge into the line of progression.

2.1. **Part Leading**. A round vertical bow is used to indicate leading or guiding, **2c**. Knust (1979, vol. 1, 9)) called this symbol the "passing state" or "passing modification" bow. At the end of the bow the modification is over. When used for deviations, **2d**, for sequential movement, **2e**, and indications such as a straight path action, **2f**, the modification to the main action is automatically over by the end of the bow. However, when used for part leading, guiding, the manner of performance may not have disappeared at the end of the bow.

2.2. **Timing of Part Leading**. The part leading will actually start to move a moment before the main movement begins; this fact is not notated. In example **2g**, the wrist leading is brief; in **2h**, leading is in effect for half of the movement; in **2i**, the leading lasts for 3/4 of the sideward gesture. In **2j**, leading is completed as the movement ends. To retain the wrist leading, a hold sign is added at the end of the bow, **2k**.

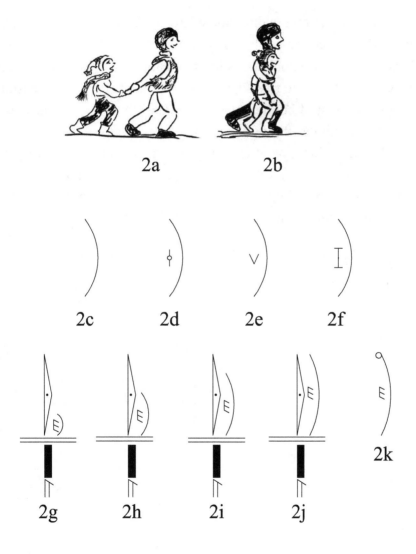

2a   2b

2c   2d   2e   2f

2k

2g   2h   2i   2j

2.3. **Duration of a Guidance**. In **2l**, guidance by the outer surface of the arm ends halfway to the forward middle destination; the inward arm rotation it caused disappears. Ex. **2m** is similar but the 'away' sign indicates the duration of the return to the standard arm carriage. If the guidance is shown to continue to the end of the bow and the inward arm rotation caused is to remain, the hold sign is added to the bow, **2n**. Compare **2n** with **2o** where the ending of the bow is a little sooner.

2.4. Depending on the direction of the movement, the effect of part leading, or a guidance can be different. Simple examples will be shown first. Leading with the shoulder, as in **2p**, disappears where the bow ends while the arm continues to rise. This can be compared with the central sequential movement of **2q**, here the initiation in the shoulder disappears as the succession continues through the arm. When lifting the arm to side middle, led by the elbow, **2r**, it is logical that the leading will disappear when the upper arm arrives side horizontal; this action is more appropriately written as **2s**. Leading with the wrist, **2t**, is usually performed with the back of the wrist, the outer surface, **2u**.

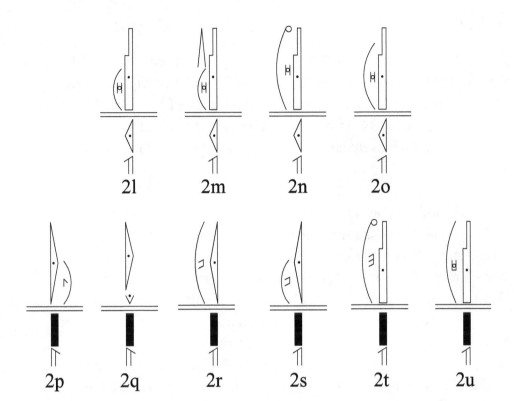

3. Guiding with Surfaces and Edges

3.1. When guiding with the thumb edge of the arm, as in **3a**, there is a sense of cutting through the air but no change in arm configuration occurs, illustrated in **3b**. If leading is with the thumb edge of the wrist, **3c**, spelled out in more detail in **3d**, there will be a bulging, **3e**. If the part leading ceases before the movement ends, then the limb will arrive in its normal state, **3f**.

3.2. In **3g** the arm rises, led first by the little finger edge of the limb with a change to leading with the palm; no time break between them is given. A sudden change can be shown by the addition of an accent, **3h**. A smooth change may start at point a) in the example of **3i**, or at b); it is significant, that the palm leading begins at the start of its bow. For **3j**, the fact is that the head leading must begin slightly before the torso moves forward, although as written, the two indications begin side by side; the head then eases unobtrusively into its normal alignment. For a quick, retained head leading, as in **3k**, the return to normal is shown by the duration of the 'away' sign that follows. Note that indication of a new movement such as the sideward gesture in **3l**, cancels the previously retained wrist leading.

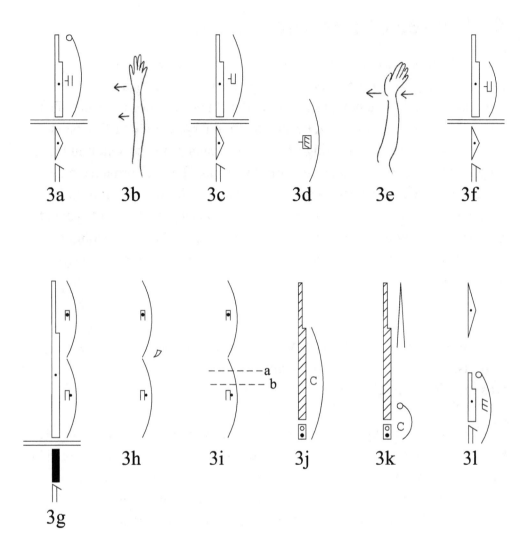

3a 3b 3c 3d 3e 3f

3h 3i 3j 3k 3l

3g

4. Degree of Leading Action

4.1. In some dance styles it is important to know whether the degree of part leading is slight or more extreme. In the simple case of the arm lowering, led by the elbow, as in **4a**, no exact performance is stated. The degree of elbow flexion could be stated, **4b**; a large degree of flexion is given in **4c**. In **4d** the lowering of the elbow causes much flexion in the elbow, followed by the rest of the arm lowering. The performance may focus on the spatial aspects: a small use of space, **4e**, will result in little spatial displacement for the elbow, while **4f** makes greater use of space, to do this the elbow needs to flex to a greater degree. These two examples focus on spatial awareness whereas examples **4b** and **4c** express body awareness.

4.2. **Initiation**. The strongly accented left leg gesture in **4g** initiates the half turn. In **4h** the chest-to-waist torso twist initiates the pirouette, the arms assisting. The delay in the rising and turning action on the left support was revealed through slow motion film analysis.

4.3. A turn may be initiated by leading with the head, **4i**; the head movement being a swift inclining and turning action, **4j**. Turning can also be initiated by other body parts, for example the shoulder. In **4k** the left shoulder initiates a half turn. This initiation is likely to be of the shoulder area with a slight rotation, **4l**. If the part leading bow ends with a hold sign, as in **4m**, the shoulder displacement will remain.

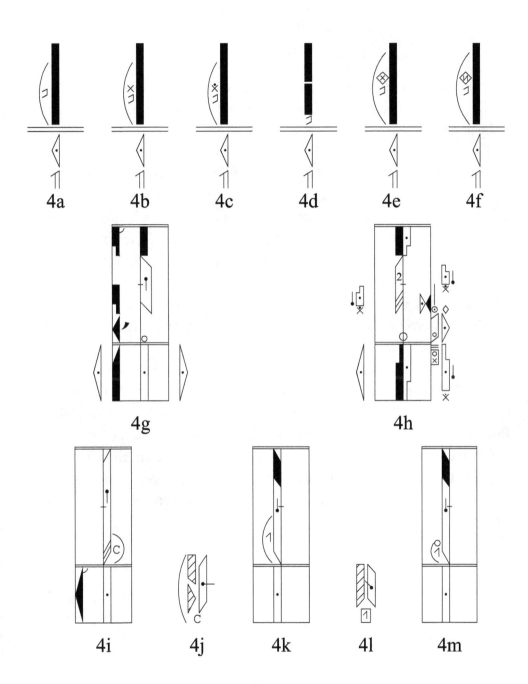

4a   4b   4c   4d   4e   4f

4g   4h

4i   4j   4k   4l   4m

5. Passive, Resultant

From active Part Leading we go to passive, part following. A passive movement is the result of an active movement by another part of the body or by another person.

5.1. **Indication of Passive**. A dotted line indicates a passive response. In **5a**, as the torso twists right and left, the arms are allowed to be affected; this requires that the arms are relaxed, a fact that is understood and not stated. Similarly, in **5b**, the hand is allowed to be affected by the arm swinging to and fro. For **5c**, the head is not carried along as usual with the sideward chest tilts but is relaxed and thus allowed to react to the chest tilts. During the turn in **5d**, the right toe contact continues passively sliding along the floor. As you walk, in **5e**, your right hand passively slides along the table.

5.2. **Duration of Passive Movement**. In **5f** the dotted passive reaction is shown to end after the main action that caused it, a little 'after-flow' is indicated. In contrast, **5g** states that the passive reaction ceases before the main movement is over. If this means that the head is back to its normal alignment, this can be stated, as in **5h**. In contrast, the passive after-flow could continue to a stated destination; in **5i** the head ends halfway to side middle.

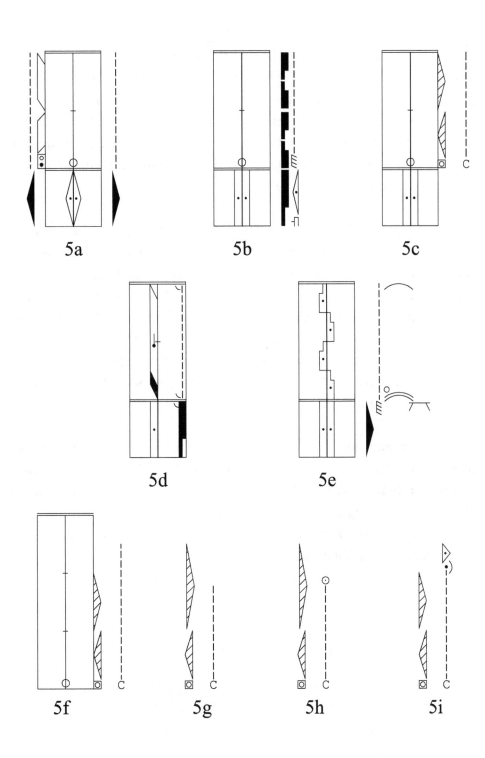

5a   5b   5c

5d   5e

5f   5g   5h   5i

5.3. **Passive Inclusion**. During the hand waving to and fro in **5j**, the arm is passively included. It is basically a hand movement but not in isolation. The hand circling sagittally backward in **5k**, is facilitated by the passive inclusion of the arm. Similarly, the overhead hand circles of **5l** are made easier by the passive inclusion of the lower arm. In **5m** the inclination of the head to forward horizontal is made easy by the relaxed 'giving in' of the shoulder section.

5.4. **With a Partner**. In partner work the man often leads and the lady follows. In a score, **5n** represents a lady, **5o** a man. In **5p** A and B are standing side by side, holding hands. As the man does a half pivot turn, she is passively led into a half circle with forward steps. In contrast, in **5q** the lady is actively circling, causing the man to perform half a turn on the spot. Note that the passive indication is written close to the turn sign to indicate the manner of performance. In **5r** a woman is being carried 'piggy-back' by the man. There are no movement indications on her staff, but a passive travelling is given.

5.5. **Resulting, Accommodating**. A slightly different result may need to be stated. In **5s** the result of the space hold during the half turn will automatically be a backward middle leg gesture. In **5t** this same ending is required but starting with the right leg diagonal low across. During the turn there is a space hold as well as a change in level; the dotted line is connected to the destination with a bow.

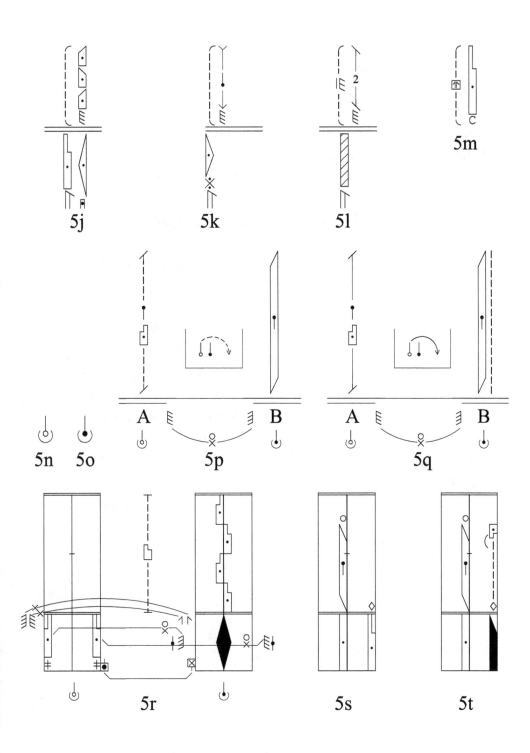

5j

5k

5l

5m

5n   5o

A   B

5p

A   B

5q

5r

5s

5t

5.6. Swiveling on both feet and lowering, as in **5u**, results in sitting on the floor in 4th position. While this destination will happen automatically, it is helpful to have the leg directions stated, particularly for whatever the next movement might be. Note the use of zed carets here. Ex. **5v** shows a half turn while sitting, rolling on the hips, changing from one 4th position to the other. Are small destinational linking bows needed in these examples? It seems self-evident that this ending is not a sudden movement but the result of the previous movement. If the performer is not flexible enough, he/she may need to adjust into the required ending position. This swiveling movement could also be stated as having spot holds for the feet, **5w**. In that case the legs might not automatically end in the stated directions and an adjustment is needed.

5.7. **Resulting Travelling**. Rotations of the legs while supporting may result in a change of position or of travelling. In **5x**, from feet together, parallel, the right leg, still supporting, swivels outward on the low heel, then inward on the 1/8 ball. This is repeated ending in a 2nd position. This change of position can also be achieved with both legs swiveling inward and outward. Leg rotations changing from weight on the low heel to the 1/8th ball can result in travelling. In **5y** the rotations are in opposition, in **5z** they are parallel, but with each rotation on the same parts of the foot; both result in travelling to the right side. These patterns occur in Russian and other European folk dances.

Passive, Resultant

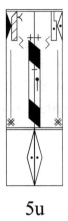

5u

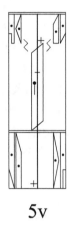

5v

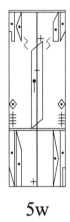

5w

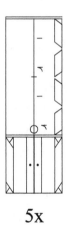

5x

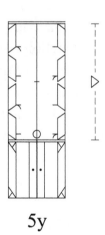

5y

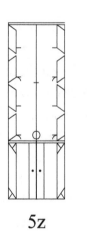

5z

6. Passive Accommodation

6.1. A passive, accommodating action is shown in **6a** where the torso leans slightly backward to facilitate lowering to the knees. The need for a destinational statement, the result, may occur after a turning or circling movement. A slow turn of the head ends looking stage right in **6b**. The active turning can end as a passive action, the ending result written as **6c**. The steps and travelling of **6d** are modified so that the performer ends in the downstage right corner.

7. Arm Gesture Ending

7.1. In any arm gesture followed by a gap, as in **7a**, the arm will remain in the direction of arrival. If a real feeling of stop, of holding, or termination is needed, a hold sign can follow the end of the direction symbol, **7b**, or an expression of stillness may follow this ending, **7c**. Stillness is like the musical reverberation which continues after the note has been played; in movement the aliveness of the action, the active energy continues although movement through space has stopped. When a sequential performance is involved, the ending is often not a stop, but may involve drifting into the ending location. To express this 'after-flow', the last part of the direction symbol is shown to be passive, **7d**. The idea of after-flow, drift, is that the limb, usually an arm, arrives almost at its destination and then flows on into the ending situation. Where lyrical, expressive movements occur, such a gentle after-flow is very expressive and often very appropriate.

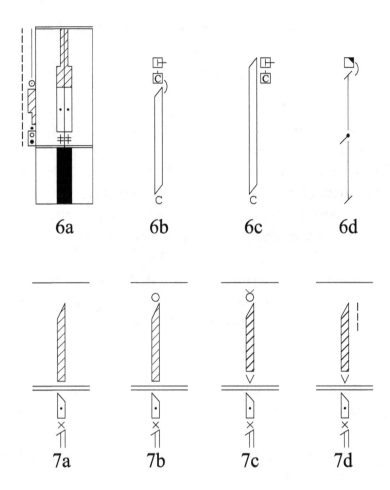

6a 6b 6c 6d

7a 7b 7c 7d

Chapter 6. Choice of Movement Description

1. Arm Gestures: Choice of Description

A sparse description of movement sequences may serve as a memory aid for the notator working at speed, but a detailed record is needed for exercises where manner of performance is necessary to acquire the desired results. For choreography expressive details may be needed to convey the meaning, the intent of the movement. This chapter explores various possibilities to illustrate the range, starting with a simple arm gesture. Examples **1a** through **1i** have the same starting position.

1.1. **Anatomical Description**. When starting with the left arm sideward, palm up, the elbow joint folds 180° bringing the hand to end above the shoulder, **1a**, illustrated in **1b**. The focus here is on the physical action of the elbow joint.

1.2. **Spatial path**. The wrist (lower arm) makes a half cartwheel path to the right, **1c**, shown in **1d**.

1.3. **Directional change**. The action is described as a change in direction for the lower arm, **1e** and **1f**.

1.4. **Shape, design**. The arm extremity is describing a half circle arc as a result of the lower arm movement, **1g** and **1h**. Here design drawing is used (see *Shape, Design, Trace Patterns,* Advanced Labanotation, vol. 1, part 2).

1.5. **Relationship approaching**. The hand approaches the head, **1i** and **1j**. Here the space hold for the upper arm is needed so that only a lower arm movement takes place.

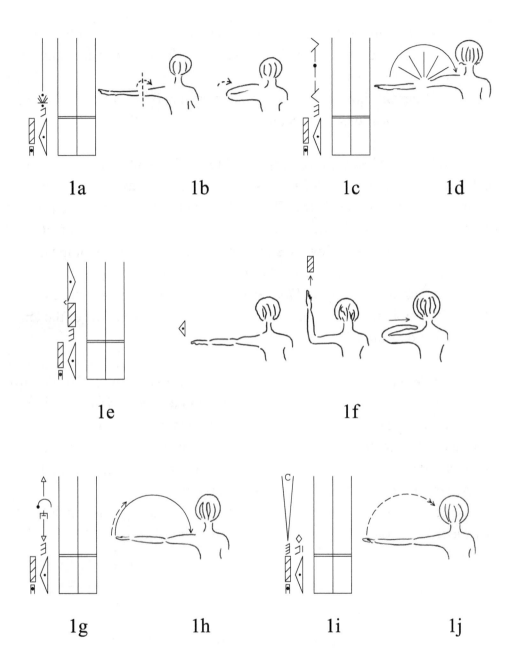

1a   1b   1c   1d

1e   1f

1g   1h   1i   1j

1.6. **Relationship – Retreating**. Here the lower arm moves away from the side middle direction, **1k** and **1l**. As in the previous example, **1i**, a space hold is needed so that only a lower arm movement takes place. The manner of performing each of these examples may be modified by timing, by dynamic indications, part leading, etc.

1.7. **Arm Gesture Crossing the Body**. The right arm gesturing to left side low, **1m**, is expected to cross in front of the body, however, this is usually specifically stated, **1n**. The arm's slightly forward displacement can be shown as **1o**, even farther forward would be the intermediate direction of **1p**, i.e., toward diagonal low. Using track pins, the placement of the arm extremity can be shown to be on the sideward centre line, **1q**, or on its more forward track, as in **1r**. (See *Floorwork, Basic Acrobatics*, Advanced Labanotation, issue 6, Appendix A.) The arm in **1s**, is side low of the left hip (Direction from a Body Part).

1.8. **Variations in the Path of an Arm Gesture**. Moving from down to side high, a 3rd degree point, **1t**, the arm will take the peripheral curved path toward its aim. In performing this path, an awareness of an intermediate direction may be important, **1u**. The performance of **1t** might include a degree of flexion at the start, **1v,** or the flexion could occur a little later, **1w**, or much later, **1x**. Another performance might be **1y**, a sequential movement led by the outer surface of the arm. Use of a straight path for the extremity is given in **1z**.

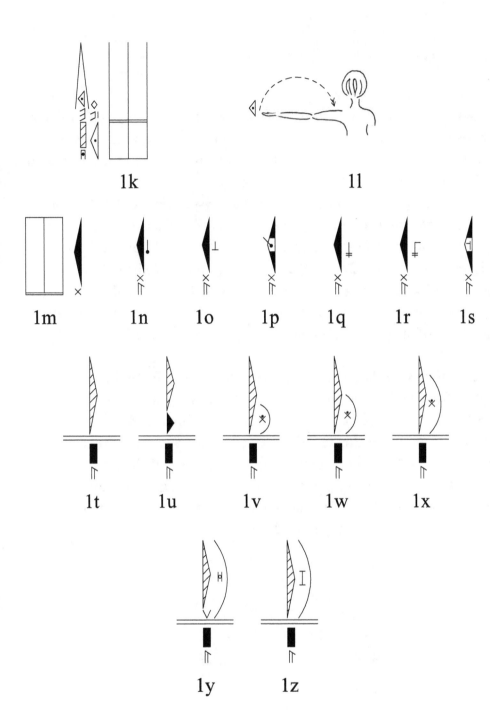

1k

1l

1m   1n   1o   1p   1q   1r   1s

1t   1u   1v   1w   1x

1y   1z

2. Supports, Footwork

2.1. The standard descriptions for level of supports: low, **2a**; middle, **2b;** and high **2c**, can be described in other terms, thereby placing a particular emphasis on one or other aspect, that is, the bent or stretched state of the knees, and the part of the foot supporting. The low level of **2a** is understood to be a *demi plié*, a degree that varies according to the individual's ability. Therefore, degrees of knee bend may need to be specifically stated. From middle level standing, **2b**, the degrees can be indicated using the 8/8 scale; at some point the middle level logically changes to low level. Ex. **2d** shows 1/8-degree knee flexion; **2e** = 1/4; **2f** = 3/8 degree with **2g** being 1/2, illustrated in **2h**. The progression continues with **2i**, **2j**, **2k** and **2l**, the last being totally flexed, shown in **2m**. Note that these stages can also be shown by the levels of the center of gravity, given in *Labanotation* (2005, 365).

2.2. **Focus on Particular Aspects in Standing**. In **2n** the usual transition from a middle level support to half toe is given. In **2o,** focus is on the change to half toe support. The high support with bent knees in **2p** could also be written as **2q,** where degree of flexion and part of foot are featured. The low support on half toe in **2r** contrasts with **2p** which has the awareness of a lifted support, whereas, in **2q** the feeling of lowness prevails despite the use of half toe. The rising to half toe of **2n** could be experienced as the rising of the center of gravity, **2s**.

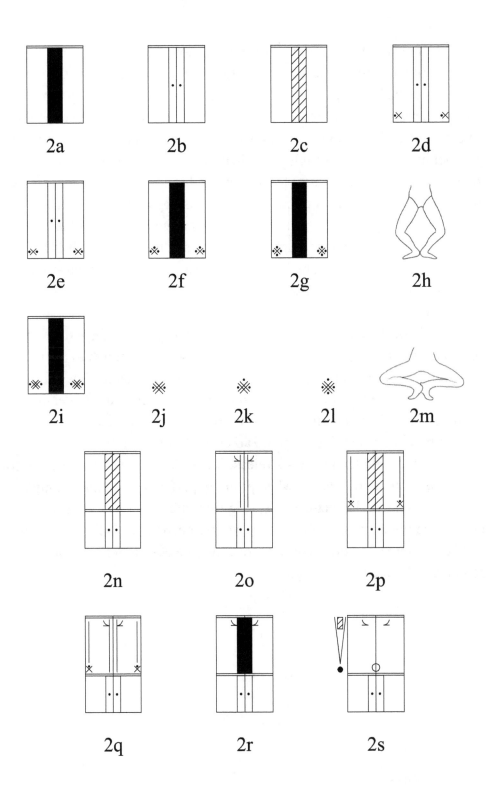

2a

2b

2c

2d

2e

2f

2g

2h

2i

2j

2k

2l

2m

2n

2o

2p

2q

2r

2s

2.3. **Footwork: Focus on Movement**. Note that to state 3rd or 5th
position, only one pin is needed. If one foot is in front, the other will
automatically be behind, two pins, as in **2t**, are not needed. Which pin to
choose can provide an awareness of what is coming next, a link between one
movement and what follows. Ex. **2u** starts in 5th position, the pin shows the
right foot in front; choice of this pin is helpful as it is the right leg that
moves next. For **2v**, the pin for left foot behind is appropriate as the left leg
will be moving. Awareness of both feet in **2w** is appropriate for what
follows as both legs are active as they are also on the landing. In the
assemblé of **2x** focus is on the right leg, whereas at the end of **2y** it is both
legs. In performing beats in ballet, if the beat should be heard then strong
accents should be added, as in **2z**.

2.4. **Foot Articulation**. In **2aa** the legs start parallel, the transition
from contact of the right whole foot on the floor moves through to the toe
and then releases. A similar progression occurs in **2ab**, the legs start turned
out, and the release becomes a stretched forward gesture. Partial weight is
featured in **2ac** where weight on the left foot is released for a moment. This
becomes more of a 'limping' step in **2ad** as the left leg briefly becomes a
gesture and the right leg features a release. The classical ballet *glissade* step
requires much foot articulation when properly performed. In **2ae** a simple
version is provided, the feet just releasing from the floor, very *terre á terre*
(close to the floor), without the over curve rise needed. In **2af** some rising is
indicated, but it is **2ag** that gives a more complete description in which the
stretching of both legs is indicated.

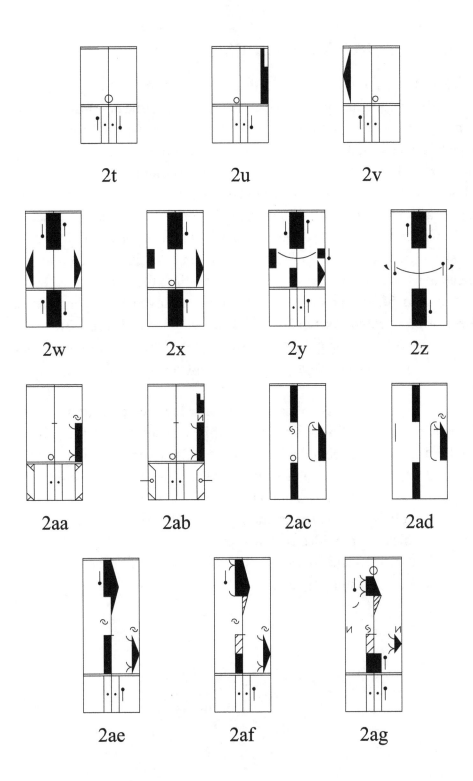

2t 2u 2v

2w 2x 2y 2z

2aa 2ab 2ac 2ad

2ae 2af 2ag

3. *Développé* Variations

3.1. Certain movements may involve some degree of leg flexion before an extension and yet not have the feeling of a true *développé* action. In **3a**, to perform the overcurve of the right leg, on its way to forward low, the path is led by the foot (the extremity); in the process the leg must bend before extending. If the leg is turned out, there is more of a *développé* feeling than if the leg is parallel, as in **3b**. When the leg begins flexed, as in **3c**, then it can be considered a *développé*. By indicating an unfolding, as in **3d**, the reader must assume a previous bend, although none is indicated. This statement could only be a form of shorthand. A slight *développé* is indicated in **3e** as the outward succession leads into the direction. Leading with the knee, **3f**, also provides a similar kind of movement. When the leg is bent before it extends, as in **3g**, a slight *développé* results. Ex. **3h** is similar to **3g** but with the unfolding providing a greater sense of développé. The standard balletic *développé* to middle level is given in **3i**.

3.2. For a *développé* to the side, outward leg rotation is needed. The following examples follow a similar line of investigation but with a different lateral sensation. The sequential movement in **3j** provides a slight *développé*. A slight leg bend in **3k** is followed by a sideward middle extension. Somewhat similar, but with the leg bent side low, is **3l**. A similar example is **3m**, the leg extending from a low *retiré* position, the unfolding indication provides emphasis on that aspect in arriving at side middle. The standard side *développé* is **3n**. In several of these examples the sense of unfolding is missing, e.g., **3g, 3l**.

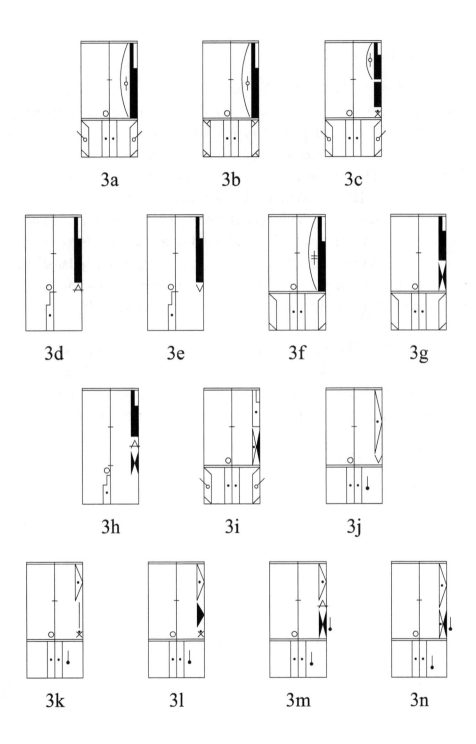

3a 3b 3c

3d 3e 3f 3g

3h 3i 3j

3k 3l 3m 3n

4. Shape Retention

4.1. A shape that is made by parts of the body or the body-as-a -whole may need to be retained. In the sequence of **4a**, the shape made by the legs in a wide low 2nd position is to be retained during the travelling jumps that follow. The statement of retaining the shape for the legs is written in an addition bracket beside the starting position and is indicated to be held until the 'away' cancellation sign at the end. Alternately the addition bracket could be extended during the length of the sequence, as indicated in **4b**, whichever is more practical. The small hold sign is distinguished from a circular shape as the latter is much larger. A high sagittal angular shape of the arms is to be retained during the forward and backward whole torso tilts in **4c**. Here again, a longer addition bracket could be used, **4d**.

4.2. A low whole torso swing is written in **4e**, the overhead arm position to be retained throughout. Here the shape retention is indicated at the start of the movement rather than in the starting position. Note the small horizontal bow connecting the rotation sign to the torso column.

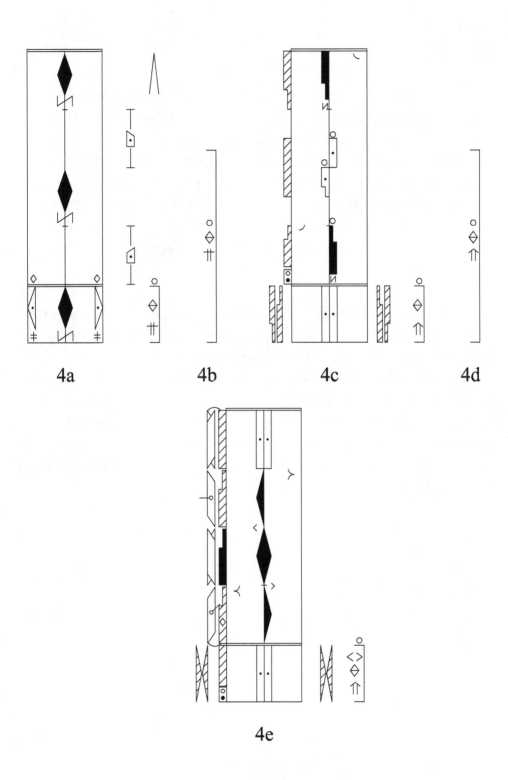

4a   4b   4c   4d

4e

5. Major Deviations

5.1. In the choice of movement description, the two deviation examples given here are worth considering. In swinging the arms around the body at low level as in **5a**, the low-level change in arm directions may not be the intention of the movement. Yet use of black pins, **5b**, seems inappropriate. Use of small blank direction symbols, as in **5c** may be the answer. A blank symbol indicates a direction to be passed through where the level is not clear and need not be stated; **5d** is a typical example. In **5e,** from diagonal high, the arm deviates close to the central body column on its way to diagonal low.

5.2. In **5f**, two things are happening at the same time. As the arm extends forward, three successions occur, each deviating horizontally from side to side, as indicated by the middle level pins. At the start of the notation the wrist is facing side middle. When palm facing directions change, wrist facing is a more practical statement. With the change to downward and upward wrist deviations (wrist bulging), **5g,** the wrist facing down description facilitates the movement. In **5h**, deviations for the lower arm are shown. Equally for **5i**, the wrist facing up is more appropriate for the repeated wrist bulging deviations.

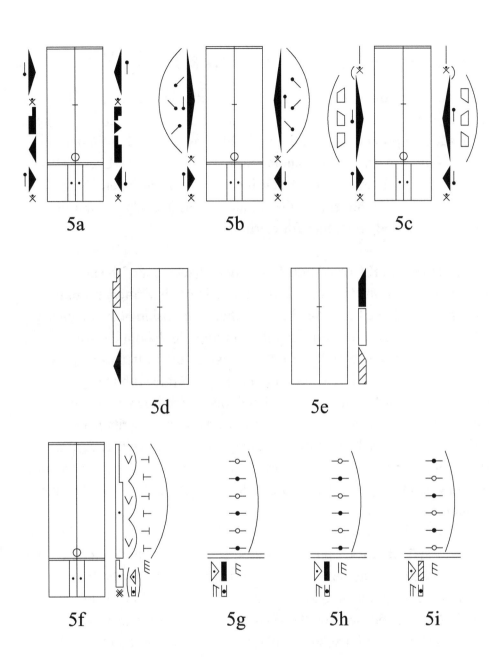

5a   5b   5c

5d   5e

5f   5g   5h   5i

6. Gestures – Direction from a Body Part

Identifying a direction according to its relationship to a part of the body, known as DBP, was adopted as a valuable device in determining the directions for supports when on all fours. This was explored in *Floorwork, Basic Acrobatics*, Advanced Labanotation, issue 6, section 8. Use of DBP for gestures is now being explored, starting with the arms, where there is the greater need. Several movement disciplines such as T'ai Chi, pantomime and ballet need a body reference for clarity.

6.1. **Horizontal Directional Reference**. Placement of the arm extremity in front of the breastbone, illustrated in **6a,** is written as **6b**, the sign for the breastbone being **6c**. In ballet this relationship occurs with a rounded arm, not indicated here. In the Bournonville School the arm extremity can be in line with the front of the waist, **6d** written as **6e**. An arabesque line is often described as the fingertips in line with the eyes, **6f**, written as **6g**. The arm extremity, the hand, may be in line with the hip, **6h** and **6i**. In sitting, the arm may be sideward of the foot, **6j** written as **6k**. Standing with the knee bent in front, **6l**, may have the arm extremity, the hand, in front of the knee, **6m**. This arm position could be described in other terms, but when focus is on the relationship to the knee, this should be the description.

6.2. **Vertical and Other Directional References**. Indication of the 'above' and 'below' may be needed. In **6n** the hand (arm extremity) is above the knee, as shown in **6o**. Similarly, the hand is below the knee in **6p** and **6q**. In **6r** the hand starts on the knee, the arm then rises to a forward high relationship to the knee, **6s**. Similarly, in **6t**, from hand on knee, the arm rises to side high of the knee, **6u**. The lady standing in **6v**, grasping the sides of her skirt, then leans forward, **6w**, with the edges of the skirt now being forward low of the hips, **6x**.

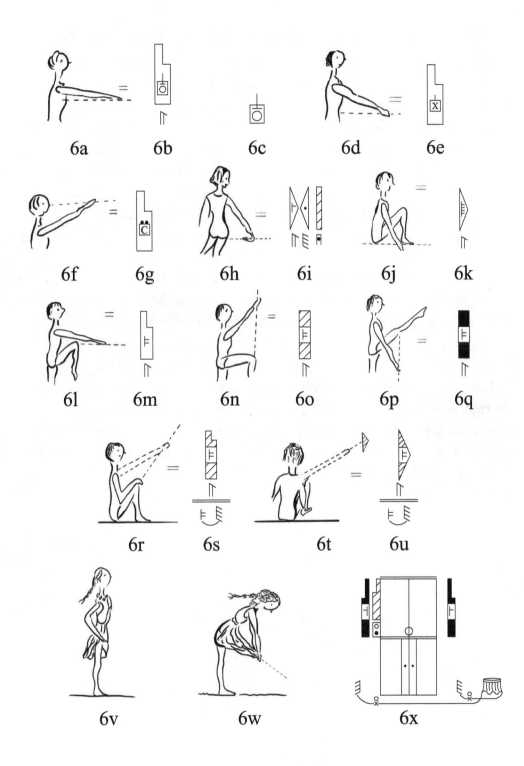

6a   6b   6c   6d   6e

6f   6g   6h   6i   6j   6k

6l   6m   6n   6o   6p   6q

6r   6s   6t   6u

6v   6w   6x

6.3. **Distance for DBP Statements**. Before resorting to specific statements of distance, the degree of flexion in the limb often gives a satisfactory indication. The illustration of **6y** shows the hand in front of the eyes, with the arm bent to different degrees. In **6z** the arm is bent to 90°, as written in **6aa**. Ex **6ab** states that the arm is sideward middle of the hip. If the limb does not bend there is no leeway regarding distance of the extremity to the point of reference, **6ac**. Through bending, contracting, folding, the hand hip relationship can be maintained, and the distance established, **6ad**. For the hand above the knee, **6ae** the distance is established by the degree of arm bend, **6af**.

6.4. **Place Directional Reference**. Use of place as a direction means that the extremity of the limb is at, for example, or very close to, the stated body part. Thus, **6ag** could be expressed as **6ah**, or **6ai** when placed on a staff. Ex. **6aj**, the right arm extremity at the left hip, would be written as **6ak** on a staff. The arms (hands) at the opposite shoulders, **6al**, the right arm in front, is illustrated in **6am**. Both arms are in place at the center of the chest, **6an**, the right hand in front is depicted in **6ao**. Next the position of **6ap** is illustrated in **6aq**, again the right arm is in front. The everyday gesture of **6ar** starts with the hands touching the head, the temples, in expressing "Oh God!" The performer tilts the head backward, the hands opening diagonally from the temples.

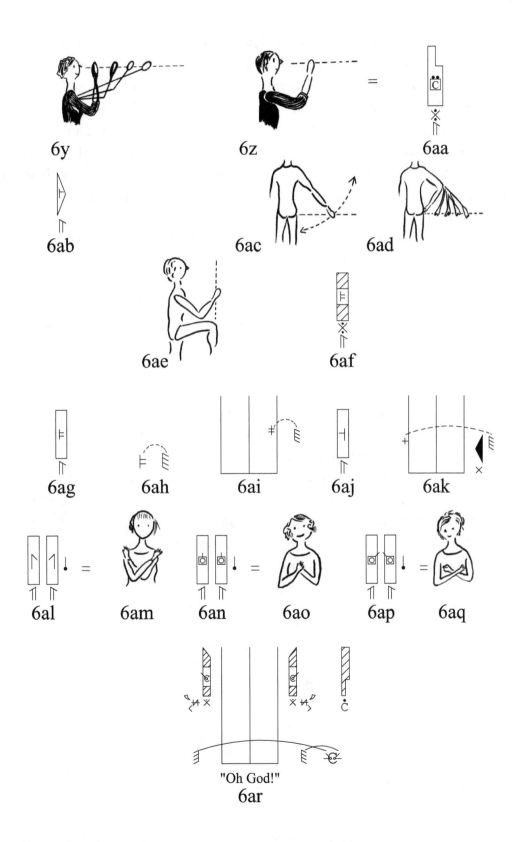

6y

6z

6aa

6ab

6ac

6ad

6ae

6af

6ag

6ah

6ai

6aj

6ak

6al

6am

6an

6ao

6ap

6aq

"Oh God!"

6ar

6.5. **Space Measurement Signs**. By using the diamond representing space, distance can be shown with space measurement signs, **6as** shows the range from very wide (far) to very near. These signs have been used to modify the size of a movement. Here they are used when focus is on the spatial distance rather than the flexed or stretched state of the arm. These spatial distance symbols can be used as pre-signs before a DBP direction symbol to indicate the distance from point to point. In **6at** the hands start on the knees. When landing in a small 2nd position, the arms move sideward of the knees, a little distance beyond the knees. Because computer symbols can be rather small, an enlarged symbol can be drawn at the side in an addition bracket, as in **6au**.

6.6. In the swaying steps of **6av**, the right hand relates to the right hip, starting very close to the hip; the normal sideward relationship to the hip is understood, no position pin has been used. On the step to the right, the hand moves slightly away from the hip, then returns to its place relationship. As the hip lifts, the arm moves to the side high relationship to the hip, slightly farther away, before returning to the hip. In these movements the arm is bent, but the degree of bending is not stated, it is unimportant. The left hand relates to the left hip in **6aw**; as the step forward increases in size, so does the forward movement of the left hip and the distance of left hand to left hip increases until each returns to place, the normal situation. The "Getting bigger and bigger" pantomime of **6ax** starts with an extended belly with the arms (hands) in front of it. During the staggering walk, the chest bends backward, and the arms move diagonally away from the belly.

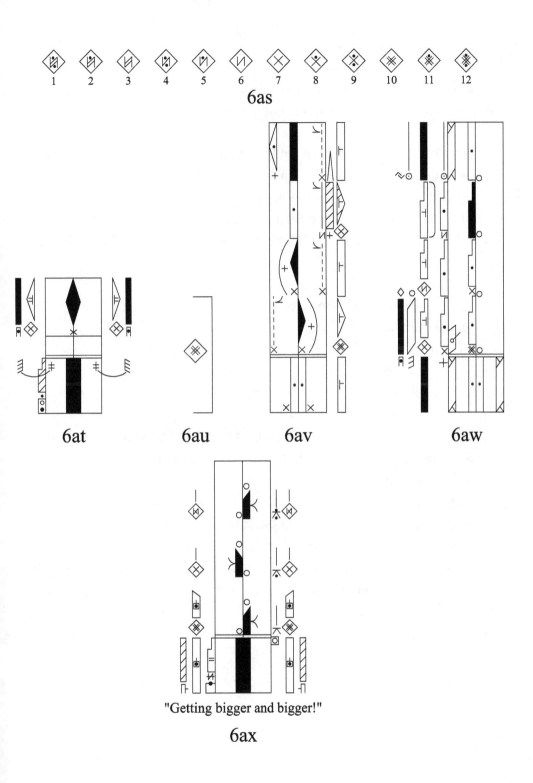

6as

6at   6au   6av   6aw

"Getting bigger and bigger!"

6ax

7. Whole Body Signs

Basic signs for the body-as-a-whole and its general sections have been found useful when, specific detail is not needed.

7.1. The three-line staff, **7a**, had been used to indicate the body-as-a-whole. The indication of **7b**, based on the figure 8 representing the torso combined with a circle representing body aspects was found more applicable to mean the body-as-a-whole. In this series, **7c** indicates the upper and lower body halves, with **7d** being the upper half and **7e** the lower half.

7.2. Ex. **7f** divides the body vertically into right and left sides; **7g** represents the right half of the body, with **7h** being the left half. The upper right quadrant is **7i**; **7j** being the upper left; **7k** the lower right and **7l** the lower left. Cross lateral is shown as **7m**, with **7n** being the right cross lateral and **7o** being the left.

7.3. The more specific signs used by specialists in Laban Movement Analysis (LMA) also represented here, express specific forms of connectivity: **7p**, breath; **7q**, core-distal (naval radiation); **7r**, head-tail (spinal); **7s** upper-lower (homologous); **7t**, body-half (homolateral); **7u** cross lateral (contra lateral). In her book *Making Connections - Total Body Integration Through Bartenieff Fundamentals* (1998), Peggy Hackney explains each of these symbols in great detail. She also provides charts with revealing explanations on physical awareness and practical application for each.

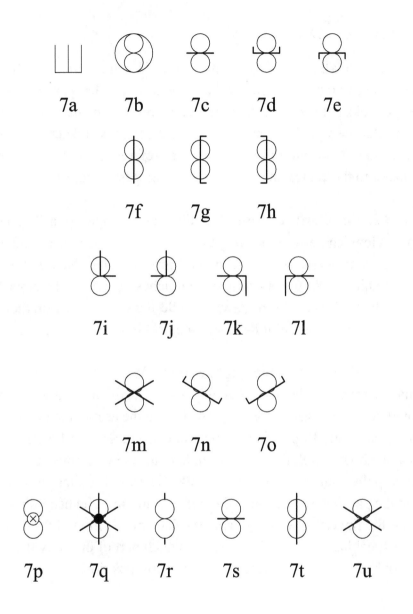

7a   7b   7c   7d   7e

7f   7g   7h

7i   7j   7k   7l

7m   7n   7o

7p   7q   7r   7s   7t   7u

8. Limb Extremity

8.1. **Relation to Body Center Line**. When a limb, in particular an arm, relates to the center line of the body, or to another part or to an object, the eye looks at the end of the limb, the extremity, the part that is involved in the relationship. The configuration of the limb will determine what will be considered the extremity. The point of reference will be that part which is closest to the center line or to a designated part or object.

8.2. **Leg Gesture Examples**. First are examples of an extended forward low leg gesture touching the floor. In **8a** it is understood that the right toe contacts the floor in its natural forward direction, i.e., forward of the right hip. In **8b** the out-turned leg touches in front of the other foot. For **8c** it is the heel that is in front, while in **8d** the knee will be on the center line. The configuration of **8e** places the heel in front of the other leg.

8.3. **Extremity Touching the Body**. When the arm hangs down, **8f**, it may be touching the body, but, when specifically needed, such contact should be stated, **8g**, the contact bow linking the arm to the body column, illustrated in **8h**. Depending on the arm configuration, different parts may touch the body. In **8i** the arm is rounded thus the fingertips are touching; this is spelled out in **8j,** illustrated in **8k**. The wrist folding of **8l** makes the wrist the part that would touch the body, as in **8m**. The hand direction of **8n** means the fingertips would touch, **8o**. The arm position of **8p** results in the elbow touching the body, **8q**. Exactly which part of the body that is touched has not been indicated, it results from the arm position.

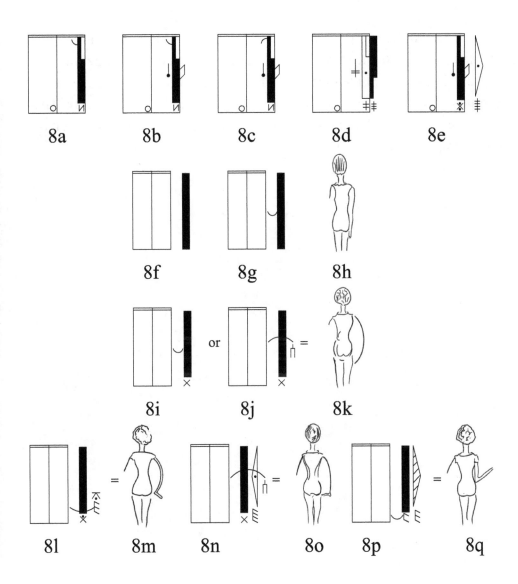

8a   8b   8c   8d   8e

8f   8g   8h

8i   or   8j   8k   =

8l   =   8m   8n   =   8o   8p   =   8q

8.4. **Relationship to Center Tracks**. Track pins are used in these next examples. In **8r** the insides of the wrists are next to the centre line, illustrated in **8s**. For **8t** the elbows are forward, next to the centre line, illustrated in **8u**. If the elbows were touching it could be written as **8v**. The position of **8w** is off centre, the wrist contact is off to the left in the track of the left arm, illustrated in **8x**.

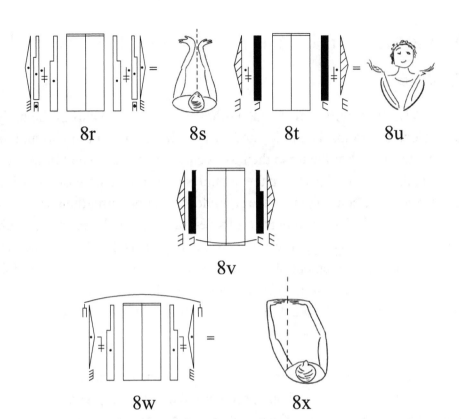

8r   8s   8t   8u

8v

8w   8x

9. Central and Peripheral Use of Body and Space

9.1. **Physically Central**, **Peripheral**. The central part of the body as a whole is the torso. The torso, and each limb, has its central part and its peripheral part. For the torso the most central part is the naval or the solar plexus; its peripheral parts are the shoulder line and the base of the spine. For the arm the central part is the shoulder and upper arm, the peripheral part is the hand. Each segment has its central (proximal) part and peripheral (distal) part. For the upper arm the peripheral part is the elbow; when that is the focus of the movement, the lower arm and hand are passive, out of the way. For the lower arm the elbow is the central part, wrist or hand the peripheral part. For the hand, the wrist the base of the hand is the central part and the fingertips the most peripheral part.

9.2. Similarly, but with less ability to articulate, the leg and its segments have their central and peripheral parts. The hip and thigh are the central part, the toes being the peripheral part. Movements of the lower leg are more peripheral than the thigh. The ankle is the central part of the foot with the toes the peripheral part. Movement exploration will reveal the degree to which an action can be relatively or markedly central or peripheral. In many instances a movement may start and remain central or may originate centrally and flow out.

9.3. **Spatially Central**, **Peripheral**. Movement within the kinesphere is spatially central when it is in the area close to the body, the torso. Imagine a vertical column around the upright torso, a column within which spatially central movements take place. In the upward direction, movements beyond the head would be emerging into the peripheral area. Peripheral space is at or near the extremity of the kinesphere. Note the following affinities: central parts of the body move more comfortably in central space. Equally the physical extremities are often involved with movement in peripheral space. The balletic use of arms and legs are good examples of this. However, the extremities, particularly the arms, often make use of central space. Equally possible is central use of the arms in peripheral space, this may occur with accompanying central torso movements.

9.4. **Indication of Physically Central, Peripheral.** The circle has been used to indicate body aspects, **9a**. In **9b** an area within the body is shown, while **9c** is the repetition sign for physical lateral symmetry. For general indications of physically central or peripheral only a half-circle is used, **9d**. A tick pointing inward toward the center indicates physically central, **9e**. The tick pointing outward states physically peripheral, **9f**. A partial arrow sign pointing outward, as in **9g**, indicates a transition from central to peripheral. Similarly, the partial arrow sign pointing inward states transitions from peripheral to central, **9h**.

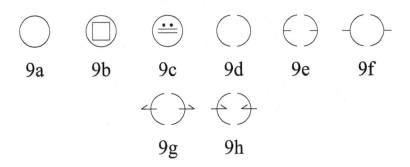

9a   9b   9c   9d   9e   9f

9g   9h

9.5. **Indication of Spatially Central, Peripheral**. The established sign for spatial aspects, the diamond, **9i**, provides the basis for symbols stating spatially central or peripheral. This diamond is best known as a space hold but is also used to indicate spatial size of a movement, as in **9j** (small size) and **9k** (large size). On occasion the diamond is used for a repeat sign indicating spatial lateral symmetry should take place, i.e., without an exchange of right and left sides of body, **9l**. Only half of the diamond is used to indicate spatially central or peripheral aspects, **9m**. The inward tick, **9n** shows spatially central while the outward tick, **9o**, shows spatially peripheral. Transition from central to peripheral is shown in **9p** and the reverse, peripheral to central is written as **9q**.

9.6. **General Movement Statements**. These signs for manner of performance can be explored with statements of 'an action'. In **9r** a physically central movement is featured, while in **9s** it is a physically peripheral action. Four physically central actions occur in **9t**, this could be written as **9u**. The three actions in **9v** are performed physically peripherally.

9.7. Specific directions are given for the left arm in **9w**, the manner of performance is physically central, an appropriate manner for these directions. In the next three examples the same spatially peripheral path is shown to be performed physically central in **9x**, physically peripheral in **9y**, and in **9z** as moving from physically central to peripheral, a comfortable manner for this space pattern.

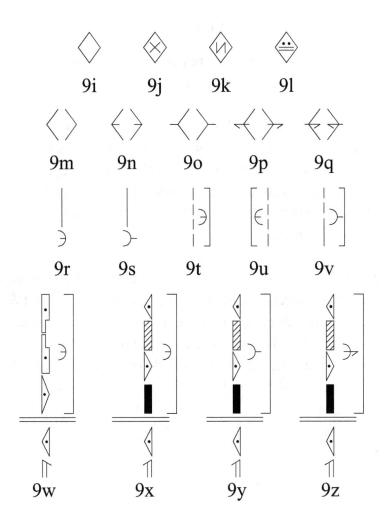

9i   9j   9k   9l

9m   9n   9o   9p   9q

9r   9s   9t   9u   9v

9w   9x   9y   9z

10. Floor Plans Prevail

10.1. When there is a discrepancy between what is spelled out in the notation and what is indicated on the floor plan, it is wise to follow the floor plan. The plan may indicate a shallow diagonal path or part of a circle which requires a more intricate description in movement terms. The following is a typical example. In **10a**, the notation indicates a straight path, but the floor plan, **10b**, indicates that dancer D enters using a curved path. By following the floor plan, the notator avoids having to spell out subtle directions for the dancer's steps or the degree of curve and a possible change of Front, the facing direction.

10.2. Through use of mini floor plans within a score, the changes in relationship of two dancers can be indicated. In **10c** the woman (W) is on the man's left. With a three step turn she moves in front of him to the other side. The notation given is quite simple, but if done literally she would bump into her partner; she has to take slightly different directions for the steps to pass in front of the man (M) and end at his right side. By an appropriate small floor plan, such as shown in **10d**, this can be clearly indicated. Dancers will adjust and do the right thing.

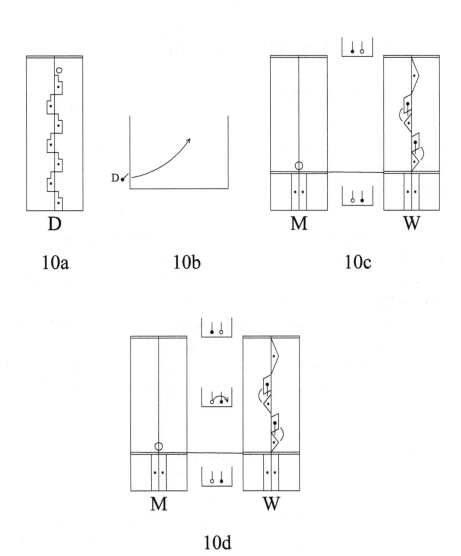

10a   10b   10c

10d

Chapter 7. Performance Details

1. Timing of a Step

The simple indication of a step, a direction symbol in the support column, can contain important information depending on what came before or what followed. It would seem of value to investigate this in depth, starting with the specific timing indication.

1.1. **Time Unit**. In marking off the vertical units of time, it is not the horizontal bar line or the 'tick' marks that show the beat, the count of 1, 2, 3, etc. These horizontal signs are dividers, the moment of the beat comes **just after** the bar line or tick mark. A small amount of space on the page has to exist to represent visually that moment, that time unit at the start of the beat, **1a**. Thus, for example, a foot hook, **1b**, or the endings of a contact bow which show the moment of contact, **1c**, need to be placed in this small area. This fact, long agreed upon, has not been clearly explained in the editions of *Labanotation*.

1.2. The count numbers should appear just above the bar line or count mark, **1d**, not before it or on it. The subdivisions of a beat: 1 y & u 2 y & u 3, etc., are presented clearly in *Labanotation* (2005, 33). The count itself – 1, 2, 3, etc., is at the start; the next division is termed 'y', pronounced 'ee', as in 'any'; the half-way point is 'and', shown as &; the last division is 'u', pronounced as in 'up'. Speaking these subdivisions and using them in scores can be very helpful.

1.3. **The Meaning of a Step Symbol**. Let us go over again what the symbol of **1e** represents. The base of the direction symbol represents (and must represent) the moment the foot contacts the floor, **1f**. This is true whatever the part of foot it might be. For the tap dancer, that is the moment the tap sound is heard, i.e., on the beat. The end of the direction symbol indicates the arrival in **1g** because this step is followed by a hold. The meaning of the end of the symbol always depends on what is coming next.

Timing of a Step

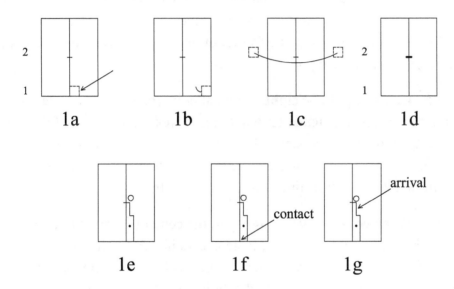

1a 1b 1c 1d

1e 1f 1g

contact

arrival

1.4. For purposes of analysis, we will spell out the unwritten but understood preparation for a step. Before a travelling step takes place, the weight is shifted to one foot. The moving leg then advances into the appropriate direction in preparation for taking weight. When nothing is written, this is understood to occur at the end of the starting position, **1h**. This gesture can be indicated by an action stroke, **1i**; note the weight is retained on the left foot while the right leg gestures. By using a zed caret, **1j**, the gesture is linked to the step. At the same time, the center of gravity (CG) moves beyond centered balance toward the new support, **1k**. This CG displacement is cancelled as the step takes place, note use here of the 'away' sign. During the step, the CG is automatically carried forward until centered over the new support.

1.5. **Centering the Weight**. At what point the weight is centered over the new support **depends on what comes next**. At the end of a **concluding step**, an arrival step, when no further transference of weight occurs, the center of weight is understood to be over the new support at the end of the symbol, the last 'time unit', as seen in **1g**.

1.6. When **consecutive steps** occur, the center of weight is always moving into the direction of the next step, as indicated by the 'p' for preparation, **1l**, and **1m**. The moment of the CG being centered occurs briefly before its displacement into the direction of the next step. **Exactly where this point of balance occurs will depend on a) the speed and b) the style of the movement**.
Because it is a passing event, it has not seemed important to pin the timing down precisely. In the case of fast, swaying steps, **1n**, the weight may never be centered over one foot, there is no time to produce full transferences of weight, it will be somewhere between the two feet. With the slower steps and throwing the torso weight from side to side, as in **1o**, a moment of being centered above the supporting base can be achieved.

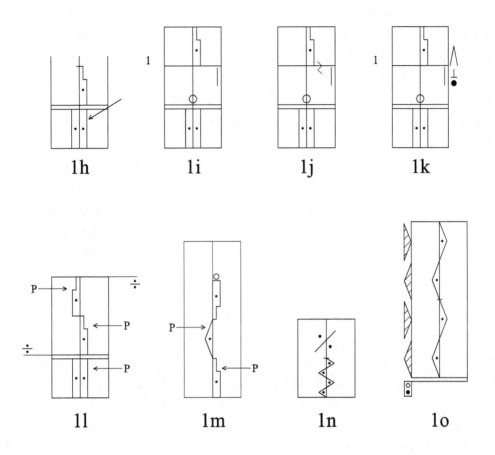

1h   1i   1j   1k

1l   1m   1n   1o

1.7. **Arrival Steps**. The ending of the step, the moment of arrival at center, can be featured in the style of walking. If there is a pause following the end of the step, it can seem abrupt, self-asserting, possibly even menacing. A good example of arrival steps is the formal step pattern at the opening of the Capulet ball in the Bolshoi Ballet production of *Romeo and Juliet*. The start of the step happens in passing, it is not emphasized, however the arrival is strong. Such timing for a step is less usual and so is not explained to beginners. Ex. **1p** shows the arrival step concluding on count 1; it began on the last count of the previous measure. This moment of arrival might be marked by the statement of centered weight, **1q**. In performing the movement, the arrival may be given an accent, **1r**, or an indication that the arrival is to be emphasized, **1s**. The above indicate the range available in Labanotation to indicate subtleties in movement performance.

1.8. **Arm Coordination in Walking**. The natural contra-lateral arm movements when walking is usually written as **1t**. This simple notation usually produces the desired movement, i.e., the natural arm swing on each step. In the notation of **1u**, the arms arrive at the beginning of each step. If the actions were extremely staccato, as in **1v**, then visually, the arm and leg placements are very clear. But when such abruptness is not wanted, the arms should use the natural swing and hence duration is needed. The notation of **1v** can be quickly modified to show duration by the addition of duration lines to the arm symbols, as in **1w**, showing where the action starts, thus providing "lollipop" symbols in which the duration line **must** be linked to the symbol that follows. Correctly notated it should be written as **1u**.

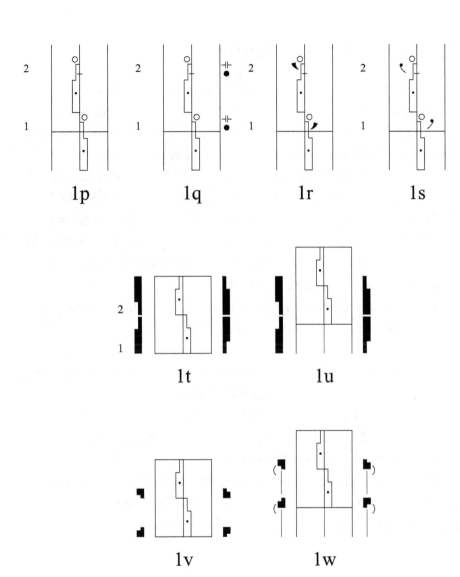

2. Timing of Palm Facing

2.1. For a forward arm gesture with the palm facing down, it is easy
to write the palm indication near the start of the movement, **2a**, but if this is
interpreted literally, what would happen to the angle at the wrist during the
rest of the gesture? Does it remain? Does the palm end facing forward low?
The rule is that **palm facing indications are valid for the duration of the
direction symbol next to which they are placed** (*Labanotation* 2005,
111). In **2b** there is no question, the palm gradually changes to facing
down. In **2c** the palm change occurs halfway through the gesture. Breaking
the gesture into two parts, as in **2d**, the automatic cancellation rule will
result in the palm returning to its standard sideward facing direction for the
second part. In **2e** a body hold sign results in the palm ending facing down.
In **2f** a space hold is used to retain the palm facing down.

2.2. Although we are accustomed to thinking in terms of palm facing,
a thumb facing indication can be more practical, especially in sagittal
gestures. At the start of **2g**, the thumb edge faces sideward, it will still be
facing side at the end of the movement, there is no need for a retention sign.
If a retention sign is needed, as shown in **2h**, it can be a body hold or a
space hold, the same movement will result. With the arm starting up, place
high, **2i**, the thumb edge is facing backward. That direction can be repeated
for the gesture ending side middle, but it is better to use a space hold, as
in **2j**.

Palm Facing

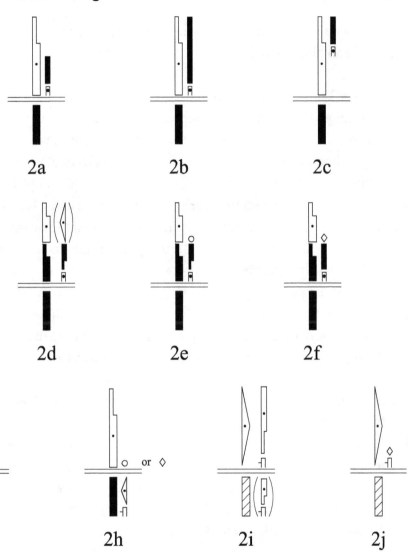

2a   2b   2c

2d   2e   2f

2g   2h   2i   2j

3. Styles of Walking

The manner of stepping, of walking, can vary according to the use of the legs, hips and also torso and arms.

3.1. **Part Leading into a Step**. In ordinary walking, **3a**, the performer is not aware of any particular 'performance', the aim usually is just to get somewhere. The performance of a step with hip leading, as in **3b**, may depend on the state of leg rotation. The hip articulation with parallel rotation, **3c**, is different from a step where turn-out is used, **3d**; here leading is more from the groin. Leading with the pelvis, as in **3e**, would be renewed with each step. By contrast, the use of a constant forward shift of the pelvis and steps on the center line, **3f**, is typical of the fashion model showing off the latest creations on the catwalk. Leading with the forward diagonal edge of the pelvis, **3g**, causes a slight pelvic rotation with a slight inward rotation of the leg, an awkward gait. For all these, the matter of timing can be important, the leading action occurring only at the start of the step and being cancelled halfway through the weight transference, **3h**.

3.2. Leading each step with the knee, **3i**, can be seen on the street, as also leading with the thigh, **3j**. Leading with the ankle, **3k**, may be more specifically the front surface of the ankle, **3l**. Leading with the foot, **3m**, may more specifically be the front of the foot, the instep, **3n**. On stage, the ballet walk leads with the toes in the preparatory leg gesture, **3o**, and then transfers from the pad of the toe to the whole foot, **3p**. Off stage ballerinas are seen to walk flat-footed, a waddle, as in **3q**.

Styles of Walking

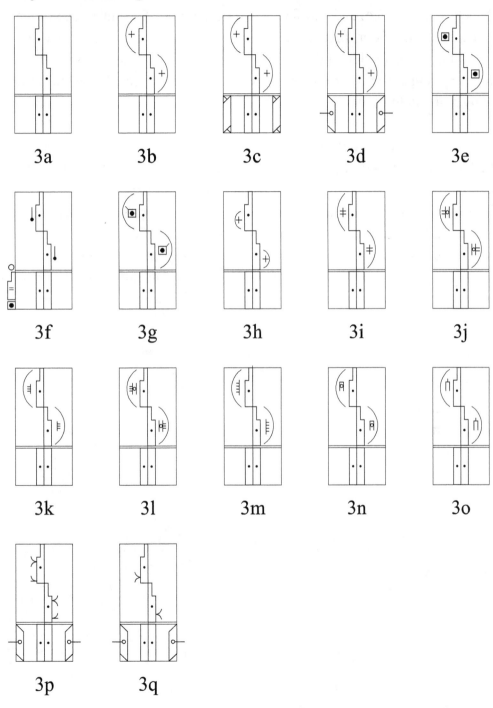

3a   3b   3c   3d   3e

3f   3g   3h   3i   3j

3k   3l   3m   3n   3o

3p   3q

3.3. The following example of a cowboy walk, **3r**, uses diagonal steps (a wider stance) and a different part of the foot. The outer edge of the foot contacts the floor, first in high level and then transfers to middle level. Thus, it is the outer side of the ball of the foot (toes) that first contacts the floor, moving to the outer border of the whole foot. Imagine being stiff after many hours in the saddle.

3.4. The following variations on a jazz walk include focus on keeping the level of the center of gravity even, thus eliminating the natural slight rise and fall that occurs in walking. Ex. **3s** indicates retention of the level of the CG together with use of parts of the foot and level changes. Similar, but with a different timing is **3t**. Note the retention of the CG level will later need to be specifically cancelled. In **3u**, there is hip inclusion and swivelling on the supporting foot as the leg rotates outward. Note the 'x' in the support column showing that the leg gesture is near the floor. Ex. **3v** is attributed to Carol Haney.

Variations in a jazz walk

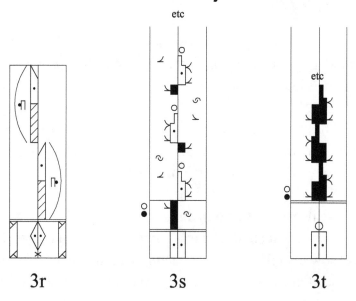

3r   3s   3t

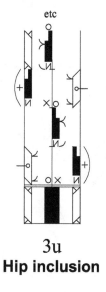

3u
Hip inclusion

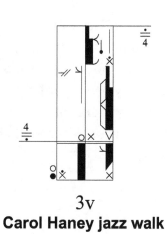

3v
Carol Haney jazz walk

4. Breathing

4.1. Breathing is analyzed and written as a movement of the lungs. The sign for the lungs is the inside of the chest, **4a**. It describes the moveable part within the chest.

4.2. The basic sign for inhaling is an increase sign, **4b**. Exhaling is expressed as **4c**. In **4d** and **4e** three-dimensional expanding and contracting are specified for breathing in and breathing out.

4.3. **Lateral, Sagittal Expansion**. The signs for spreading and closing can express what should be experienced. In **4f** inhaling with lateral expansion is shown, while **4g** states exhaling with lateral closing in. Inhaling with sagittal expansion, **4h**, might more appropriately be written as **4i**, the expansion being specifically forward, this being shown by thickening the forward part of the symbol. Vertical expansion and contraction are based on the indication for 'above and below', **4j**; thus, **4k** is spreading vertically and **4l** is vertical closing in.

4.4. **Regions of Breathing**. A certain region for breathing may be designated. Breathing 'into the belly' is written as **4m**, using the sign for the moveable part of the pelvis. Although three-dimensional breathing is shown, it will mainly be forward with the diagonal and sideward areas also involved. Breathing with expansion in the chest is shown in **4n,** the moveable part; when both sides are to be expanded while breathing, then **4o** would be written.

Breathing

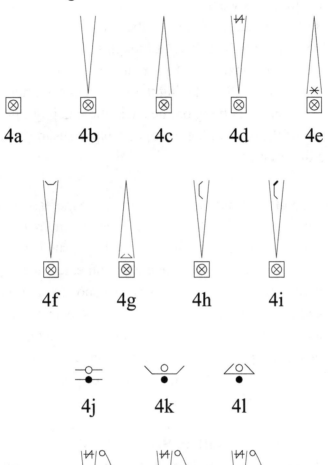

4.5. **Combined Movements**. Even if breathing is analyzed as a movement of the lungs, as we have seen, it can also entail movements of moveable parts of the trunk, in particular the chest. Ex. **4p** indicates a contraction of the chest on the exhale as though squeezing the air out of the lungs. The result of the inhaling in **4q** is that the front of the chest is expanded three-dimensionally. Having the arms backward helps focus on this expansion. In **4r,** while lying on the back, the inhaling can result in a lateral expansion of the back of the torso; this expresses the idea of 'breathing into the back'.

4.6. **Timing of Breathing**. The length of the increase and decrease signs indicate the duration. Ex. **4s** indicates quick in and out breathing, while **4t** shows a slow intake of breath followed by a sudden forceful exhale. In a score where time spans have been indicated, the appropriate length can be given. If the timing of a particular movement is connected with inhaling and exhaling, those indications can be placed to the left of the staff taking the place of counts and measure numbers. In **4u** the demi-plié occurs while inhaling, and the return to normal standing occurs during exhaling. If freedom in timing is desired, the Time Sign for 'no indication of timing', **4v**, can be used.

4.7. **Use of Nose or Mouth in Breathing**. Many breathing exercises specify when the breathing should be through the nose, **4w**, or the mouth, **4x**. For speed writing, these signs can be simplified to **4y**. Inhaling through the nose is shown in **4z** and exhaling through the mouth in **4aa**.

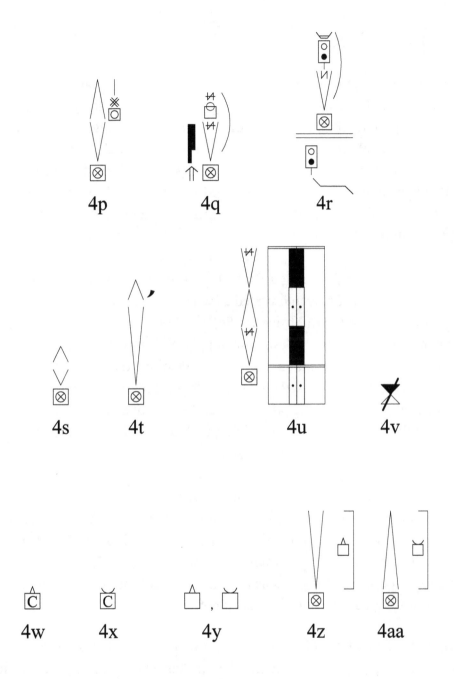

4p 4q 4r

4s 4t 4u 4v

4w 4x 4y 4z 4aa

5. Focus

In a dance, the movements can be accompanied by an expression of inner or outer focus on the part of the performer. Outer focus is typical when the performer engages with the audience, looking at them, perhaps smiling, certainly relating with them. In his abstract ballets, George Balanchine wanted his dancers to be facially expressionless, concentrating only on the movements, never 'playing to the audience'. In certain Asian dance forms, the performer has an inner focus, the facial expression, the eyes being focused inward.

5.1. **Looking, Facing a Direction**. A direction given for the front of the head, the face, **5a**, is interpreted as where the person is looking, e.g., forward for **5b**, to the right side for **5c**, etc. Looking far into the distance is shown in **5d**. Specific 'looking', gazing, is shown by the eyes without involvements of the head, **5e**, these may be looking diagonally to the left, **5f**. The eyes can be focused on a particular object, or they may be unfocused, in a non-seeing way, as when looking at a complex design on a page to find the three-dimensional picture hidden within. The question of focus is related more to the focus of the eyes.

5.2. **Point of Interest**. The indication of inner and outer focus is related to the concept of the Point of Interest, thus the symbol of **5g** is used. Ex. **5h** indicates outward focus, with **5i** being inward focus. The degree of focus, the intensity, can be expressed by distance signs, **5j** being very far and **5k**, very near. This gives us a distant outward focus, **5l**; and **5m**, a very near inward focus, deep inner concentration.

5.3. **Duration of Focus**. An inward or outward focus may appear briefly during a dance or be established for the whole dance. The addition bracket can show the timing. In **5n** a marked distant outward focus accompanies the arm gesture; as the feet close and the arm lowers, the focus is over.

At the start of **5o**, the inward focus is shown to be maintained for the whole dance. Cancellation can be shown with the back-to-normal sign, **5p**, or the 'away' sign, **5q**.

Focus

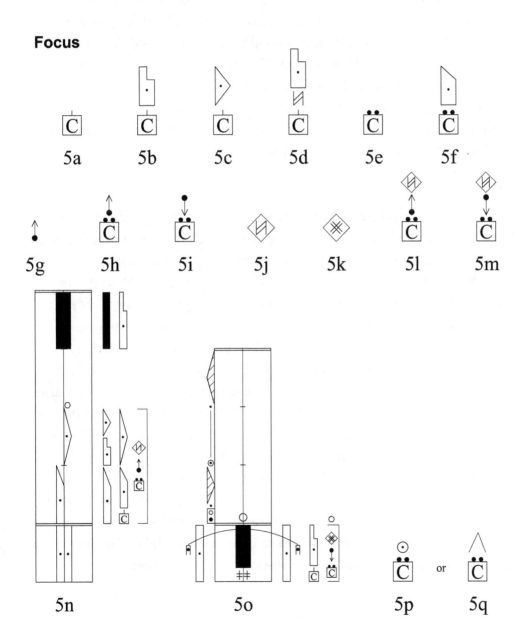

Chapter 8. Path Variations

1. Revolving on a Path

1.1. Revolving on a Straight Path. Revolving around oneself while traveling on a straight path is written as **1a**. Historically this movement was written as **1b** (see Knust 1956); it was called a "straightened out curved path", the idea being that the amount of turning (change of Front) that would have happened on the curved path is happening on a straight path. This seemed a clumsy explanation when no circular path was involved. Thus, the symbol of **1a** was adopted. When such revolving occurred on a circular path, **1c**, the instruction is clear; the old usage of **1d** was seen as confusing.

1.2. Swivel or Non-swivel Steps. In walking a large circle, **1e**, the feet are naturally placed on the curving line of the circle and on each step a slight blind turn (non-swivelling) takes place. With a very small circle, **1f**, some swivelling will naturally occur. If no swivelling should occur, then the space hold sign is placed alongside each turn sign, as in **1g**, indicating what we term a 'blind turn'. In this example, if one started with parallel feet, the blind turn would result in a marked inward twist for the right leg. In ballroom dance such blind turns are preceded by the appropriate degree of leg rotation as each step is taken so that the blind turn that follows causes the leg smoothly to return to parallel, as indicated in **1h**. Revolving on a straight path without swivelling can be shown as **1i** or the simpler **1j**, one space hold being enough. If, specifically, each step should swivel, it is written as in **1k**, the heel barely lifted off the floor. More specific foot hooks can be indicated. Placed on the path sign, the indication would be **1l**, or the simpler **1m**. Note: the term "a turn with friction" was discarded because the word friction can refer to static friction or sliding friction; therefore, the terms **'swivel'** and **'non-swivel'** were adopted.

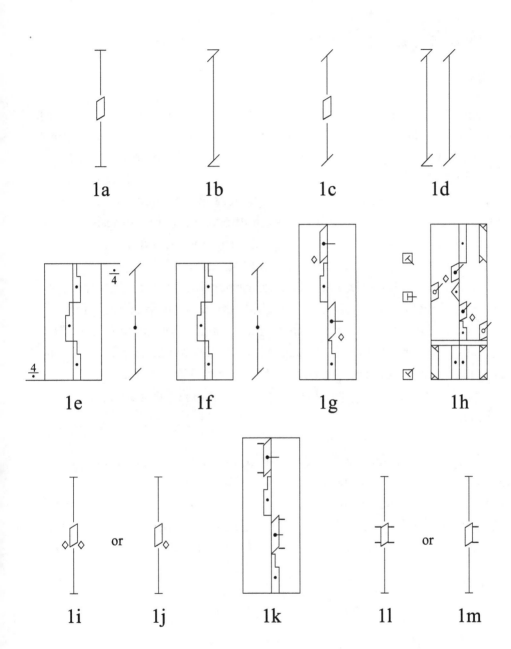

1a   1b   1c   1d

1e   1f   1g   1h

1i   or   1j   1k   1l   or   1m

2. Walking a Circle Without Change of Front

2.1. This form of circling was given in the *Labanotation* (1970, 195), but was not included in the text published in 2005, it is therefore presented again here. Eight steps with an appropriate change of direction for each step, as in **2a**, will produce a circular path with no change of Front. Walking a half clockwise circle with eight steps, **2b**, produces a half change of Front. In **2c** the half circle includes a half revolution resulting in a total of one turn, thus ending facing the original direction. In **2d** the half revolution in the opposite direction cancels out the half change of Front produced by the half circle path. The performer follows the circle through changes in direction for each step. The indication of this pattern, originally written as **2e,** was changed to the more immediately clear statement of **2f**, the front of the torso being given a space hold, thus remaining facing Front during the eight steps. This was simplified to **2g**. The circling is accomplished by adjusting the direction of each step so that a circular path is followed.

2.2. Note that for the direction where the performer is facing, the room or stage orientation, the word 'front' is given a capital 'F' to distinguish it from the 'front' of the body. Also, note that the black pin for the amount of circling in **2c** is replaced in **2d** by the appropriate number, in this case 1/2. This is because of the absence of change of Front which the black pin would indicate.

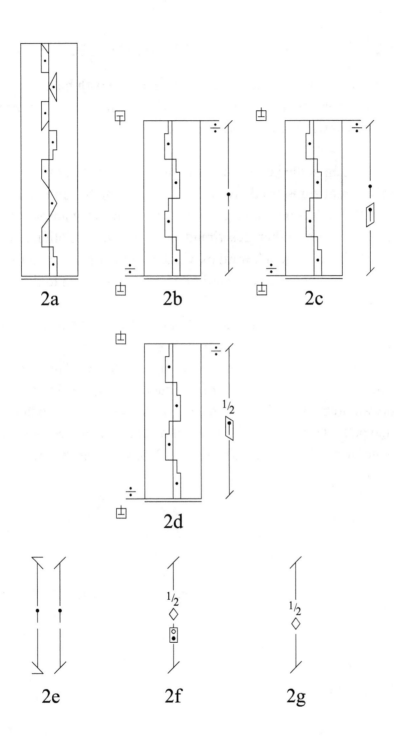

2a   2b   2c

2d

2e   2f   2g

3. Relating to the Direction of the Path

Movements may relate to the direction of the path being travelled, the direction of progression. This is particularly useful for circular, curving or meandering pathways when there is a line of people.

3.1. Ex. **3a** is the key for the Direction of the Path. From this, the appropriate Front signs are derived: **3b** shows facing the direction of the path; in **3c** the path is on your right, while **3d** indicates your back is to the direction of the path. When describing a movement in relation to the path, the key of **3e** is used. A sideward movement to the right in relation to the path is **3f**, with **3g** being a backward movement in relation to the path.

3.2. Ex. **3h** indicates a space hold in relation to the path. Usually, a space hold refers to the directions in the room, but as these usually are not applicable for paths that curve, a special sign is needed. The sign of **3h** can be simplified to **3i**. In the meandering sequence of **3j,** the left arm changes from forward to backward and then again to forward, the limb being on the line of the path. Here the resulting direction has been added as well as the 'front' sign in relation to the path (Knust 1979, vol.1, 80-82, 303-308).

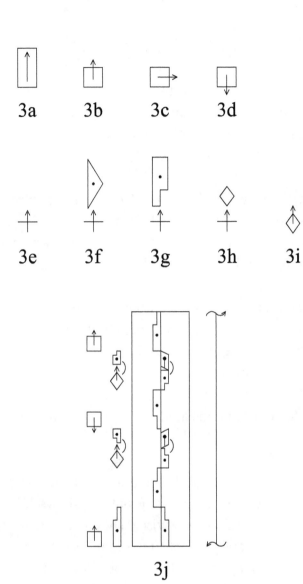

3a   3b   3c   3d

3e   3f   3g   3h   3i

3j

Chapter 9. Use of Pins Survey

This chapter aims to set forth and clarify the uses of various kinds of pins and their application. Although presented previously in *Spatial Variations,* Advanced Labanotation, issue 9, the following investigation includes some different perspectives.

1.1. **Relationship Indications**. The first use of black pins is in indicating *relationship* of one part of the body to another, as when a crossing step occurs. The reader may need to know whether the stepping leg crosses in front of the supporting leg or behind, **1a**.

1.2. Pins are also used to show the relationship of the feet when standing: first position, legs side by side, **1b**; third position right foot front, **1c**, fifth position right foot front, **1d**. Tight rope walking is shown in **1e**. Similarly, these pins are used to show the relationship of the arms to the torso. In **1f**, the arms cross in front of the body, the left arm in front of the right. In **1g**, the rounded arms are in front of the body; in **1h** they are at the sides.

2.1. **Degree of Turning**. Black pins also show the degree of pivot turns, that is, the degree of change of Front; **2a**, shows 1/4, 1/2, 3/4, a full turn and so on when turning clockwise. They show the relationship of the new Front to the previously established Front. Black pins indicate *motion;* the amount of turn in relation to the previous Front. These pins are also similarly applied to circular paths, **2b**.

3.1. **Statement of Front**. The Front signs indicate the direction in the room, or where on stage the performer is facing. They combine the area sign for the room with a flat pin or 'tack', **3a**. When placed within a turn sign the tack pin indicates the room direction to be faced at the end, i.e., the *destination*, **3b**. This room direction destination can be applied also to the head, **3c**, and other appropriate body parts.

1. Relationships (Positions Signs)

Crossing Step

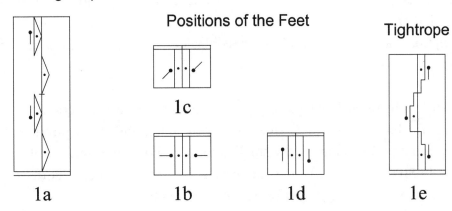

Positions of the Feet

1c

1a   1b   1d

Tightrope

1e

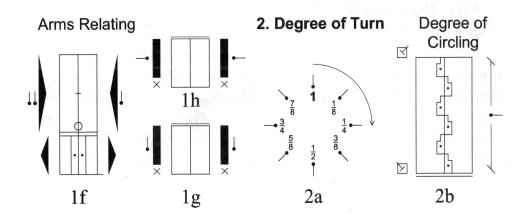

Arms Relating

1f   1g

1h

2. Degree of Turn

2a

Degree of Circling

2b

3. Front Signs

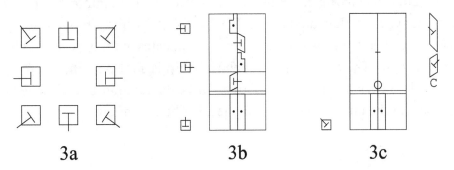

3a   3b   3c

4.1. **Degree from Unrotated, Untwisted State**. A white pin inside a turn sign indicates the destination for the rotation, judged from the unrotated state for that part of the body. In **4a** the right leg rotates 1/8 to the left from parallel, then 1/4 to the right, judged from parallel. This white pin description states a *destination*, whereas black pins indicate *motion*, the amount of movement.

5.1. **Shifting**. The equal sign = is used to indicate the action of shifting the body parts a unit. In **5a** the equal sign is added to a pin (here to a tack, a flat pin) to show a very small amount of horizontal shift for the chest. In **5b** the head shifts in a circular pattern. In **5c** the pelvis shifts side to side. Such shifts can be performed in any direction.

6.1. **Indication of Performer**. Pins are used on floor plans to indicate the performers: **6a**, a black pin for a male; white for a female and a tack for either. When placed at the start of a score, or within a score, these same pins are drawn within a circle, usually in a not-quite-closed circle, **6b**, to indicate an individual performer. This same encircling is used to indicate a couple, **6c**, or a trio, etc. The double circle of **6d** represents 'each one'; it can be added to a white pin to indicate 'each female'. When combined with a Meeting Line, **6e**, it states "Each one has a person in front." In **6f** the performer has a female in front; in **6g** there is a person behind you.

7. 1. **Minor Directional Indications**. For each major direction and level there is a corresponding pin that indicates a small, minor movement of the same type, as illustrated in **7a**. For example, a white pin pointing forward relates to a forward high sign and indicates a minor forward high displacement. The **direction of a relationship** is shown in **7b**, where the left hand touches the head from above. In **7c** the relationship of the legs as they beat in the air is shown with the left leg below the right.

4.Degree from Untwisted State

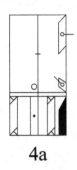

4a

5. Shifting

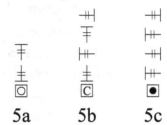

5a   5b   5c

6. People, A Person, Couple, Each Person

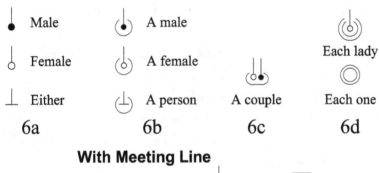

6a   6b   6c   6d

With Meeting Line

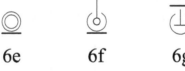

6e   6f   6g

7. Minor Directional Indications

Direction of Relationship

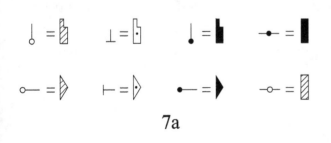

7a

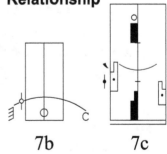

7b   7c

8.1. **Minor Movements; Distal or Proximal Reference**. Minor displacements of the extremities are shown with pins. In **8a** the arm lowers and lifts slightly, judged from the understood **distal center**, the end of the arm. In **8b** the **proximal center** description is given, judged from the base of the limb, the pins representing very diminished versions of **8c**. The choice of pins usually indicates from which point of view the movement is being judged. In **8d**, the distal pins show the arm moving slightly forward and backward; the proximal description is **8e**. A small clockwise arm circle is described with distal pins in **8f**, starting out to the side. With the arm up, the hand waves, **8g**, the direction being judged from the fingertips (distal description). In **8h** the head makes a small circle starting forward, judged from the **proximal center**. The larger movement to which it relates is **8i**.

8.2. **Indication of Distal Reference**. To specify distal reference, a small stroke is added near the end of the pin's shaft, as indicated in **8j**. In **8k**, the pins used are judged from the top of the head. This is the same movement as **8h**. Note the 'away' cancellation sign at the end. In **8l** the forward displacement is cancelled by the pin for center, another way of cancelling. For the head in particular, some notators prefer to describe such displacements from the proximal center, as in **8h**, and similar to **8i**, though smaller.

8.3. The vibrating of the lower arm up and down in **8m**, uses a proximal description. To be specific, the lower arm sign can be indicated, as in **8n**; this is a distal description. If the wrist itself is to move, the wrist sign should be indicated; **8o**, shows the wrist joint lifting and lowering, i.e., bulging in those directions. For clarity, the Distal stroke on the pin shaft can be added.

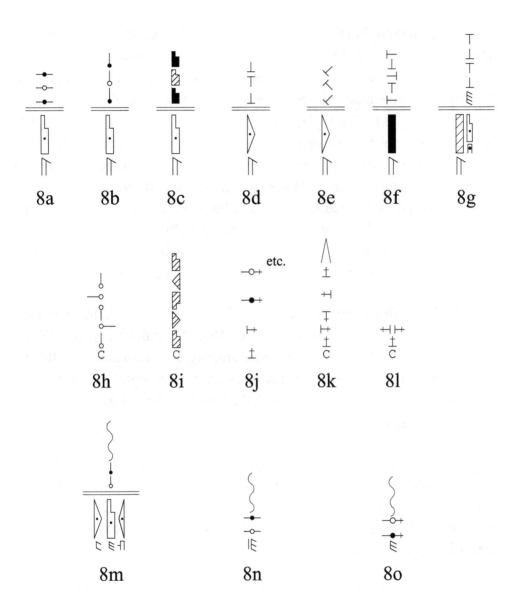

9.1. **Intermediate Directions; Degree of Turns**. Points between the main directions are shown by placing the appropriate pin within the main direction symbol, **9a**. These pins relate to the adjacent main direction, thus 1/3 way from side middle toward side high is shown by adding a white pin pointing sideward (a side high pin) within the side middle sign, **9b**. Slightly above that will be shown with a side high symbol with a sideward flat pin (side middle pin) inside, **9c**. In **9d** the right arm, slightly lower than forward middle level, is also in front of the body. In **9e**, the left arm is up but slightly forward. Intermediate degrees of turning are shown by combining two pins: **9f** shows 1/16th degree of turn to the right; **9g** indicates a 3/16th rotation to the right from the previous location. In **9h**, the 1/16th rotation to the right is judged from the understood normal situation for that limb.

10.1. **Modified Positions, Steps**. Feet together, but slightly apart is written with sideward displacement tacks, **10a**. A modified 2nd position is given in **10b**, the right foot being placed slightly backward and the left foot slightly forward. In 5th position, **10c**, the right foot is slightly separated (forward) from the left. Walking with the feet more apart than normal, a 'wide gait', is shown in **10d**.

11.1. **Deviations from a Gestural Path**. Pins are used to indicate minor deviations as the limb follows the basic path indicated. In **11a** the arm rises to place high, deviating to the left and then to the right on its pathway. In **11b**, as the arm moves to the side it makes a downward, upward then downward wave on the way to its destination.

12.1. **Direction of Arm Successions**. Directions of arm successions are shown with appropriate pins: in **12a**, the action happens with a forward deviation; in **12b** it is a downward motion. Overlapping successions can occur, as in **12c**.

9. Intermediate Directions

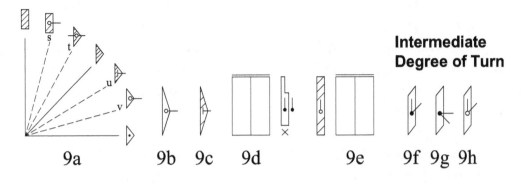

Intermediate Degree of Turn

9a　　　　9b　9c　　9d　　　　　9e　　　9f 9g 9h

10. Modified Positions, Steps

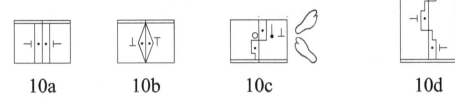

10a　　　　10b　　　　10c　　　　　　　10d

12. With Successions

11. Deviation for a Gestural Path

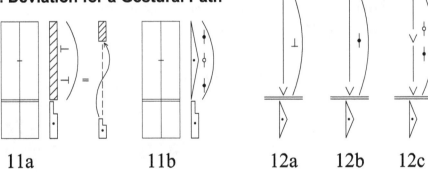

11a　　　　　11b　　　　12a　　12b　　12c

13.1. **Track Pins**. Because of the width of the torso the destination of the arm extremity may need to be described in terms of the possible tracks for the arms, **13a**; next to the center line is shown by adding dots right and left. The arms may be forward but in line with the normal track for the other arm, **13b**, which illustrates the *port de bras* Balanchine often used in his choreography. (See later discussion on track pins applied to ballet arm positions in Section 17.)

14.1. **Parts of the Head**. Placement of the appropriate pin in the C head sign indicates the various parts of the head. The following are the main parts needed: **14a**, the chin; **14b**, the nose; **14c**, the forehead; **14d**, the top of the head; **14e**, the eyes; **14f**, the mouth; **14g**, the left cheek, and **14h**, the right ear. Such parts of the body are given in detail in Chapter One.

15.1. **Fixed Points in the Room**. Ex. **15a** is the key for a Fixed Point in the room or on stage. Directional pins are used to indicate different parts of the room, **15b**. These may be used to indicate where a performer is looking, or where an arm gesture might be directed. Flat pins, reduced to ticks, indicate the horizontal points around the room, **15c**. Some specific points are: **15d**, lower left front corner; **15e**, the center of the ceiling, which may also be written as **15f**; **15g**, upper right front corner; **15h**, between left front corner and center.

3. Track Pins

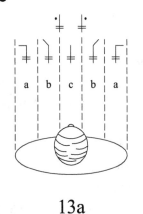

13a

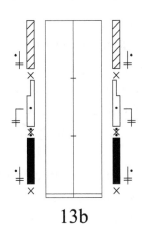

13b

14. Parts of the Head

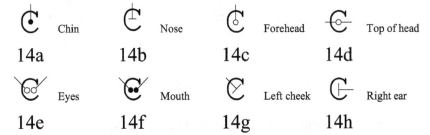

Chin — 14a

Nose — 14b

Forehead — 14c

Top of head — 14d

Eyes — 14e

Mouth — 14f

Left cheek — 14g

Right ear — 14h

15. Fixed Points in the Room

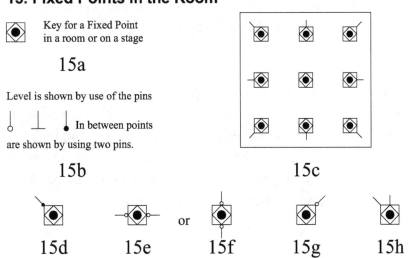

Key for a Fixed Point in a room or on a stage

15a

Level is shown by use of the pins

In between points are shown by using two pins.

15b

15c

15d   15e   or   15f   15g   15h

16.1. **Polar Pins**. There are instances where the standard directional pins do not serve. When a limb is in an intermediate location, determining which pins to use can be a problem. For these and when minor displacements occur while a limb is moving, Polar Pins should be used. They are explained in detail in *Spatial Variations,* Advanced Labanotation, issue 9, section 23. Here we give a brief explanation and examples that were not given previously.

16.2. Polar Pins are based on the idea of our planet with its north and south poles and the longitude and latitude directions. On any longitudinal point we are aware of rising (away from the pull of gravity), **16a**; or sinking (toward the pull of gravity), **16b**. For any latitudinal point the directions are clockwise, **16c**, or anticlockwise, **16d**. Spoke-like horizontal displacements are away from the body's core, **16e**, or toward it, **16f**. The following are the set of Polar Pins: **16g**, longitude rising; **16h**, longitude sinking; **16i**, latitude clockwise; **16j**, latitude anti-clockwise; **16k**, outward spoke-like displacements (bird's eye view), and **16l**, inward spoke-like displacements.

16.3. Starting with the bent arm forward toward diagonal high in **16m**, it displaces slightly to and fro, clockwise and anticlockwise. With the same starting position in **16n** the displacement is spoke-like, out and in horizontally. In **16o** the arm is down, half-way to side low, from there minor rising and sinking displacements occur.

16.4. **Repeated Displacements**. In **16p**, the minor rising and sinking displacement is repeated after a gap. This can be shown with a repeat sign. This same displacement may be constantly repeated, shown in **16q** by a wavy line for the hand. The smaller the wavy line, the faster the movement. A Polar Pin description can be repeated while the arm is moving, **16r**, the clockwise, anticlockwise displacements are relevant in each location.

The Idea of Polar Pins

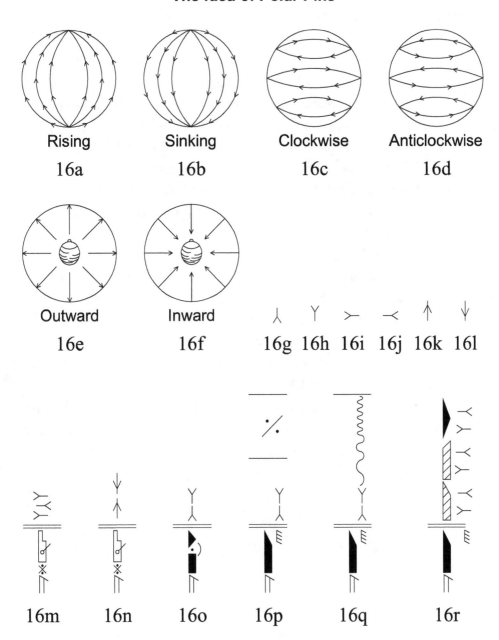

Rising	Sinking	Clockwise	Anticlockwise
16a	16b	16c	16d

Outward	Inward
16e	16f

16g 16h 16i 16j 16k 16l

16m   16n   16o   16p   16q   16r

17.1. **Pins for Ballet Arm Positions**. There are differences in the placement of the arms in the different Schools of Classical Ballet, the Russian, Italian, French and English. By using the appropriate pins, these differences can be shown. Initially, black pins were used for arm positions as in the diagram of **17a**. Ex. **17b** shows the arms slightly rounded hanging below the shoulders, illustrated in **17c**. This position is called '*bras au repose*' in the French School, and 'First Position' in the Cecchetti (Italian) Method. If position pins were used, it would be as **17d**. In **17e** the extremities of the arms are in front of the body, shown in **17f**. The arms in ballet can be held slightly forward, shown by the forward pointing tacks, **17g**, or this can be as much as **17h**. This position is called '*bras bas*' (English) or '5th *en bas*' in Cecchetti and 'preparatory position' in Russian style. For the forward arm position, the general statement of **17i** should more accurately be written with the arms lower than horizontal, **17j**, shown in **17k**, or even as low as **17l**, the black pin inside the forward symbol indicates $1/3^{rd}$ toward forward low. This position is called '5th *en avant*' in Cecchetti, and sometimes 'the gateway' (English) since it is the position so often passed through in *ports de bras*. The position called '1st' in the French School, has the arms as low as **17m,** illustrated in **17n**. Arms overhead, **17o**, illustrated in **17p**, is termed '*5th en haut*' in French and Cecchetti, and '*third position*' in Russian. The arms could be a little more forward, **17q**, or even as in **17r**. This position is also known as '*bras en couronne*' (as in a crown).

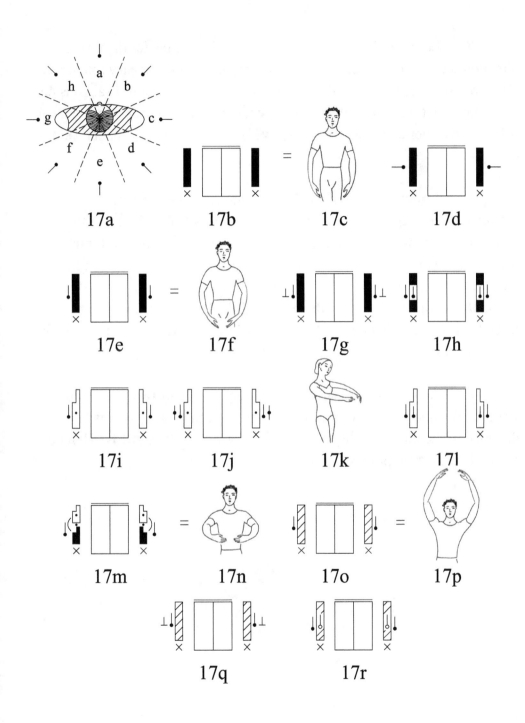

17a

17b = 17c 17d

17e = 17f 17g 17h

17i 17j 17k 17l

17m = 17n 17o = 17p

17q 17r

18.1. **Intermediate track possibilities**. Track Pins for the forward direction were given in Section 13; **13a** is repeated here for easy reference. The more specific intermediate track possibilities are given in **18a**: (i) is on the center line (i.e., within the center track; (ii) is next to the center line; (iii) is between center and diagonal track; (iv) is between the diagonal and side track.

18.2. Tracks for the diagonal directions, as in **18b** and for the sideward directions, **18c**, can also be used. Because of the body build, diagonal and sideward tracks are much narrower than the forward track. While for the diagonal directions, diagonal pins should be used to indicate the 'lanes', as in **18d**, for practical purposes vertical pins, are used, **18e**. Thus, **18f** becomes **18g**, and **18h** becomes **18i**. The same applies to the lanes for sideward directions: **18j** becomes **18k**, **18l** becomes **18m**, and **18n** becomes **18o**.

18.3. Indication of the arm immediately overhead **18p** can also be written as **18q**, on the center track. The arm up can be specified as being in the track of the left arm, **18r**, or in its own normal track as in **18s**. Diagonal placements are also possible, as in **18t**.

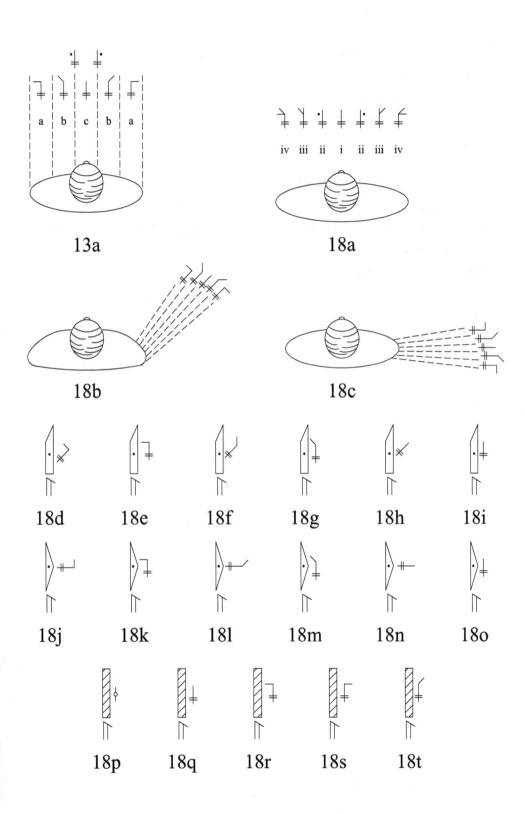

13a

18a

iv iii ii i ii iii iv

18b

18c

18d

18e

18f

18g

18h

18i

18j

18k

18l

18m

18n

18o

18p

18q

18r

18s

18t

18.4. In **18u** and **18v** the arms are on the forward center line, the right arm above the left. The inwardly rotated arms of **18w** have the fingertips next to the center line. Raising the arms through the lanes of the opposite shoulders, **18x**, illustrated in **18y,** is a style used by Balanchine in his choreography.

18.5. **Distance Between Fingertips**. This varies in the different Schools of Ballet: they may be almost touching, **18z**, illustrated in **18aa**; or the width of the face apart, **18ab**, illustrated in **18ac**; or they might be **18ad** placed in the diagonal tracks of the body. In actual application, **18ab**, is the one most likely to be used.

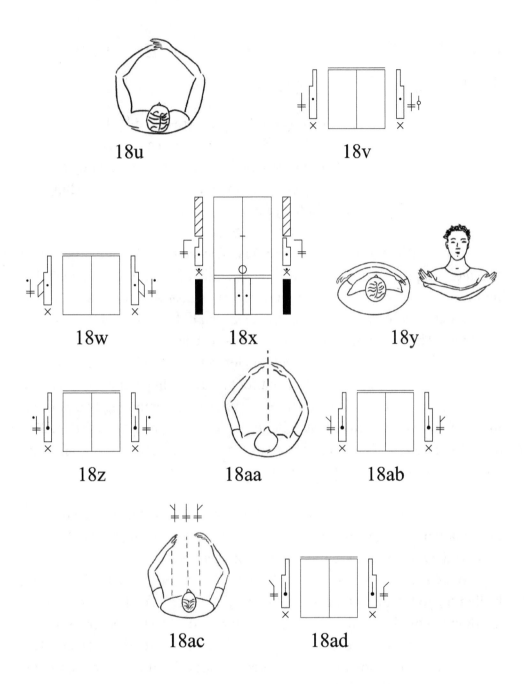

18u

18v

18w

18x

18y

18z

18aa

18ab

18ac

18ad

Chapter 10. Closed Positions of the Feet
1. General Considerations

This chapter is based mainly on the paper presented by Dr Sheila
Marion, formerly Director of the Dance Notation Bureau Extension at Ohio
State University, at the 1979 International Council of Kinetography Laban
(ICKL) Conference. Research has also drawn on the work of our Hungarian
colleagues, the late Mária Szentpál, János Fügedi and Gábor Misi.

1.1. **With Symmetrical Rotations**. Closed positions with the feet
together, supporting in place, beneath the center of weight, with the whole
foot contacting the floor, **1a**, are modified by the conventional use of black
pins to indicate the relationship of the feet. In all these positions the feet are
touching. The understood meaning of **1a** is feet side by side, stated in **1b**.
Fifth position, the right foot in front, the left foot behind is shown in **1c**.
For third position, **1d**, shows the right foot in front. In practice on§12ly one
pin is needed. Intermediate positions are shown by combining two pins, as
in **1e**, **1f** and **1g**, etc. Note that ballet terminology is being used for 1st, 3rd
and 5th regardless of the rotated state of the legs. The use of black pins for
these positions relates to the Standard Cross of Axes, **1h**.

1.2. **Analysis of Specific Positions**. Researchers have given close
examination to the length and width of the average foot and the angles
produced by the line joining the centers of each foot. In actual practice we
tend to focus on the relationship of the parts of the feet to each other, heel to
heel or toe to toe for first position, these being more visually obvious. In
the drawing of **1i,** and all subsequent drawings, the black heel represents the
right foot, with the white heel being for the left foot. Ex. **1i**, **1j**, **1k** and **1l**
all illustrate 1st position in a few different rotational states. Note the use of
a black heel to indicate the right foot.

Closed Positions of Feet

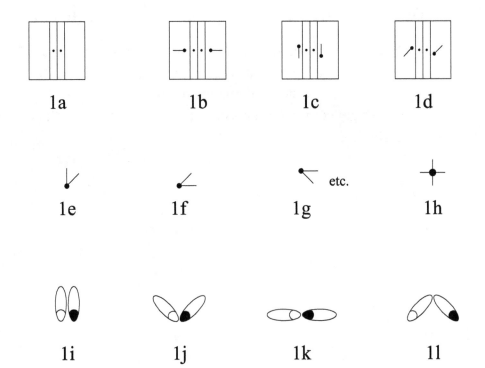

1a   1b   1c   1d

1e   1f   1g etc.   1h

1i   1j   1k   1l

2. Closed Positions of the Feet with Symmetrical and Asymmetrical Rotations

Chart I: Symmetrical Rotations. This chart shows symmetrical states for both legs using black pins which relate to the Standard Key. In the left top corner of the left vertical column the rotational state of the legs is shown. In the top right corner of each square a black pin indicates the position for the right foot.

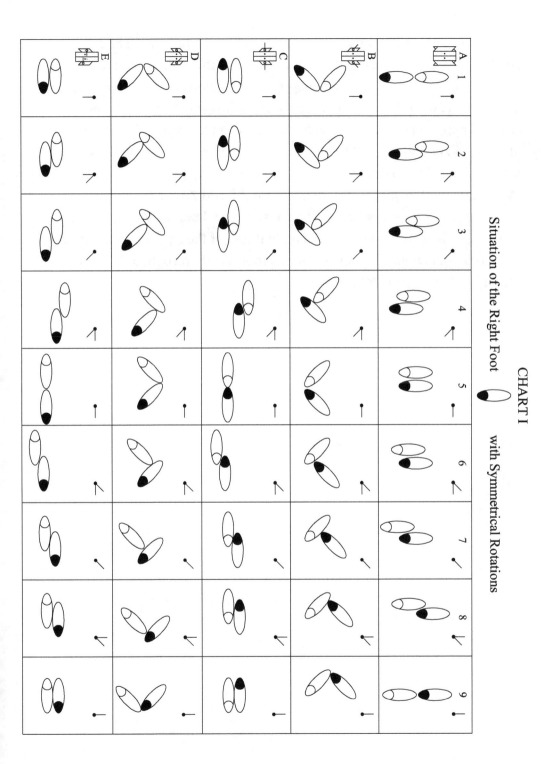

CHART I

Situation of the Right Foot with Symmetrical Rotations

Chart II: **Fifth Position, Asymmetrical Rotations**. The 5th position is shown in each case for the right foot in front, as are the subsequent charts. In this chart the top line indicates the rotational state for the right leg, the left leg is indicated in the left vertical column. The analysis applied rests on the line between the center point of each foot. In the case of A2 and A4, without an awareness of the center points for the feet, these could be seen as a shifted A1 and A5, written with a 'tack' pin to indicate a slight displacement, as in **2a** for A2 and **2b** for A4. Such modifications can be applied to other instances where the visual message requires it. Note the highlighted diagonal line of the squares from 1A down to 5E drawing attention to the positions most easily recognized. This is also applied to the subsequent charts.

CHART II

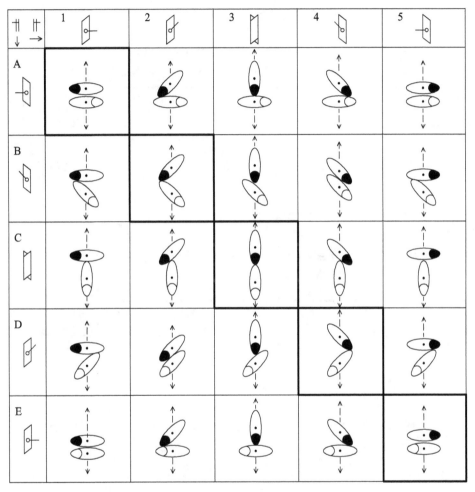

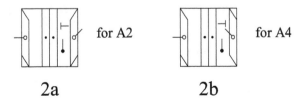

for A2   for A4

2a   2b

Chart III: **Third Position in Front**. In this series, the heel or toe relationship to the instep for 3rd position is not readily visible, although the line connecting the center point of each foot is followed.

CHART III

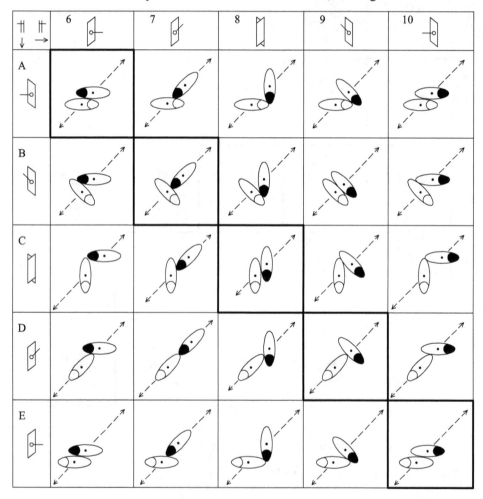

using ✛ Analysis: Centre of Right Foot Directly in Front of Centre of Left Foot, 45° angle

Chart IV: **The Side-by-Side Relationship**. The analysis of the line between the center points of the feet may not readily give the image of the feet being side by side; in the highlighted squares the message is clear.

CHART IV

using ├─ Analysis: Centre of Right Foot
Side of Centre of Left Foot

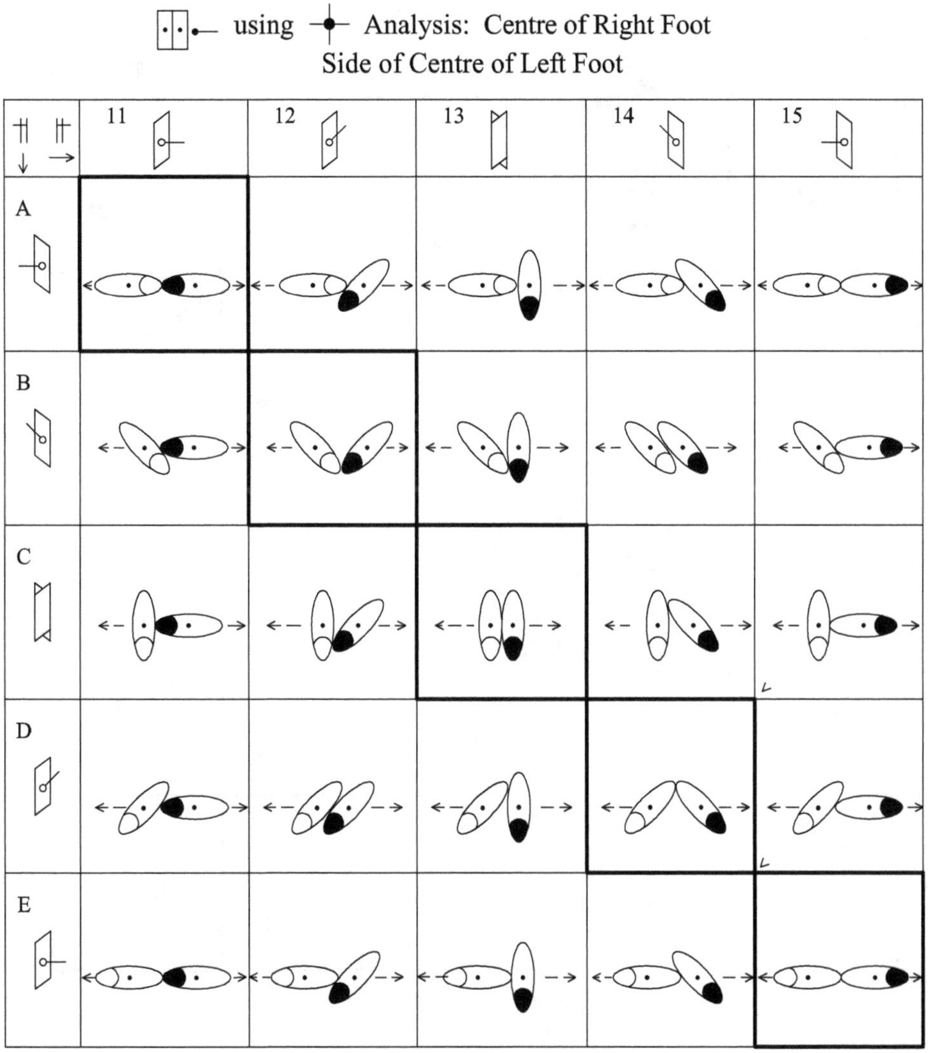

Chart V: Third Position Behind. This is comparable with Chart III.

CHART V

using ━●━ Analysis: Centre of Right Foot
Diagonally Behind Centre of Left Foot, 45° angle

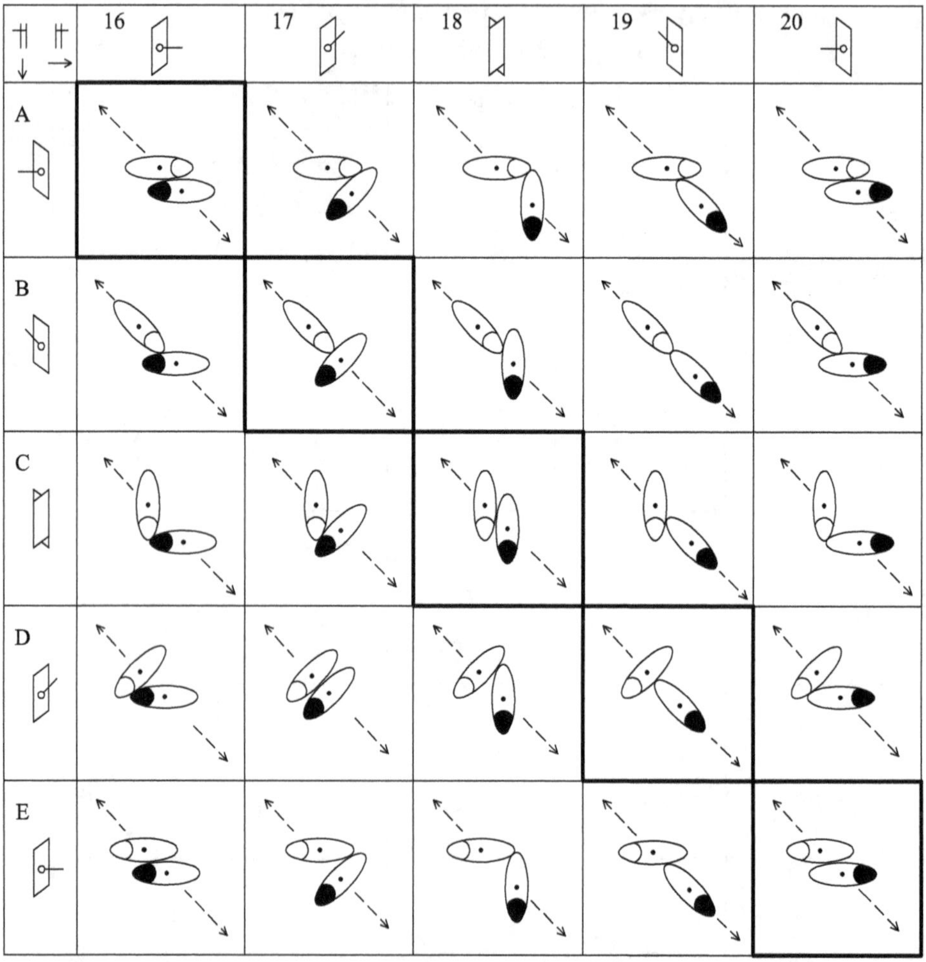

Chart VI: **Fifth Position Behind**. This is comparable to Chart II.

CHART VI

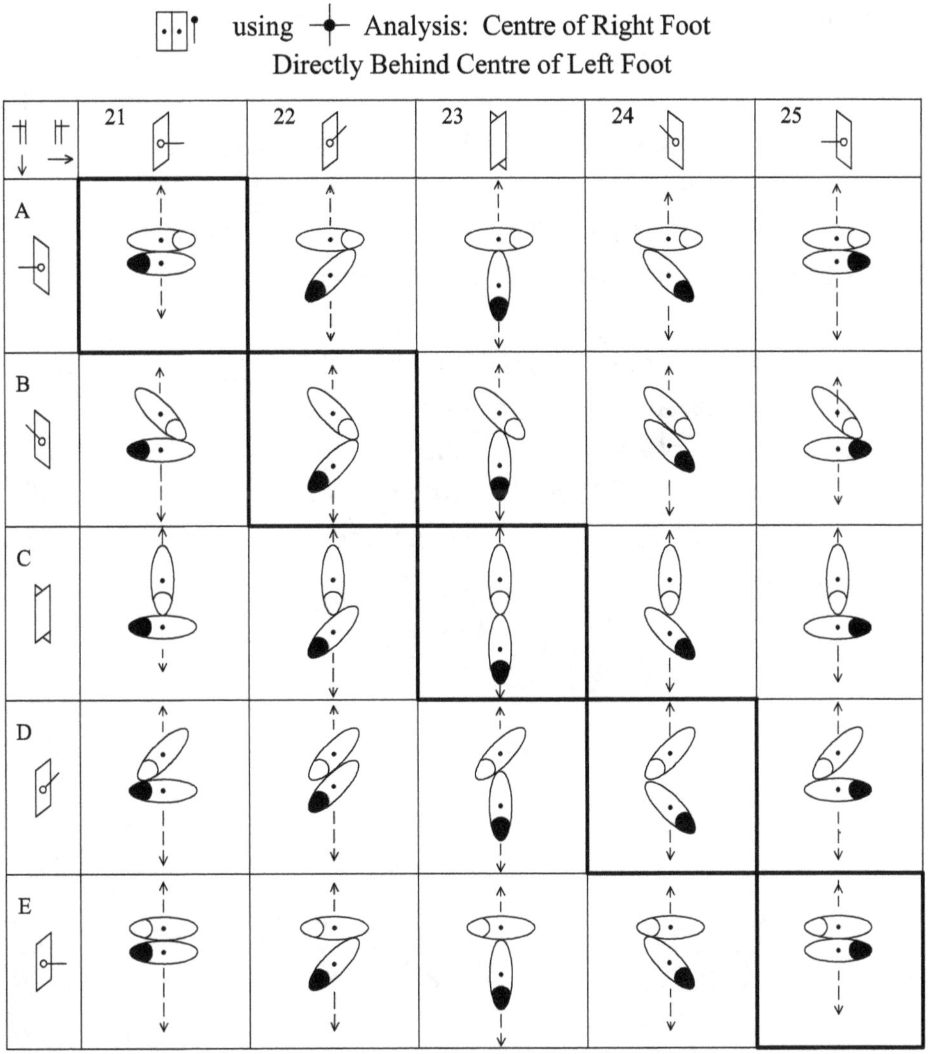
using
Analysis: Centre of Right Foot
Directly Behind Centre of Left Foot
21
22
23
24
25
A
B
C
D
E

Chart VII. The next charts follow the same investigation but from the point of view of a **Local Body System of Reference, 2c**, which applies to whatever body part is being dealt with. In this case it is the feet for which white pins are used instead of black pins for foot positions. Because these examples are of the feet, the 'Local' is understood to refer to the feet, the relationship of one foot to the other, heel to heel, toe to toe, etc. There is no relationship to Front, where the body is facing in the room.

Body Twisted Part Key. This term, derived from twists in the torso (where is Front?), is not equally applicable to other parts.

Use of pins. In turn signs, **2d, black pins** show degree (amount) of turn. **White pins, 2e,** show the destination of the turn, the new Front. For Positions of the Feet: **black pins** show the relationship of the feet judged from the Standard Cross of Axes, **2f; white pins** show the relationship of the feet to one another, **2g.** From the pin one knows that a different system of reference is being used.

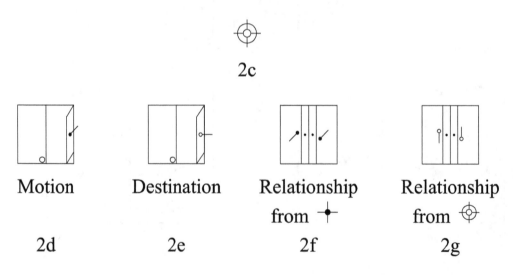

2c

Motion   Destination   Relationship   Relationship
                                         from ┼   from ⊕

2d   2e   2f   2g

Chart VII. The 5th position, right foot in front.

CHART VII

Using ⊕ Analysis: Right Heel in Front of Left Toe

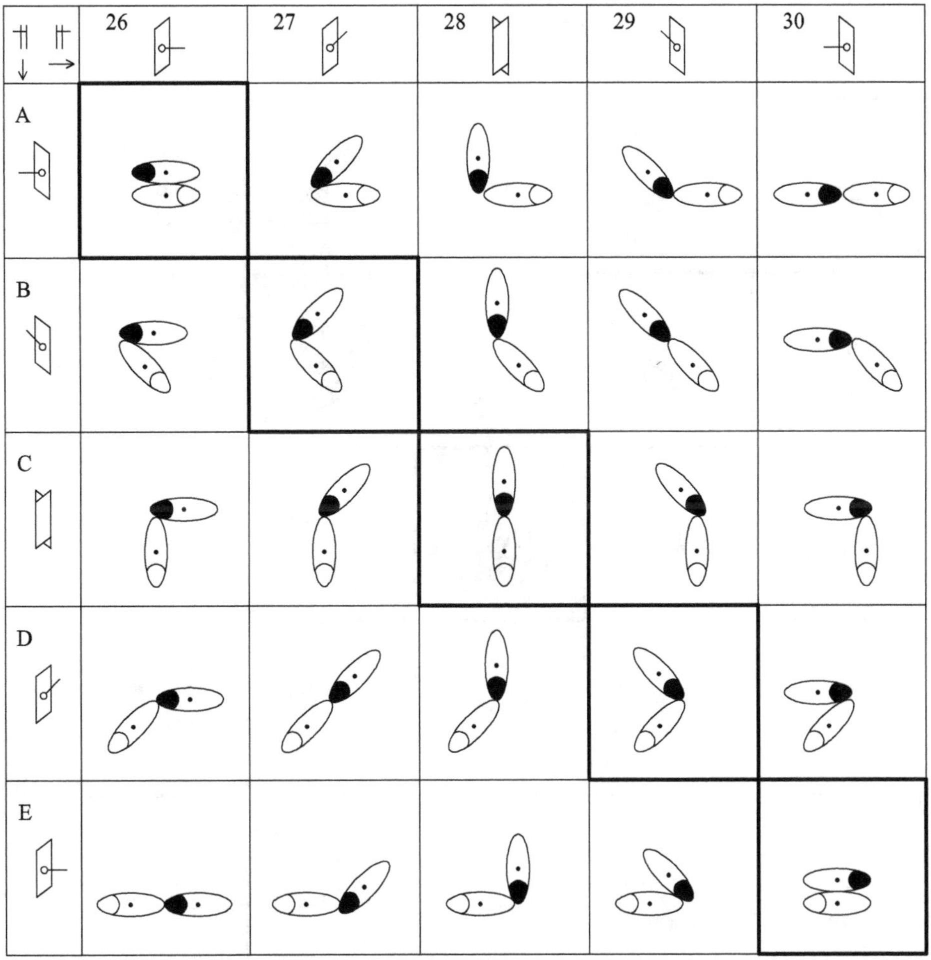

Chart VIII. The 3rd position front.

CHART VIII

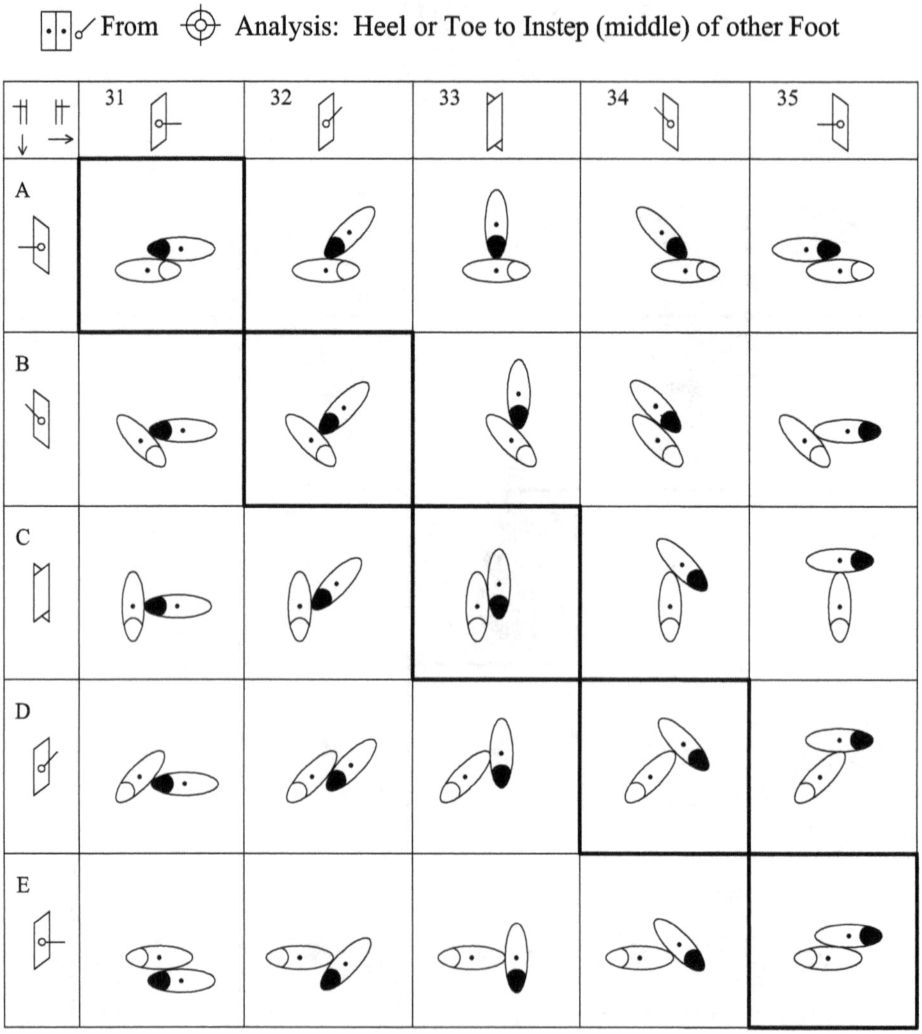

From ⊕ Analysis: Heel or Toe to Instep (middle) of other Foot

Chart IX. The side-by-side relationship.

CHART IX

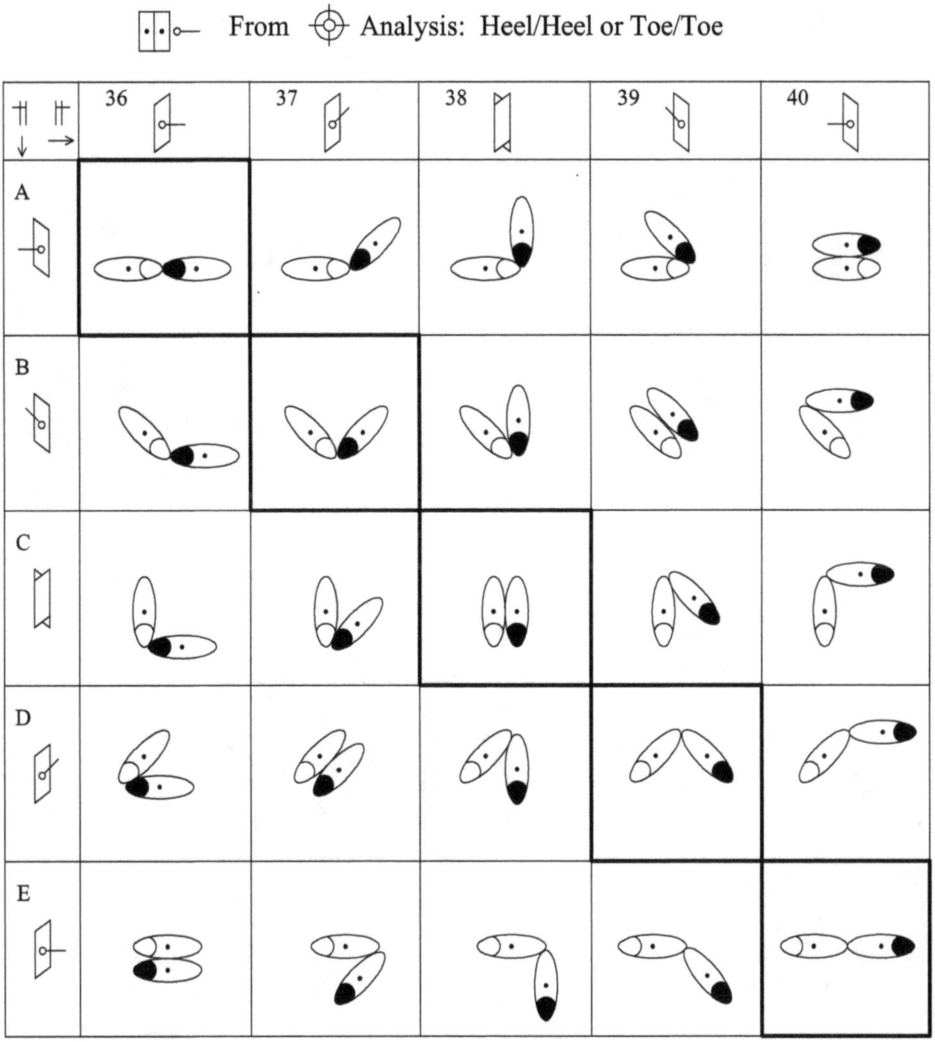

Chart X the 3rd position behind.

CHART X

From ⊕ Analysis: Heel or Toe to Instep (middle) of Other Foot

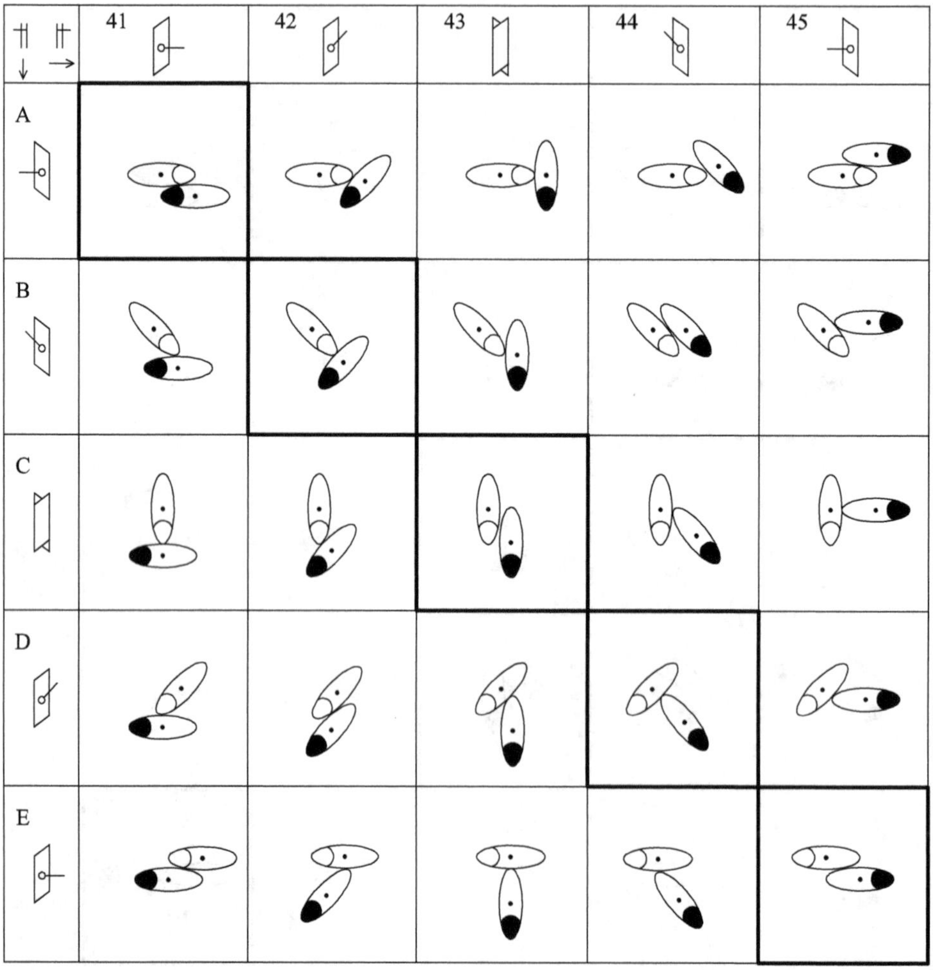

Chart XI. The 5th position behind.

CHART XI

From ⊕ Analysis: Right Toe behind Left Heel

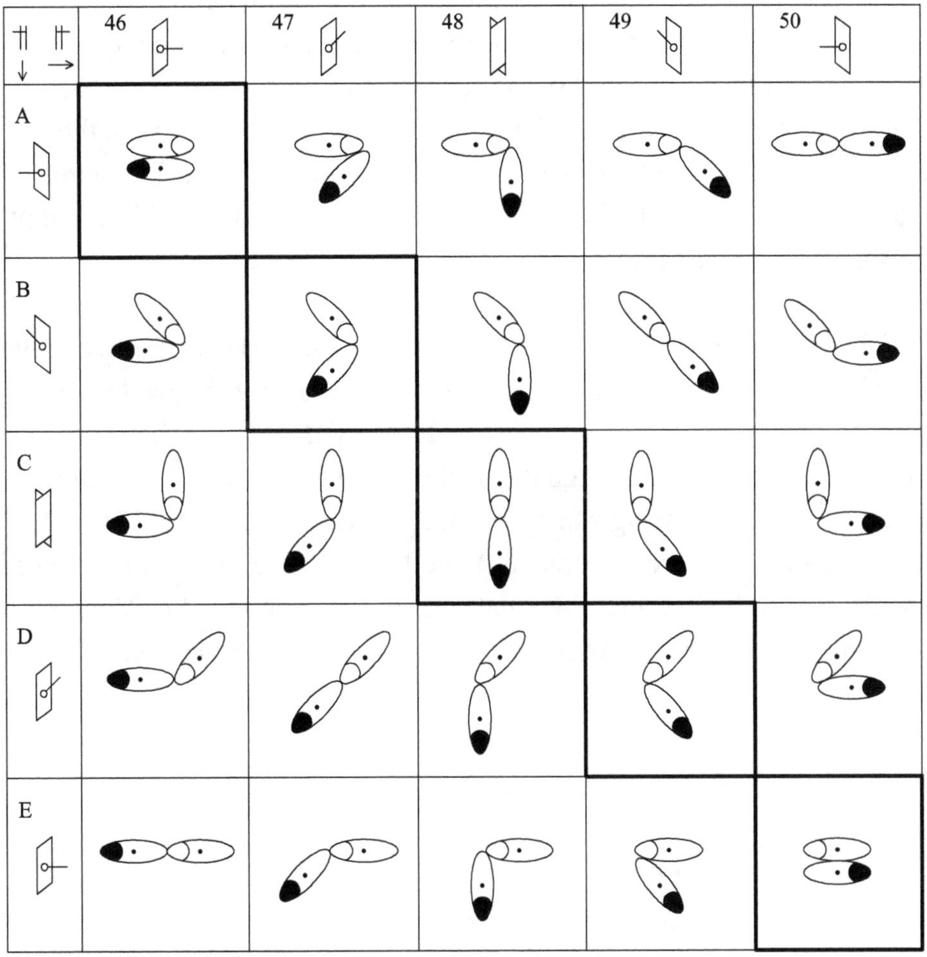

3. Foot Positions for Touching Gestures

3.1. A leg gesture touching the floor, often with the ball of the foot, can have similar relationships to the supporting foot. The term 'Mixed Surfaces' has been used for such positions, the touch can be made by any part of the gesturing foot, from the toe to the heel. Usually the touching gesture does not take weight. For the sake of simplicity, these support/touch mixtures will be referred to as 'closed positions' with the side-by-side relationship being called 1st, the diagonal relationship being called 3rd, and so on. As before, the left foot has a white heel with the right being shown as a black toe or heel.

3.2. **Distance of Touch from Supporting Foot**. There are two views on this: **View A** – when the touching part is placed next to or touching the supporting foot it should be written as such; **View B** – the toe (ball, etc.) touch should be placed as though the heel were to be lowered (or had just been raised). The following examples illustrate this difference. The ball of the foot touching in place (1st position), **3a**, has the View A interpretation of **3b**, **3c**, **3d**, depending on the rotational state of the right leg. For View B the placement would be **3e**, **3f**, **3g**, allowing room to lower the heel.

3.3. Placement of the 1/2 ball touching, **3h**, for View A is **3i**, **3j**, **3k**, and for View B, **3l**, **3m**, and **3n**.

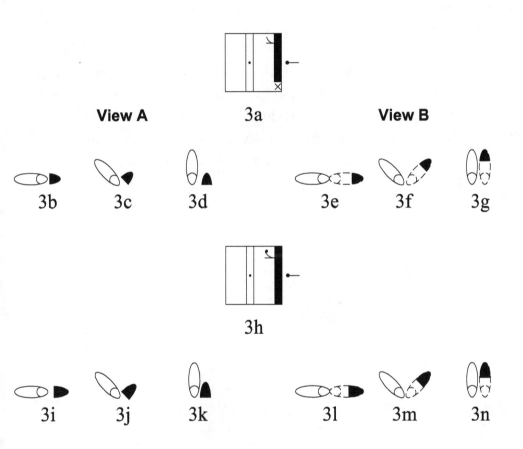

View A 3a **View B**

3b 3c 3d 3e 3f 3g

3h

3i 3j 3k 3l 3m 3n

3.4. For the 1/8 ball, **3o**, more of the sole of the foot is shown in the drawings. In View A the outward rotation of **3p**, even with a slightly bent leg, the touch cannot be exactly next to the other foot, there needs to be a separation. However, with the turn-out of **3q**, the touch can be placed next to the left heel, as it is also for **3r**. It is interesting to see that in View B the placement, **3s – 3u**, remains the same as in **3l – 3n**.

3.5. For a heel touch, **3v**, outward rotation poses no problem for View A, **3w**, **3x**, **3y**, or for View B, **3z**, **3aa**, **3ab**. But with inward rotations, the gesturing foot is in the way for achieving a close heel touch, as illustrated in **3ad**, and **3ae**, the placement has to be more like View B. Once parallel rotation is reached this problem no longer exists, **3af**. Drawings **3ag**, **3ah**, **3ai** illustrate View B.

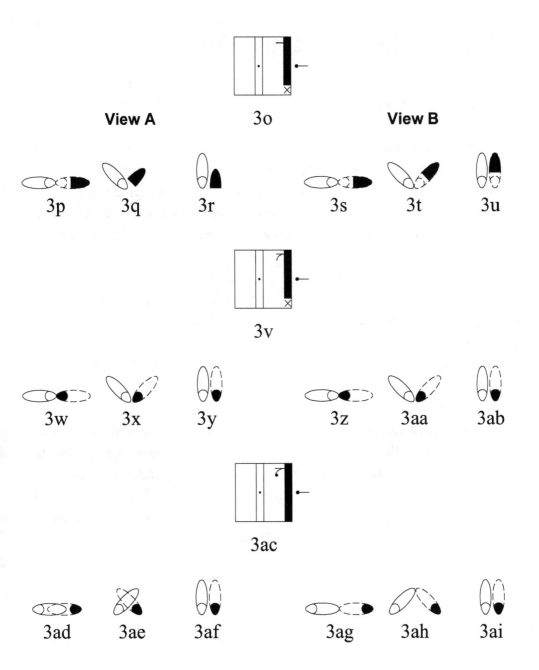

View A　　　3o　　　**View B**

3p　　3q　　3r　　　3s　　3t　　3u

3v

3w　　3x　　3y　　　3z　　3aa　　3ab

3ac

3ad　　3ae　　3af　　　3ag　　3ah　　3ai

4. Touch, then Lower the Foot

4.1. In **4a** an isolated touch is followed by a step forward. If a toe or ball of foot touch is to be followed by a lowering of the heel, for those using View A, a warning is needed to indicate that the touch is linked to what comes next, be it immediately or a little later. The reader then knows where to place the contact. For this information a 'refer forward' caret is use, **4b**. In **4c** the touch is written with a 'refer forward' caret at the end of the symbol; there is a pause and then the whole foot contact is shown. Use of a 'zed' caret attached to the new support symbol can reinforce the message.

4.2. **Touch Near Support: for View B**. With the extreme turn-out of **4d**, the ball of the foot touch needs a double X in the support column to indicate a very small distance, thus placing the touch closer to the heel, **4e**. With a moderate turn-out, the pin used in **4f** indicates a position between a 3rd behind and a fully behind relationship, **4g**. This would allow the heel to drop should that follow.

4.3. **Use of Local Body Key**. When the analysis is of the relationship of one foot to the other, white pins are used for the positions. The following examples, **4h, 4i** and **4j** show the feet in 5th position in parallel rotations, illustrating that wherever the feet are pointing the relationship of foot to foot is the same. Similarly, in the 1st position use of the same parallel rotations, **4k, 4l** and **4m** produces the same foot relationship.

4.4. **Preference for View A or View B**. Because of the intricate use of footwork with changes in rotation, part of foot contacting the floor and distances from the other foot, the Hungarian users of Laban's notation system have found View B more practical for their needs. The forms of dance encountered by users of Labanotation have indicated that View A is more appropriate. Note use of refer forward caret in **4c**.

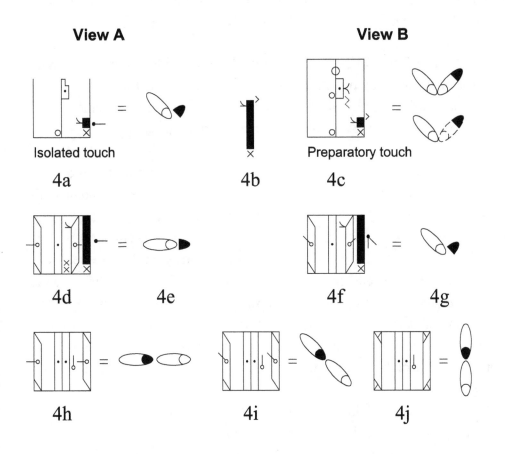

Chapter 11. Time Signs

Since Labanotation indicates timing through the length of the symbols, why was there a need for Time Signs? Mária Szentpál and Ann Hutchinson Guest had both encountered the need, they then worked together and eventually the Time Signs were accepted at ICKL in 1991 in Budapest. Note that in the following exploration, the numbering follows that on the Chart for Aspects of Time (see pp. 278-279).

1.1. **The Basic Time Signs**. Derived from the idea of an hourglass, the basic sign for Time, or Timing is **1a**; the sand is at the top. The full hourglass, **1b**, represents **duration**, the time available for a movement. Aspects of **speed**, **tempo**, are based on the empty hourglass, **1c**.

1.2. When the aspect of time is not relevant or is not part of the picture, as when listing the contents of a movement phrase or of a dance, the symbol is crossed out, as in **1d**. If freedom in each aspect of timing (speed, rhythm, beat) is needed it can be indicated as **1e** or **1f**. Exactness in timing in each aspect is stated as **1g** or **1h**; in each case the symbol for a specific use of time can be placed either below the Time Sign or at the right side. A return to general, 'normal' timing is shown with a back-to-normal sign, **1i**. Where timing has been relatively free, a Time Dot indication, **1j**, can show exactly when an action should occur. Another useful device in a dance score is a treble clef sign to indicate to take the music as the cue, **1k**.

2.1. **Duration**. The time available for a movement may be little, a brief duration, **2a**, very little, **2b**, or extremely brief, **2c**. Or duration may be extended: **2d** states a long duration, **2e** a very long duration, and **2f** an extremely long duration. Freedom in duration is stated as **2g**. Exactness is shown as **2h**. Not exact is **2i**. The relationship in timing between movements can be stated: **2j** states equal durations, with **2k** indicating uneven, unequal durations.

Time Signs

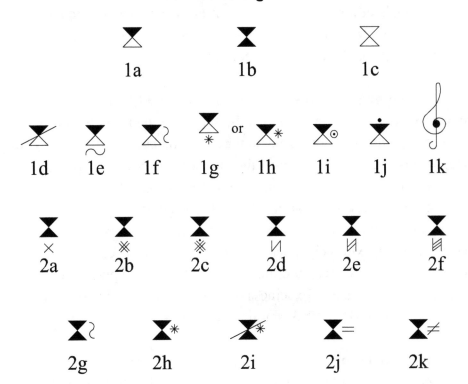

2.2. **Variations in Duration**. Increasingly less time available results in movement becoming faster; in **2k** the duration is diminishing. In **2l** the duration is increasing, thus the movement is getting slower. For use in direction symbols or turn signs these indications can be reduced to the wedges of **2m** and **2n**. The amount of accelerando, i.e. increasingly less time is given in **2o**, and increasingly more time is **2p**.

3.1. **Tempo; Variations in Speed of Movement.** The tempo of the basic pulse (beat) may be fast or slow. In music, tempo is often indicated by a metronome marking giving the number of crotchets (quarter notes) per minute, **3a** indicates 100. The lower the number, the slower the piece; the higher the number, the faster. In movement, the passage through space (the pace) may vary. Note the following: **3b**, little speed; **3c**, very little speed; **3d**, extremely slow. In contrast quick, much speed, is shown as **3e**; **3f** is very quick and **3g**, extremely quick. Freedom in use of speed is shown as **3h** or **3i**. Here there is a reminder that the modifier can be placed below or at the right side of the sign. Exactness in speed is indicated by **3j**. Even speed is indicated by **3k**, with **3l** stating uneven in speed.

3.2. Variations in Speed are shown as follows: accelerando, increasing the speed, getting faster, is **3m**. This may be abbreviated to the wedge of **3n** (taken from the basic sign) making it suitable for placement inside a direction symbol, in a turn sign, etc. Ritardando, decreasing in speed, getting slower, is **3o**, with **3p** being the abbreviated sign. Degrees in changing speed can be shown: **3q**, a very little increase; **3r**, a little; **3s**, much increase. These same indications can be applied to a decrease in speed, **3t**, being a slight decrease. Note that use of as much time as possible results in being as slow as possible. Use of as little time as possible results in movement as fast as possible.

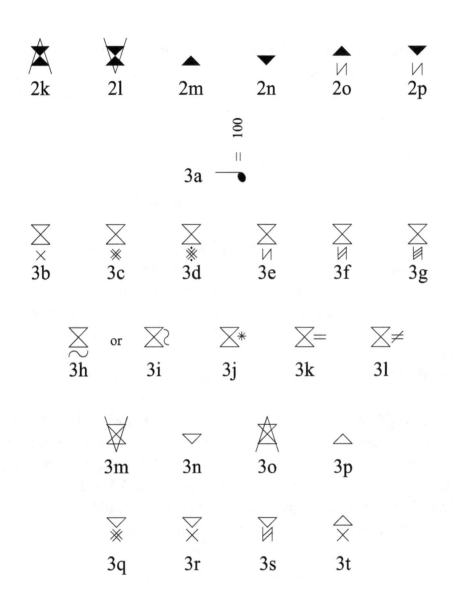

4.1. **A Rhythm**. is composed either of **even beats** with **changes of accent**, or it is a pattern of **two or more units of different lengths**. The basic sign is a diamond shaped music note, the top half black, the lower half white, example **4a**. 'Any rhythm' is shown as **4b**; an exact rhythm, **4c**; a constant rhythm, **4d**; and changing rhythms, **4e**.

5.1. **Beats**. The symbol of **5a** indicates 'a beat'; **5b** states 6 beats; the ad lib. symbol in a circle, **5c**, means 'any number' of beats.
Even beats are shown as **5d**, with uneven beats being **5e**.

6.1. **Meter**. The basic grouping of beats, the Meter (Measure), is indicated in **6a**, with **6b** an alternative, showing meter in the staff; here it is 2/4 meter. Any meter is indicated as **6c**, with **6d** stating use of an even, constant meter. Changing meters is shown as **6e**. Statement of meter is indicated as **6f** for 3/4 meter, **6g** for 6/8, **6h** for 4/4, and so on. Dances that consist mainly of foot work, stamping rhythmic patterns, even when performed without music, usually have a metric basis.

7.1. **Application in the Movement Score**. The wedge-shaped indications for changes in speed can be placed within the notation symbols. In **7a** the forward movement decreases in speed. This could be for an arm gesture, **7b**, or a transference of weight, **7c**, for turning, **7d**, or for travelling, **7e**. These indications can be put in a bracket to cover more than one symbol, as in **7f**. The wedge for increase in speed can be similarly indicated.

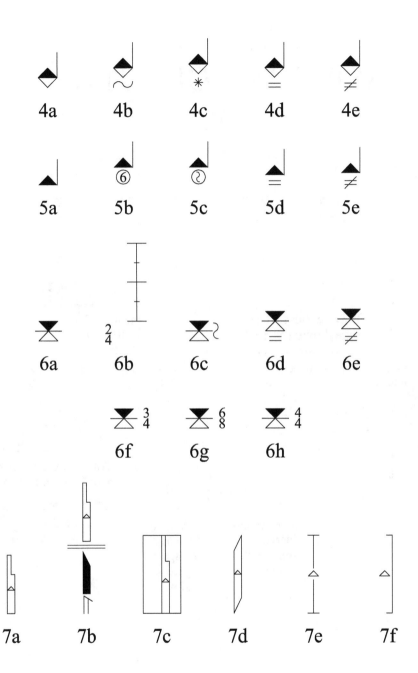

4a 4b 4c 4d 4e

5a 5b 5c 5d 5e

6a 6b 6c 6d 6e

6f 6g 6h

7a 7b 7c 7d 7e 7f

CHART FOR

ASPECTS OF TIME

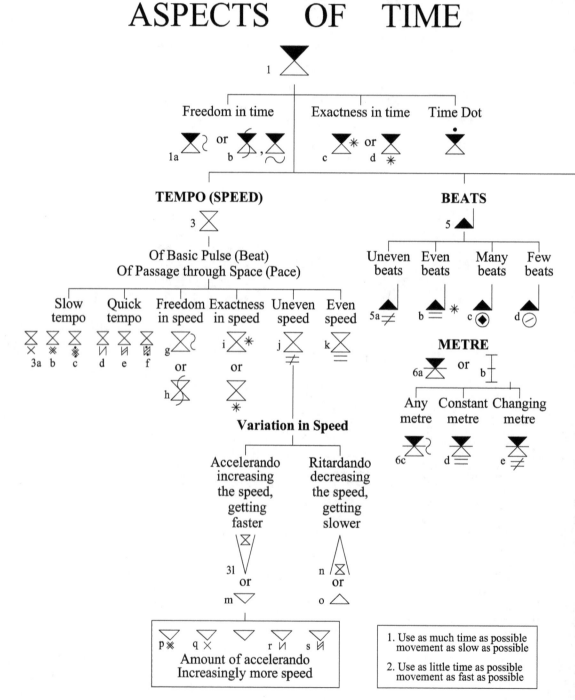

1

Freedom in time   **Exactness in time**   **Time Dot**

1a   or   b   ,   c   or   d

TEMPO (SPEED)   **BEATS**

3   5

Of Basic Pulse (Beat)   Uneven   Even   Many   Few
Of Passage through Space (Pace)   beats   beats   beats   beats

Slow   Quick   Freedom Exactness Uneven Even
tempo   tempo   in speed in speed   speed   speed   5a   b   c   d

3a   b   c   d   e   f   g   i   j   k   **METRE**

            or   or   6a   or   b

         h   Any   Constant Changing
                               metre   metre   metre

Variation in Speed   6c   d   e

Accelerando   Ritardando
increasing   decreasing
the speed,   the speed,
getting   getting
faster   slower

31   n
   or   or
m   o

p   q   r   s
Amount of accelerando
Increasingly more speed

1. Use as much time as possible
   movement as slow as possible

2. Use as little time as possible
   movement as fast as possible

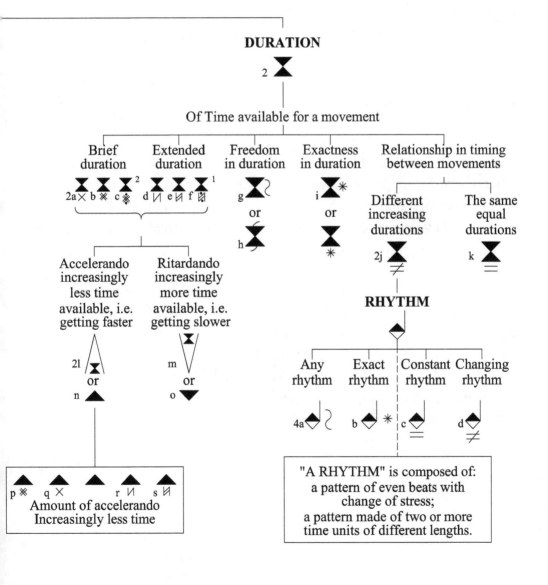

DURATION

Of Time available for a movement

| Brief duration | Extended duration | Freedom in duration | Exactness in duration | Relationship in timing between movements |

2a× b※ c✳ d⋈ e⋈ f⋈

g. or h.

i. or

Different increasing durations

2j ≠

The same equal durations

k =

Accelerando increasingly less time available, i.e. getting faster

Ritardando increasingly more time available, i.e. getting slower

2l / or n

m or o

RHYTHM

Any rhythm | Exact rhythm | Constant rhythm | Changing rhythm

4a | b | c = | d ≠

p※ q× r⋈ s⋈
Amount of accelerando
Increasingly less time

"A RHYTHM" is composed of:
a pattern of even beats with
change of stress;
a pattern made of two or more
time units of different lengths.

Chapter 12. Use of Ad Libitum Signs

The meaning and use of the *ad libitum* sign have varied in practice in Labanotation and also Kinetography Laban. This chapter presents a clarification and proposed solutions for each particular need. Credit must be given to Ray Cook whose thoughtful 2001 ICKL paper on the subject included dictionary and thesaurus meanings. The most appropriate ones are:

Any, More or Less, Approximately, Similar, Either, Free, Unspecified.

Laban took the symbol from mathematics where it means 'approximate', 'nearly'. With the development of more specific signs in more recent years, how the *ad libitum* sign (shortened to ad lib.) is to be interpreted, can be more specifically stated.

1.1. **The ANY Meaning for the Ad Lib. Sign**. The vertical ad lib. sign, **1a**, can also be drawn horizontally, **1b**. Used in Motif Notation for general statements of choice, we have: any direction **1c**; thus, **1d**, any middle level direction; **1e**, any high-level direction, and **1f**, any low-level direction. Any level in the vertical dimension is **1g**, which gives us: **1h**, any forward level; **1i**, any side level, and so on.

1.2. The sign of **1j** means a tilting, inclining action, also termed 'taking a direction': **1k** states any tilting act, while **1l** means any forward high inclination. The action of shifting a body part is **1m**, any shift is shown as **1n**, with **1o** being any forward shift. A rotation in the form of a twist of a body part, **1p**, gives us **1q**, any twist, with **1r** stating twist right or left. Rotating a limb as a unit, **1s**, can be shown to apply to any part, **1t**, with choice of right or left rotation being **1u**.

1.3. Certain symbols representing the idea of 'any' have not had the 'any' sign attached, for example, 'any spring', **1v**; there has been a request that this be **1w**. Any movement for the legs while in the air is **1x**, while **1y** shows the right leg to do any movement.

1.4. The symbol of **1z** represents the body-as-a-whole; **1aa** shows an action for the whole body; in **1ab** any action is stated. The indication of an appropriate gesture, **1ac**, can be shown to be any gesture, **1ad**. An action leading to a new support, **1ae**, could be indicated to be any action, **1af**. A shape, **1ag**, can be indicated to be any shape, **1ah**, **1ai** or **1aj**.

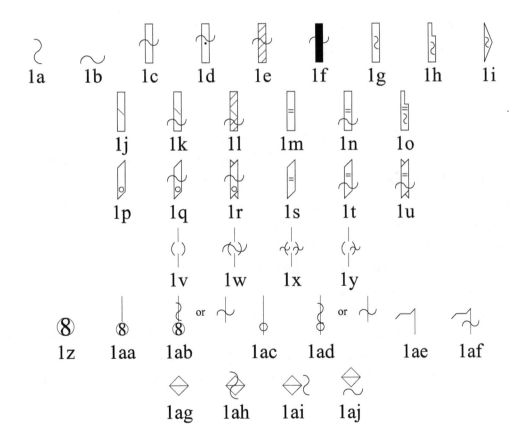

2.1. **"Any" Modifying Other Symbols**. The vertical line (stroke) by itself means 'An action', **2a**. This may be an appropriate action (when in context) or may mean 'any action', specified in **2b**. The need for this distinction came from Labanotation in canceling a hold sign in the support column. In **2c** the legs do the appropriate action to spring into 1st position. Here the action stroke does not mean 'any'. Ex. **2d** indicates that, in springing into 1st position the legs may do anything. **2e** states 'any number of repeats'; **2f** indicates 'any amount of turn'. Any pathway, any form of travelling, is shown in **2g**, with **2h** specifically meaning meandering. 'Any number' is **2i**. Any form of flexion is **2j**; **2k**, shows any form of extension. In **2l**, any degree of contraction, the vertical ad lib. sign takes the place of dots used to show the degree. This is useful when arm flexion may need to change or adjust, as in ballroom or other partner dance forms. **2m** shows any amount of elongation. To indicate any form of flexion to any degree, a small ad lib. sign is attached below the symbol, as in **2n**. Similar placement of the ad lib. sign in **2o** indicates any extension to any degree.

3.1. **Any, Free, Applied to Structured Labanotation**. An ad lib. sign placed in a starting position, **3a**, indicates freedom in the preparatory position. In the arm columns, **3b**, it states the arm movements are open to the performer. In a score a large ad lib. sign placed over a section of an empty staff, **3c**, indicates the performer may improvise in a manner fitting to the context of the piece. During the running steps of **3d** the arms may move freely. While the arms are held overhead in **3e**, the foot work can be the choice of the performer.

3.2. The pattern given in **3f** may vary freely. Alternatively, the ad lib. sign can be placed in an addition bracket, **3g**. The directions for leg flexion and extension movements in **3h** are open to choice. The number of repeats

in **3i** is left open. In performing **3j** the amount of turn is open to choice. The
level of the arms in swinging forward and backward in **3k** is open to choice.

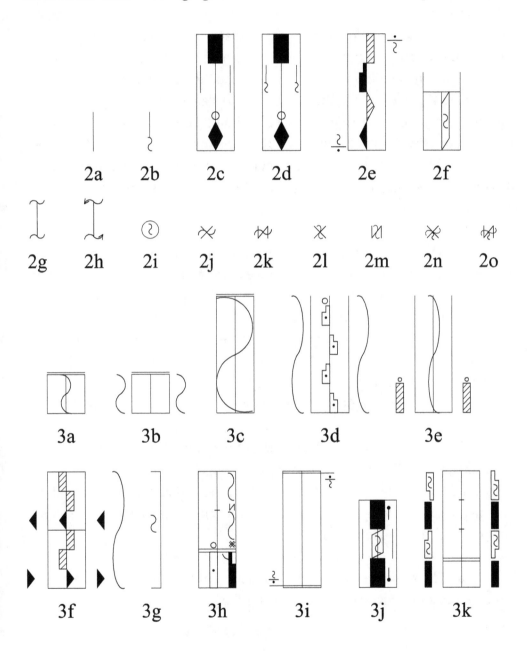

2a　　2b　　　2c　　2d　　　　2e　　　2f

2g　　2h　　2i　　2j　　2k　　2l　　2m　　2n　　2o

3a　　　　3b　　　　3c　　　　3d　　　　3e

3f　　　　3g　　3h　　　　3i　　　　3j　　　　3k

4.1. **Specific Modifications**. The elongated ad lib. sign, **4a**, shows general freedom in performing a movement. Specific freedom in timing is shown in **4b**; placed next to a movement sequence it means the timing is open to interpretation. Freedom in use of space is shown by **4c**. The sign for 'any body part' is **4d**: thus **4e**, is a movement of any part of the body; **4f**, any area, and **4g**, any limb. The combined shoulder and hip sign meaning 'any joint', **4h**, is applied to the ad lib. sign to state choice of any joint, **4i**. The sign for 'total freedom in all aspects' should be **4j**, the sign formerly used to mean freedom in timing. Note that the timing freedom of **4b** can be more specifically stated: **4k** shows freedom in duration of the movements; **4l**, freedom in speed; **4m**, freedom in rhythmic pattern; **4n**, freedom in meter used.

5.1. **Meaning 'Something', 'An Aim'**. The ad lib. sign can represent 'something', which later may be clarified as a person, an object or a part of the room. A motion toward something is **5a**, with **5b** being a motion away from something. This can also be applied to travelling, **5c** being travelling toward something, with **5d** being travelling away. In circling away from something, **5e**, the performer may have to adjust the circular path to provide the desired 'away' result. The 'aim', the 'destination' is shown in **5f** where travelling is to arrive somewhere.

6.1. **Meaning 'Either'**. Very useful for Motive Notation and Labanotation are the following: the sign for 'either' is **6a**; in **6b** either hand is indicated; **6c**, either wrist; **6d**, either elbow; **6e**, either shoulder (note the drawing of this to avoid it looking like an arrow); **6f**, either foot; and so on, applicable also to the limbs, arms and legs.

6.2. The signs for stepping on left and right foot, **6g**, can be stated as either left or right, **6h**. The indications for the gestures of gathering, left and right, **6i**, are indicated to be open to choice, **6j**; similarly scattering **6k**, is open to choice in **6l**. The choice to either gather or scatter is shown in **6m**.

'Specific Modifications'

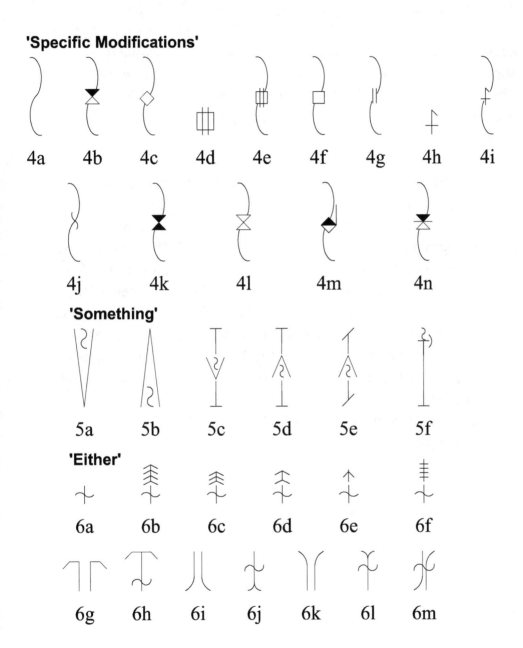

4a   4b   4c   4d   4e   4f   4g   4h   4i

4j   4k   4l   4m   4n

'Something'

5a   5b   5c   5d   5e   5f

'Either'

6a   6b   6c   6d   6e   6f

6g   6h   6i   6j   6k   6l   6m

6.3. The rotation signs of **6n** and **6o** indicate in general 'turn either right or left', except when it is used in the leg gesture column where it indicates 'neither left nor right' i.e., a parallel state for the legs. A cartwheel rotation right or left is shown as **6p** with **6q** being a forward or backward somersault. Because the 'any' indication is missing on these signs, people have questioned whether **6r**, **6s** and **6t** would not be better. The paths related to these rotations are as follows: **6u**, circling clockwise or anticlockwise; **6v**, a cartwheel path right or left; **6w**, a somersault path forward or backward.

7.1. **Meaning 'More or Less'.** When placed next to a direction symbol, **7a**, the meaning is 'more or less'. When adjacent to a direction symbol, the ad lib. sign can be drawn shorter, as in **7a**, or drawn longer, **7g**; the meaning is the same. This freedom contrasts with **7b** where the 'exact' symbol calls for a precise performance. Closer to **7a**, but with a different message, is **7c**, a gesture in the area of forward high. Placement of the ad lib. sign can give a different meaning: in **7d** it refers to the arm direction; in **7e** it refers to the thumb direction; to refer to both the ad lib. sign is placed in a bracket alongside the notation, **7f**. In **7g** the right arm is more or less side low and then the left arm more or less down. Starting from a kneeling position, the hold on the center of gravity sign in **7h** indicates staying at the same level, but in **7i**, the similar sign allows natural resiliency to occur while taking the steps.

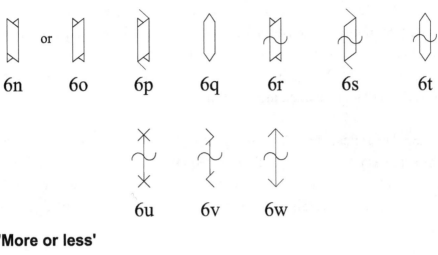

6n   6o   6p   6q   6r   6s   6t

6u   6v   6w

'More or less'

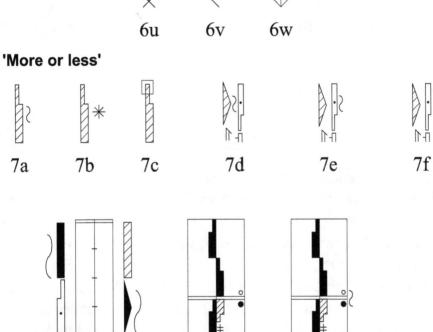

7a   7b   7c   7d   7e   7f

7g   7h   7i

7.2. The feet in **7j** are more or less parallel, there is some freedom; in **7k** the degree of circling need not be exactly 3/4. In **7l** the shape of the circling may not be precise. Note that the indication of **7m,** which gives the message of "See the floor plan" can be a practical device where the floor plan clearly states the needed information.

7.3. The repeat sign, **7n,** states perform in a similar way, i.e., more or less the same as person A. The sign for 'equal', **7o,** shown with a slash (meaning 'not') in **7p,** indicates not to be equal; in **7q** we have 'more or less equal'. Used with Front Signs, as in **7r,** a little freedom is allowed; **7s** states "any front".

8.1. **Wavy Lines**: '**Continue in the Same Manner**'. The use of a vertical wavy line, **8a**, was thought to be consecutive ad lib. signs, but the basic meaning is to 'continue this pattern' when it follows clearly indicated movement. The density of oscillations in the wavy line can indicate relative speed, **8b** being much faster than **8a**. A familiar use is **8c** in which the meaning is "Continue to run forward freely." Ex. **8d** indicates freedom in step timing (i.e., running through the music) in addition to continuing to run forward freely. Another frequent use is for very fast *bourrées* on *pointe* in classical ballets, as in **8e**. Continuously waving of the hand is given in **8f**. In contrast, nodding the head in **8g** occurs once, then, after a pause, twice more. Note use of horizontal dotted lines to define the movement to be repeated and the subsequent timing. The patting movement of the hand in **8h** is shown to continue very rapidly.

'More or less' continued

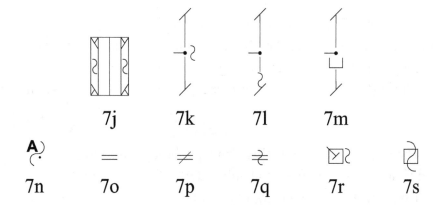

7j	7k	7l	7m

7n	7o	7p	7q	7r	7s

Continue in the same manner

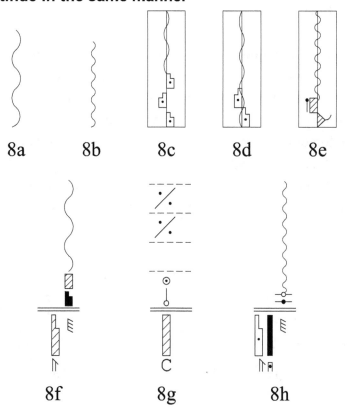

8a	8b	8c	8d	8e

8f	8g	8h

Chapter 13. Dynamics

1.1. The ebb and flow of energy in the body affects the quality and impact of a movement. The interplay of tension and relaxation within the muscles, the increase in force and the letting go, provide a range of movement 'coloring'. How and why these changes take place may rest on many factors.

Note: The development of analysis and symbology used in Labanotation is quite separate from Laban's *Effort* (1947). That was developed for factory workers who could not relax or drop energy while at work, thus relaxation, limp, droop, etc. were not included in his initial development of Effort.

1.2. **Accented Movements**. A sudden, brief increase in energy produces an accent, giving that moment more importance. An accent may be slight or may be marked, a strong accent. The sign for an accent was derived from music notation where a note is accented to mark a pattern or a more expressive, forceful sound. Ex. **1a** shows a slight accent while **1b** indicates a strong accent. The signs point in toward the movement they are describing. A single accent may occur at the start of a movement, **1c**, in the middle, **1d**, or at the end, **1e**. More than one accent may occur during a single movement, **1f**.

Dynamics

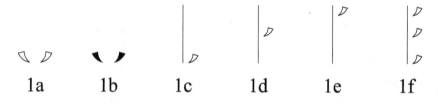

1a   1b   1c   1d   1e   1f

2.1. The Concept of 'Par'. Par is that level of energy needed to accomplish a particular movement efficiently without wasted effort or insufficient energy. Jumping requires more energy than walking, sitting requires less energy than standing. We can easily observe when someone uses too much or too little energy. The reasons for a rise in energy may vary. Stamping, like jumping, takes added energy. The reason for stamping may be to mark a musical rhythm. In practical cases, use of body weight can contribute to the downward thrust. A rise in energy could be caused by an emotional need, perhaps when one is angry. A drop in energy may also have different causes. A carefree attitude may produce relaxed, freely swinging movements. Tiredness may cause an inability to reach Par.

2.2. The concept of Par is illustrated by a horizontal dotted line, **2a**. Usually, the energy level of Par is understood to be in effect, and nothing need be indicated. However, to indicate a return to Par, the sign of **2b** is used. A rise in energy above Par is shown by an upward curve, as in **2c**. A lowering, a drop in energy is shown by a downward curve, as in **2d**. The general statements for the degree of rise or drop in energy are: a white circle for a slight degree, **2e**; a black circle for a marked degree, **2f**. These are placed on the appropriate curved bow. A rise in energy may be for practical purposes, lifting a heavy object, or sawing wood.

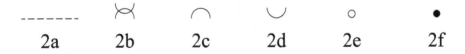

| 2a | 2b | 2c | 2d | 2e | 2f |

2.3. A slight rise in energy, as in being alert, aware, is **2g**; a marked rise in energy, strong, forceful, **2h**; a slight drop in energy, relaxed, weak, **2i**; a marked drop in energy, droop, limp, flop, **2j**. These symbols are placed next to the movement indication they qualify.

2.4. **Emphasis**. An emphasis in a movement lacks the suddenness of an accent but gives a stress, an importance to the movement. The signs for emphasis, **2k** for slight and **2l** for marked, are derived from **2g** and **2h**. A lack of emphasis indicates that an action is unimportant, the focus of the movement is elsewhere. Ex. **2m** states slightly unemphasized with **2n** the same to a greater degree. In the sequence of **2o** the lowering of the right arm is not to be noticed, the left arm gesture is important.

3.1. **Relation to Gravity**. The force of gravity is with us all the time. In our Par relation to gravity, we use the amount of energy needed to remain upright, standing, the amount needed for our daily tasks. We may give in to gravity, that is, allow gravity partially to take over, through tiredness, or through a sense of hopelessness. The exaggerated case being when all muscular tension lets go, as in fainting. We fight gravity in lifting objects, in lifting ourselves when we climb stairs, or when jumping, springing high off the ground.

3.2. The line of gravity is visualized as an imaginary vertical line, **3a**. This imaginary line is centered on the upward or downward bows. The white or black circle for amount, when centered in the curved bow, indicates a rise or drop of energy in relation to gravity. A slight rise in energy against gravity, uplift, buoyant, is **3b**; a marked rise in energy against gravity, an upward pressure, is **3c**. A drop in energy to make use of gravity, **3d**, provides a sense of weight, a weighty, ponderous gesture perhaps; **3e** indicates a marked drop in energy in making use of gravity, a sense of heaviness, a heavy stance, a heavy gesture using the weight of the limb, the torso weight dropped toward earth.

3.3. How we make use of gravity in movement is not always understood. Four categories need to be considered: 1) practical, functional need; 2) the result of an emotional state; 3) the need for a physical sense of body mass; 4) the production of sound, as in stamping a rhythm.

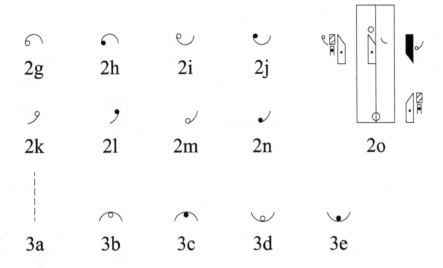

4.1. **Practical, Functional Use.** In his teaching, Laban always expressed strong movement in a downward direction, thus making use of the natural affinity with gravity. For practical purposes, we hammer a nail downward, making use of gravity. Hammering a nail into the ceiling is much harder as we must fight gravity. By resisting gravity, using 'uplift', the ballet dancer on *pointe* minimizes her weight. Spanish dancers combine a high lift in the torso and upper arms with earthy stamping. The folk dancer expresses an earthy quality by an appropriate degree of giving in to gravity. In contrast 'silent' stamps, require an uplift control at the moment when the foot would contact the floor. The wrestler lowers his center of gravity by pressing his weight downward, thus using gravity to maintain stability. How we sense body weight is determined by how we actively relate to gravity.

4.2. **Holding the Arms – Above, Below Par.** The interplay between resistance to gravity and giving in to its pull can be experienced with the arms. Holding the arm out to the side at shoulder height, as in 2nd position, **4a**, can become quite tiring. If the imagination provides a row of tiny balloons holding the arm up, the weight of the arm is not felt, there is constant uplift, **4b**. If these imaginary balloons start to rise (a greater pull against gravity), **4c**, the arm will begin to float upward. The imagination affects the muscles.

4.3. When the normal degree of muscular energy used to hold the arm up gradually drops, **4d**, the arm begins to relax, its 'tone' drops, the 'lifted elbow', used in several dance forms, drops and one becomes aware of the weight of the arm. Soon the whole arm sinks, giving way to gravity, **4e**. Sensing the weight of the arm, moving it with this awareness, produces a quality, a sense of weight, that is observable by the audience.

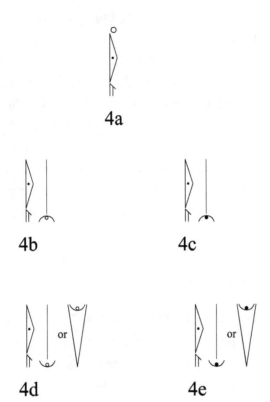

4a

4b   4c

4d   4e

4.4. Similarly, the weight of the torso can be used functionally or expressively. In pushing a heavy object, engaging the body weight can help significantly. We are familiar with the words, "Put your weight behind it." In **4f**, the action is spelled out in detail; the use of torso weight and the abbreviated sign for pressure are placed in an addition bracket. For a light object, only the hand and arm muscles are needed. The heavier the object, the more body weight and force needs to come into action. In certain body configurations muscular tension can allow us to control the natural reaction to gravity. Consider, for example, the normal backward compensation (slight shift) that occurs to maintain balance when leaning the torso forward horizontally in a standing position, **4g**. This compensation can be eliminated by muscular training. The use of strong uplift, even when lowering the body spatially, can produce a controlled action, constant resistance to gravity, **4h**. The observer sees only a slow, controlled movement.

5.1. **Use of Gravity in Swings, Analysis of an Arm Swing**. An arm (or leg) gesture can make a downward curved path without changing the par relationship to gravity, **5a**. Here the action can be compared to the motion of a clock pendulum. However, a natural, human arm swing, as in walking, has a changing relationship to gravity and a different timing.

5.2. When an arm is held out to the side, and arm tension is totally relaxed, the limb will drop quickly and swing past the body center line across to the other side, **5b**. If the drop is immediately followed by a gradual return to par, a harmonious swinging movement results. If an uplift occurs during the swing, **5c**, with some guidance, the arm can be taken into an over-curve to complete the circle. Note the difference between moving **toward a state, 5d**, and **arriving at that state, 5e**. The degree of using and fighting gravity can vary, as can the timing. In the notation of **5f**, total flop is shown at the start as the arm suddenly drops down with a light accent and the flop quality makes the arm very heavy. The question of control may also come into the picture, **5g** being the sign for free flow and **5h** the sign for bound, guided flow.

The downward path in **5i** begins with free flow and a slight giving in to gravity, then, the arm moves across to the other side with uplift and increasing guidance (bound flow).

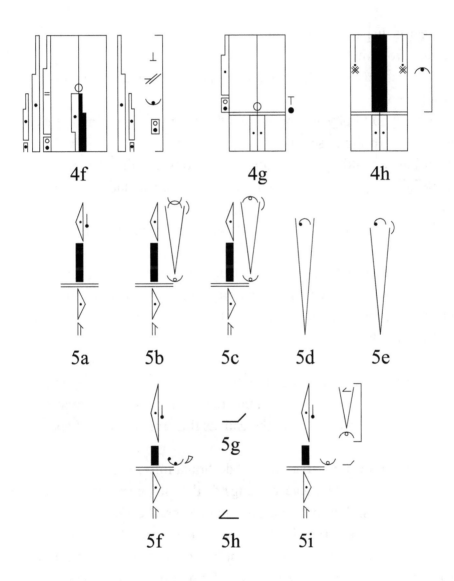

4f   4g   4h

5a   5b   5c   5d   5e

5f   5h   5i

5g

6.1. **Muscular Relaxation**. Dropping the muscular energy below par will allow the pull of gravity to take effect, this is inevitable. But it may or may not be the intention of the performer, and this intention is important. Energy drop, relaxing the muscles, may occur:

- when fear is dispelled after fright;
- as release from the tension of worry;
- after listening anxiously (nothing to worry about, shoulder and neck muscles relax);
- when letting go of physical pressure, after holding something in place;
- after peering, trying to see (neck muscles relax);
- after sitting very still, perhaps from fear as to what might happen, a natural fighting gravity situation (the buttocks, back, and abdomen muscles relax);
- after fear of being hurt (the danger is over, general relaxation).

Laughter, especially exaggerated laughter, is a mixture of tension and relaxation. This rise or lowering of muscular energy may occur for practical reasons while coping with everyday life or may be used expressively for a theatrical event.

7.1. **Timing of Dynamic Indications**. Any dynamic marking can be placed at the point in an action when that quality occurs. This could be at the beginning, in the middle, or at the end, as illustrated in **1c**, **1d** and **1e**.

7.2. **Use of Vertical Brackets**. Additional information is often placed in a vertical bracket, placed alongside the movement(s) to which the information belongs. For dynamics, the angular bracket, **7a**, refers to a physical use or state; a curved bracket, **7b**, derived from the drawing of a heart, **7c**, is used to indicate feeling, emotion, inner intent. Good spirits, an optimistic feeling, is shown in **7d**. A specific part of the body being qualified can be stated within the bow; in **7e**, it specifically states that the arms are to have uplift.

7.3. **Duration of Dynamic Indications**. How long a dynamic quality is maintained is shown by the length of the vertical bracket in which it is placed. Within this bracket the stated dynamic will be constant. In **7f** and **7g** a brief duration is shown; in **7h** and **7i** it is maintained for a longer time. When an increase or decrease sign is used, the length of that sign indicates how long the stated quality should grow or diminish, i.e. become established or fade away. Ex. **7j** shows a short duration; in **7k** it takes considerably longer. These indications apply to both physical and emotional aspects, the latter illustrated in **7l** and **7m**, an increase in strong feeling.

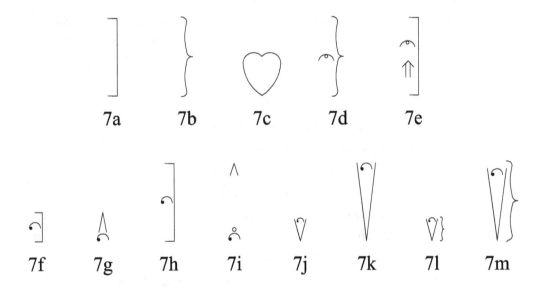

7a   7b   7c   7d   7e

7f   7g   7h   7i   7j   7k   7l   7m

8.1. **Cancellation**. When no dynamic indication is given, the performance is expected to be at the level of par appropriate for that particular kind of action. Cancellation of a dynamic indication occurs when another dynamic aspect has been indicated, as in **8a**. A movement that follows a statement in a vertical bracket, **8b**, will have an understood return to neutral, that is, to an unstated par. However, when a direct statement is needed, the par symbol can be used to indicate a return to that state. In **8c** a return to par is shown to occur quickly. The return to par is of a slower duration in **8d**, where the description is of going away from heaviness ending with par.

9.1. **Resilient, Rebound Movements**. The qualities of resilience, rebound, can occur in gestures as well as in steps. In each case it involves a slight 'there and back' action which combines a slight accent and a 'let go'. The slight rise in energy of the accent, **9a**, is often followed by a slight relaxation, **9b**. The accent sign always points in toward the movement it is describing.

9.2. **Resilient Steps**. The simple pattern of a step to the side followed by a closing step can be performed with a rebound on each step. One simple version can be **9c**, the step being followed by a slight knee bend, the closing following the same. A more fluent performance of this could be **9d**, while a more energetic version, **9e**, uses a straight leg on each step followed by a slight bend. This may also be performed by closing with weight on both feet, as in **9f**. The reverse pattern would be a step on a slightly flexed leg followed by a normally straight leg, **9g**. Weight could also be on both feet for the closing, **9h**, which also shows stretched legs.

9.3. Emphasis could be placed on the knee action, giving a different focus, as in **9i**. A slight knee-focused version of **9e** could be **9j** in which, from being stretched, the knee is shown to relax. A different focus could be the slight momentary lowering of the center of gravity, **9k**. Note the weight placement in **9l** in contrast to **9k**.

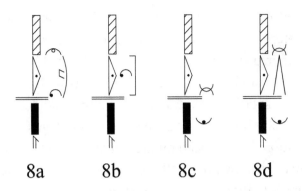

8a   8b   8c   8d

Rebound

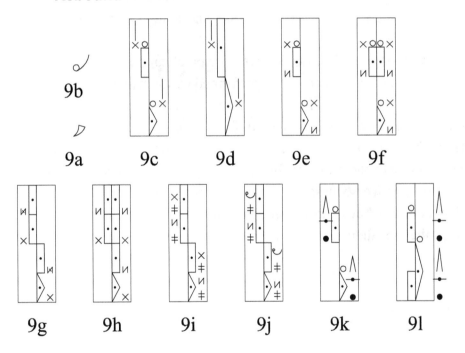

9a   9c   9d   9e   9f

9b

9g   9h   9i   9j   9k   9l

9.4. **Rebound Quality**. The above examples provide the facts of resilient, rebound steps, but have not stated the quality. A rebound is caused by a quick increase in energy, an accent, followed by a relaxation, **9m**; the accent may be slight, as in **9m**, or marked, as in **9n**. Or the rebound may be the reverse, a sudden relaxation followed by a sudden accent, **9o** and **9p**. These signs are combined to produce the rebound signs of **9q**, accent first, and **9r**, relaxation first. Placed on the left side, these are **9s** and **9t**. Low, rebound steps are shown in **9u**, these could be trudging steps. In **9v** the reverse is indicated. Placement of the rebound symbol in a bracket indicates that each step is to be performed with that quality, **9w**. Such rebound steps are found in European folk dances, notably in Hungary.

10.1. **Resilient Hand Gestures**. For practical or expressive reasons, resilient, rebound actions are often performed by the hands. Ex. **10a** could be bouncing a ball, the temporary minor downward displacement could be written as **10b**. In contrast, with palm facing up, the ball could be bouncing upward, **10c**, or as indicated in **10d**. In contrast, the gesture of **10e** could be a small version of the message for people to get up. With palm facing down, **10f**, the reverse message "Sit down" might be intended. Note that the distal tick has been added to the pins in **10a** – **10f**. If distal ticks are missing, the pins themselves reveal the analysis used.

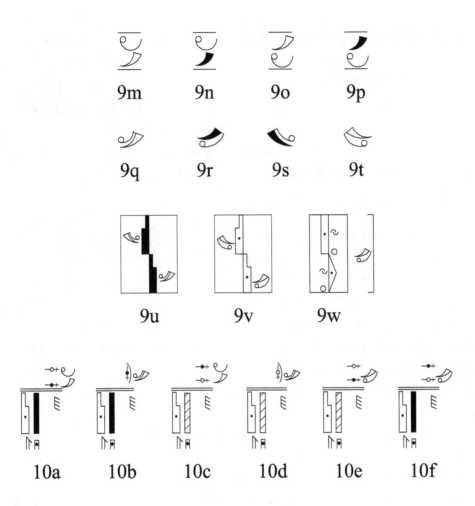

Chapter 14. Minor and Additional Points

1. Size, Distance

Many indications for the size of a position of the feet, the distance of a step, have been covered, in Labanotation textbooks and specifically in *Spatial Variations,* Advanced Labanotation, issue 9, section 40, p336. Here are presented a few less usual examples, but first a quick resume of the general picture.

1.1. **Statement of Relative Distance**. By placing the appropriate signs within a diamond, as in **1a**, a general statement of distance is given. Any distance is shown in **1b**. In **1c** each hand is sideward of the other and addressing each other. The distance between them is not stated, placement of the arms and the degree of arm flexion can pin down the location to a certain degree. Additional information can be given by using the distance signs; in **1d** they are shown to be very near. The degree of nearness can be stated within the dotted horizontal bow, very near being expressed by **1e**.

1.2. When use of the addressing sign is not appropriate, the sign used in draughtsmanship and carpentry to measure distance, 1f, can be used; it can also be written vertically, **1g**. In **1h** the right hand is above the left knee; the left knee is below the right hand and the distance is stated as being fairly far apart. What is not stated here is where the arm and leg are spatially, they could be in a low area, off to one side, etc., many configurations are possible; we only know the spatial relationship of those two body parts. The illustration of **1i** gives a comfortable, non-contorted location.

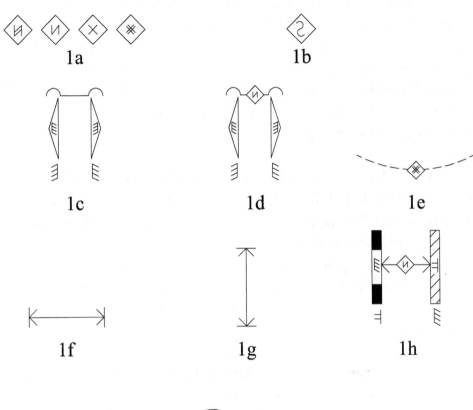

1i

1.3. **Statement of Specific Distance.** In his development of Kinetography Laban, Knust established indications for specific distance. A number in a square indicated the number of step-lengths, his basic unit of measurement (see Knust 1979, vol. 1, 249). Ex. **1j** (Knust 1979, vol. 2, 114, Ex. 670a) states 7 step-lengths. In **1k** (ibid., Ex. 670c) the distance of the leap is 3 step-lengths. In **1l** (ibid., 140, Ex. 844d) person 'y' is more or less 4 step lengths to the right of person 'x'.

1.4. Knust placed statements of specific distance to the left of the staff. Ex. **1m** (ibid., 114, Ex. 670b) indicates that 1 equals one meter, or 1 may indicate 0.75 of a meter. With the appropriate distance for '1' being established, the required distance can be measured accordingly. Ex. **1n** indicates how the proposed sign for distance could be used: the leap is to cover two meters. In **1o** the distance between person A and person B is about 4 feet, the apostrophe after the number being the standard sign for measurement in feet.

1.5. **A Forward Split.** The ultimate in length of step in the forward direction is the forward split. The front foot slides out until the hip is supporting on the floor, the distance is the length of both legs. In the notation of such a split, **1p**, the distance forward is given as triple wide plus, but it is the destination that completes the instruction. Note that the non-specific 'U' contact sign is used for the sliding as the part of the foot involved changes. The lowering of the center of gravity is also given for confirmation, although not really needed. Another question of distance arises when the leg is sliding on the barre in a stretching exercise. While facing the barre, standing very close, with the right leg sideward, resting on the barre, as in **1q**, the leg slides along the barre as it extends far sideward, the pelvis included, and the center of weight (gravity) shifts a great distance to the right. The actual distance achieved depends on the flexibility of the performer. In measure 2, the return to the upright situation involves the path of the center of weight shifting to the left until it is in its normal place high situation. At the same time the pelvic inclusion disappears, the leg returns to its normal side extension and the sliding has ceased.

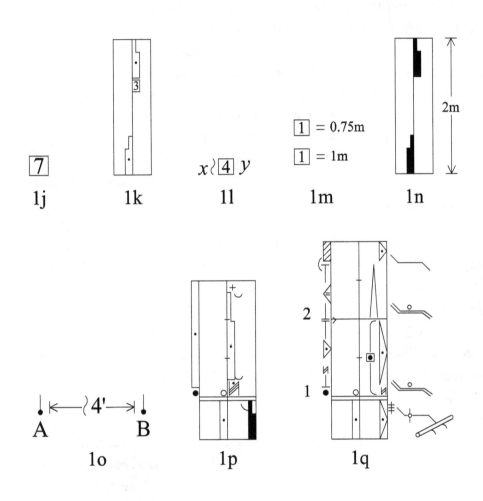

2. Natural

From the beginning, consideration needs to be given to what is understood as **natural**, **normal** or **standard** for positions of the body and basic movements. **Natural** is considered to be each individual's comfortable manner in standing and moving. **Normal** is a statistical term meaning that based on a large sampling, i.e., a group, and the average manner of performing the movement. **Standard** refers to a defined manner of performing a movement. In a system of movement notation is it practical to have certain details of performance established as Standard. This does not preclude the use of other non-standard descriptions, this flexibility being essential for a system that records many different forms of dance, training exercises, body development and other aspects.

2.1. **Standing in Place**. A standard interpretation exists in the basic notation of standing in place, **2a**. In Labanotation it means feet together, heels touching – a stylistic convention and not a natural placement. The place symbols should mean vertically below each hip, thus feet slightly apart. A simple notation can indicate each of these, **2b** being legs touching, and **2c** indicating each support to be displaced slightly to the side. An even more specific statement is that of **2d** where 'Direction from Body Part' (DBP) is used by placing a hip sign within each place symbol.

2.2. **Degree of Leg Rotation**. Originally Labanotation established a basic, understood degree of leg rotation, it was then found better to state in each instance the degree needed for each particular exercise or score. When nothing is stated the performance of **2a** is open to individual interpretation. The precise degree of outward or inward rotation can be indicated, **2e** states parallel feet; **2f** states a 45° outward rotation. For a score that is known to be classical ballet, the outward leg rotation of **2g** can automatically be understood even if it has not been stated at the start or in a glossary. The degree of rotation that is natural for each individual can be indicted as **2h**.

2.3. **Carriage of the Arms**. The arms are normally relaxed with soft elbows and wrists, **2i**. Regarding facing of the palms, because the arms are flexible, and people's natural arm carriage varies, to facilitate matters Labanotation has established a Standard direction for palm facing for each major direction: down, **2j**; forward horizontal, **2k**; and up, place high, **2l**, for each of which the palm faces 'in'. For side horizontal the Standard is palm facing forward, **2m**. These are automatically understood and provide a reference point for rotary actions of the lower arms.

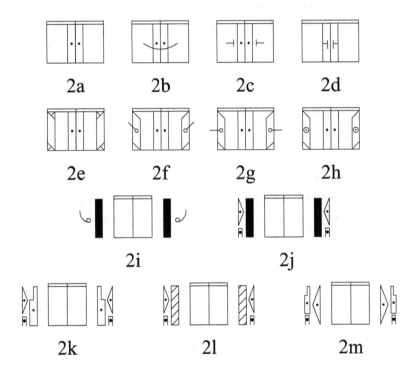

3. The Away Cancellation

3.1. A new movement indication usually cancels the result of a previous indication. The four specific signs for cancellation are: **3a** meaning 'back-to-normal' for that part of the body; **3b**, the 'away' sign, and **3c** the release sign to cancel forms of contact. To cancel a space hold or a spot hold **3d** is used.

3.2. The back-to-normal sign may mean to return to the normal state for that body part; in **3e** the flexed arm returns to its normal state. In **3f** the inclined torso returns to its normal upright situation. Statement of return to place high, **3g**, places focus on awareness of the direction. In **3h**, from looking up the head returns to its normal situation.

3.3. The inverted V for 'away' states that the result of a previous indication is no longer in effect. It is used when a back-to-normal indication is not appropriate or less appropriate. The clenched fist in the starting position of **3i** disappears as the arm rises to side middle. The thumb facing direction when the arm is up, in **3j**, is cancelled as the arm moves forward diagonal. In **3k** the forward torso tilt is cancelled as the chest inclines to the side. The sideward folding of the chest in **3l** needs to be cancelled to produce a normal torso alignment. The retained degree of bent legs during the high steps in **3m** is cancelled when the feet lower to place middle. A very slight bouncing action on each slow step in **3n** is indicated.

3.4. A very pertinent example of the value of the 'away' sign comes from Veronica Dittman's score of *Nun Better* (Pedro Alejandro, 1992). In **3o** the side middle leg gesture should not remain during the low turn, it should 'dissolve' in preparation for the backward step that follows. An action stroke tied with a zed caret to the following step, **3p**, would give the wrong message. The idea is to relinquish the previous, not to plan for the next.

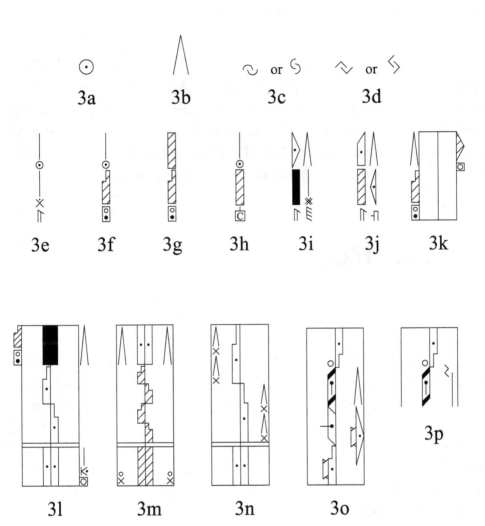

3a

3b

3c

3d

3e   3f   3g   3h   3i   3j   3k

3l   3m   3n   3o   3p

4. As Much as Possible

4.1. In some circumstances the instruction can be to perform a particular action to the unspecified degree of "as much as possible". The infinity sign, **4a**, is used to express this idea. Thus, in **4b** the torso folds forward high as much as possible. In **4c** the amount of turning should be as much as possible. The distance between the hands in **4d** should be as much as possible. The number of repeats of a movement phrase may be unspecified with the ad lib. signs, **4e**, or an infinite number may be indicated, **4f**.

5. Place Middle for Gestures

The following material is not advanced Labanotation but is a topic that has not been covered in any of the textbooks.

5.1. **Arm Gestures**. The direction place middle for the arm means that the extremity, the hand, is at the base, the shoulder. This description serves as a simple statement, the exact placement of the arm may depend on what came before. No indication of state of rotation is given. As a starting position, **5a**, the elbow will probably be down, the hand somewhere close to the shoulder. In **5b** the starting position of place high could result in the elbow ending somewhere down out to the side, or down by the sides; in **5c** the elbow can easily end sideward, as also in **5d**.

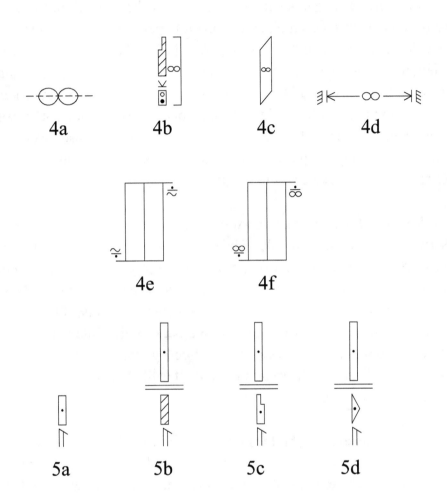

4a   4b   4c   4d

4e   4f

5a   5b   5c   5d

5.2. The basic gymnastic exercise of **5e**, makes use of returning to place middle between each direction; no exact performance is required, hence the place middle indication is quite suitable. In **5f** both arms start to the left, then pass hands close to shoulders on the way to the opposite side. In passing from forward to backward middle, **5g** indicates the hand should pass close to the shoulder. Addition of the black pins for 'in front' means that in **5h** the hands will be at the center line of the body, close together. Generally speaking, the place middle indication is used as a simple description when exactness is not required.

5.3. **The Legs**. In a similar way the foot close to the hip can be described as being place middle. The legs being less flexible than the arms the usage of place middle is less appropriate but provides the needed idea. In **5i**, the right leg moves from forward through place to backward. How close the foot will come to the hip depends on the flexibility of the performer. The leg kicks forward, side and back in **5j**, while in **5k** the pattern includes hops to the side with the free leg tucked close to the hip. What is not indicated is the rotational state; it is likely that the knee will be forward or diagonal rather than side.

5.4. In this excerpt, **5l**, the arms come in while the torso is bent, then extend out sideward as the torso returns to normal. The sequence of **5m** features the direct, central path of the arms as they move from up to down or vice versa.

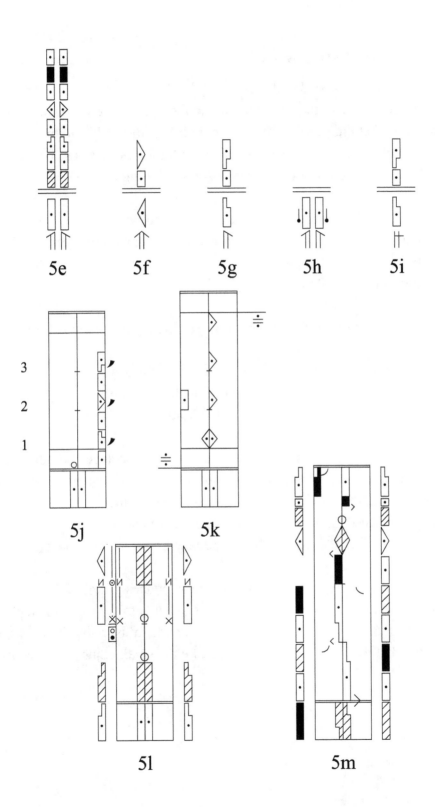

5e 5f 5g 5h 5i

3

2

1

5j 5k

5l 5m

6. Center of Levity

6.1. At the Jooss-Leeder Dance School in the 1930s the instruction included reference to the heavy point and the light point in the body. It was understood that the pelvis is the 'heavy point' in the body and the chest the 'light point'. The chest was considered the light point because of the lungs, the filling of the lungs with air which gives a feeling of lightness or rising.

6.2. In 1936, when Hutchinson began studying the Laban notation system, the 'heavy point' was somewhat mixed up with the **center of gravity** (CG); the same sign was used for both. Laban gives the following explanation in his 1928 book (16,17):

> "Center of gravity"– Starting point of the leg movements (in the pelvis).
>
> "Point of Elevation" – Point from which the arm movements are made (thought of as in height of the breastbone).
>
> "Weight'– Center of gravity of the body.

6.3. The awareness that the CG is a point of balance and not a body part came much later. Instead of the sign for the pelvis, **6a**, the sign of **6b** was adopted at the 1965 ICKL conference. Deeper investigation – a visit to the Science Museum in London – revealed that in some forms of movement, sport in particular, the CG can lie outside the body. It is a moveable point.

6.4. A movement led by the CG, **6c**, produces a slight fall. This is quite different from **6d** in which the pelvis leads into the forward step. A pelvic shift, **6e**, need not change the balance line in the body; it is usual and expected that the rest of the body will make the small adjustment needed to keep the line of balance.

6.5. The center of levity has no relationship with laughter, nor does it relate to the center of gravity, thus the term 'light point' is more appropriate. The following examples give an idea as to the meaning of 'light point'. As the arms open up in **6f**, the front of the chest expands. In **6g** the upward arm gesture is accompanied by the chest rising. An opening of the arms backward in **6h** is accompanied by the upper front of the chest. Breathing in and expanding the chest enriches the opening of the arms sideward in **6i**. An action of the light point may coincide with a loss of balance, **6j**.

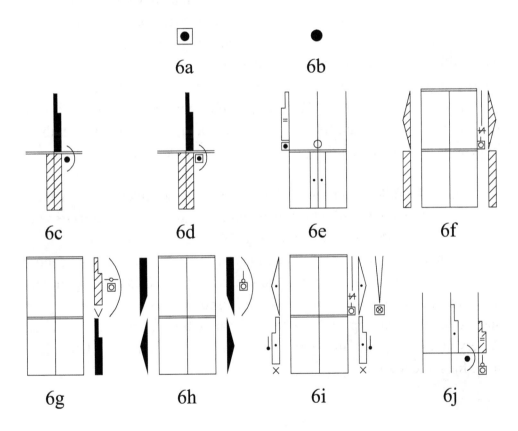

6a   6b

6c   6d   6e   6f

6g   6h   6i   6j

7. Stillness

A pause, a break, a stop, a stillness, these are not new items for consideration but an in-depth look at each can be revealing.

7.1. **A Pause**. A continuous flow of movement is shown in **7a**, there is no gap between the symbols. In **7b** there is a small gap between each direction indicating a momentary break in the flow, a hesitation perhaps, a breath pause. In a ballet *port de bras* this pause may have the value of establishing that position for a moment before moving on. The gap is increased in **7c**, a definite break, perhaps an enjoyment of that direction. The swift movements of **7d** give a very different message. The use of energy to be so swift and stop, changes the expression. One is reminded of the doll dancing in the ballet *Coppélia*, sudden, abrupt. In a human it might be a startled reaction, and 'oh!' expression. In a dramatic situation, with both arms moving, it could express anger, or even despair.

7.2. The following presents known facts but considered now with regard to their expression. Fluent walking forward, as in **7e**, contrasts with the slight break in the forward travelling, **7f**, which might express hesitation, a slight uncertainty. Note the need for the hold sign for supports to counteract the rule that a gap in the support column means going into the air. Use of this retention sign: 'o' will be discussed later. In **7g** the separation between steps is 1/2 a beat, a definite break, a moment of arrest. A very quick step, **7h**, can express a great reluctance to travel, a holding back for some reason.

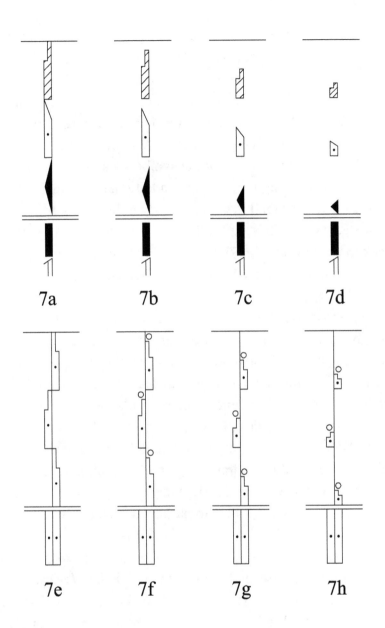

7a   7b   7c   7d

7e   7f   7g   7h

7.3. A sudden ending to a sequence may provide a conclusion, an impact to provide a strong statement. Think of the soft shoe tap dance that ends with "Shave and a haircut – two bits!" and an extended arm gesture toward the audience, **7i**. Such a gesture is a definite 'stop', it is held until the applause begins. Also using a definite stop, a freezing, occurs when moving into poses, as in playing 'statues'. Here the retention sign can be used, as in **7j**. The gap at the end of the symbols states the cessation of movement, but the hold sign provides the additional message "Do not move". This retention sign, known as a 'body hold', is used to indicate that a particular state is to be held, as in **7k**, where the fist is held until cancelled by the back to normal sign. In **7l** the hands are to be held until the release sign indicates to let go, the cancellation for retained relationships.

7.4. **Stillness**. What is stillness in terms of movement? Movement has ceased, but there is still an aliveness, an energy still present, the expression of the previous movement continues, 'beaming out' in a way that can be observed. In music the note is sounded on the piano and the note continues to reverberate, the sound continues to 'sing on'. In movement, stillness conveys the same idea. How is stillness used in choreography? The present-day choreographic style is of endless movement. Even in earlier decades the beauty, the dramatic impact of stillness was rarely use. Jerome Robbins was an exception. He understood the value of the 'pregnant pause'. He used stillness to particular effect in his ballet *The Age of Anxiety* (1950).

7.5. Stillness is the second item on the list in the *Movement Alphabet* (Hutchinson Guest 2006): 1, An action of some kind; 2, Stillness, an absence of movement. We have seen that an absence of motion can be just a gap, an empty moment, an 'end of the road'. The symbol for stillness, **7m**, was developed from the long existing retention sign, the 'body hold': O, with the V for out-flowing added. In Motif Notation it has particular value in instilling the awareness of different forms of movement and how a stillness that follows can continue to express that movement. In **7n** travelling forward is followed by stillness. The rise (movement up) after turning in **7o** is followed by stillness. In structured notation use of stillness is left more up to the performer; where a pause exists, stillness can be indicated, as in **7p**, where the high position with feet together can be followed by stillness, rather than just a hold sign.

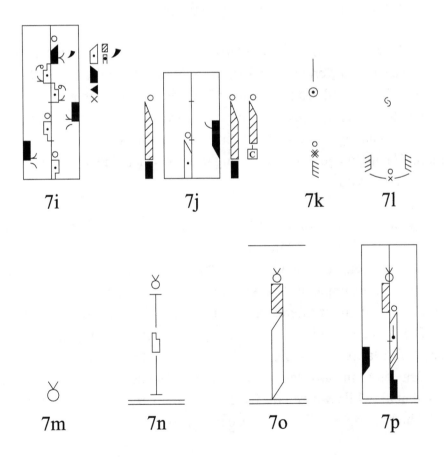

7i   7j   7k   7l

7m   7n   7o   7p

8. Looking, Gaze and Focus

8.1. **The Action of Looking**. The action of looking is indicated as the face sign followed by a particular direction; it is understood that the eyes are naturally included. Such looking usually involves an action for the head. In **8a** the head will turn to the right to face side right, in **8b** the head inclines forward to look down.

8.2. Looking at a person can be expressed with the addressing sign, **8c**, or by the simple indication of **8d**. The change in head alignment will depend on where person B is in relation to the performer.

8.3. **Gaze**. The term 'gaze' refers specifically to the eyes which may glance or gaze into different directions without the head moving. In **8e** the gaze is straight forward. In gazing up, **8f**, the direction is actually more likely to be forward high, just as in looking down, **8g**, it is more likely to be forward low. Gazing to the side, **8h**, might not get beyond the diagonal direction. Gazing diagonally up, **8i**, might occur when one is sceptical about something said.

8.4. **Inward and Outward Focus**. The eyes may be in their natural, forward directed placement, but the focus of the mind can be inward or outward. Such focus may be very important for the expression of the mood of the dance, for example, a strong inward focus can produce a trance-like expression. The Point of Interest arrow indicates this outward or inward focus. The diamond, indicating spatial aspects, is used to show the degrees, the sense of distance. Thus, very far inward focus, **8j**, can be almost a trance. The lesser inward state is given as **8k**. The neutral, normal state is expressed at **8l**, while **8m** and **8n** indicate far and very far outward focus, both of which involve a slight increase in energy.

Looking - Gaze

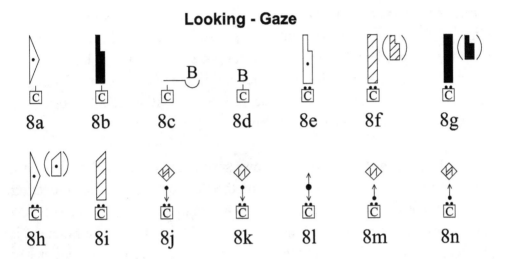

8a   8b   8c   8d   8e   8f   8g

8h   8i   8j   8k   8l   8m   8n

9. Unit Timing, Exact Timing

In the development of Labanotation, Unit Timing was generally used; in time a more specific indication of timing was developed, known as Exact Timing. These have been presented in *Labanotation* (2005, 183, 247, 313 and 441). Additional thoughts and usages are presented here. The many discussions on the subject have centered around the fact that Unit Timing is simpler to read and easier for beginners. Here we will discuss Spring Points, a simple step given to children.

9.1. **Spring Points**. Ex. **9a** shows springing onto the left foot and at the same time touching the right foot on the floor on count 1, then repeating onto the other foot landing on count 2. The notation is simple, but to perform exactly what is stated, i.e., to point and land at the same moment, is physically hard. In fact, what the body does is to land just before count 1 and then point on count 1. Each beat, each count can be divided into four, as illustrated in **9c** (see p.208, 1.2). Thus, in **9b** the landing occurs on the 'u' before the count.

9.2.   In the Unit Timing example of **9d** the arms and leg move fluently from one position to the next. If arrival exactly on the count is important, the notation should be as **9e**, i.e., Exact Timing. When hands clap, the indication needs to be written exactly when the contact occurs; in **9f** the claps are on count 1 and count 2. If foot movements occur at exactly the same moment, then Exact Timing is needed but with very short symbols. This usage allows for easier reading but gives the impression of sudden movements.

9.3. In **9g** the movements arrive on the appropriate count, but being brief, suggest staccato actions. To show a lengthening in time, the Time Sign for duration is placed in a vertical bow with the wide sign below it, meaning more duration, i.e., not so separated, more sustained, legato.

9.4. **Keys for Unit and Exact Timing**. Ex. **9h** is the indication for **Unit Timing,** while **9i** states that **Exact Timing** is being used.

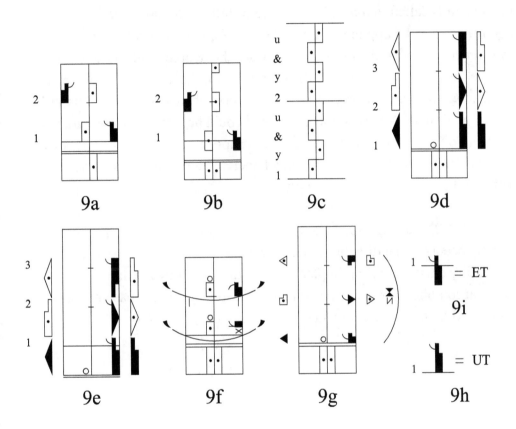

10. Limb Falling

10.1. A falling movement, as in **10a**, is shown by the center of gravity leading into the direction of the new support. In ballet this movement is called 'a *tombé*'. This idea of falling, or momentarily losing control can also be applied to the limbs. In **10b** the arm starts up and then falls down. In dynamic terms the arm loses the degree of effort holding it up, the 'let go' results in the center of gravity for the am arriving down, at place low. In a similar way the head may lose all energy and fall forward, **10c**. The timing of this dropping the head could be slower, a more gradual 'letting go' as in **10d**. In **10e** the elbow is supported by the table, the lower arm then falls to the side. From a low kneel, the torso might fall sideward, **10f**, the right hand taking the weight.

10.2. Returning to falling for the whole body, as in **10a**, this action usually occurs into a direction, often far from the point of support. The possibility exists of falling in place, **10g**, a difficult movement, usually being accomplished by clowns who are able to displace the base of support and to fall on the same spot usually onto the side of the body.

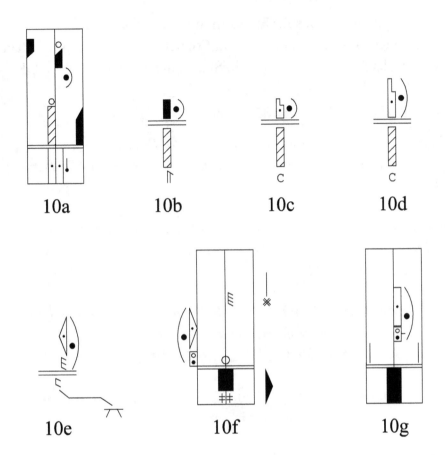

10a 10b 10c 10d

10e 10f 10g

Bibliography

Cook, Ray. "Indications for Freedom of Interpretation." In Proceedings of the 22nd International Council for Kinetography Laban (ICKL) Biennial Conference, Ohio State University, Columbus, OH, July 26-August 2, 2001, 45-53. https://ickl.org/wp-content/uploads/2016/04/Proceedings_2001_TXT.pdf

Hackney, Peggy. *Making Connections: Total Body Integration through Bartenieff Fundamentals*. New York: Gordon and Breach, 1998.

Hutchinson, Ann. *Labanotation or Kinetographie Laban: the System of Analyzing and Recording Movement*. 2nd ed. London: Oxford University Press, 1970.

Hutchinson, Ann. *Labanotation or Kinetographie Laban: the System of Analyzing and Recording Movement*. 3rd ed., rev. New York: Theatre Arts Books, London: Dance Books, 1977.

Hutchinson Guest, Ann, and Claudia Jeschke. *Nijinsky's "Faune" Restored*. The Netherlands: Gordon and Breach, 1991.

Hutchinson Guest, Ann, and Rob van Haarst. *Canon Forms*. Advanced Labanotation, vol 1, part 1. London: Harwood Academic Publishers, 1991.

Hutchinson Guest, Ann, and Rob van Haarst. *Shape, Design, Trace Patterns*. Advanced Labanotation, vol. 1, part 2. London: Harwood Academic Publishers, 1991.

Hutchinson Guest, Ann, and Rob van Haarst. *Kneeling, Sitting, Lying*. Advanced Labanotation, vol. 1, part 3. London: Harwood Academic Publishers, London, 1991.

Hutchinson Guest, Ann, and Joukje Kolff. *Sequential Movements.* Advanced Labanotation, issue 4. London: Dance Books, 2003.

Hutchinson Guest, Ann, and Joukje Kolff. *Hands, Fingers.* Advanced Labanotation, issue 5. London: Dance Books, 2002.

Hutchinson Guest, Ann, and Joukje Kolff. *Floorwork, Basic Acrobatics.* Advanced Labanotation, issue 6. London: Dance Books, 2003.

Hutchinson Guest, Ann, and Kolff, Joukje. *Center of Weight.* Advanced Labanotation, issue 7. London: Dance Books, 2003.

Hutchinson Guest, Ann, and Joukje Kolff. *Handling of Objects, Props.* Advanced Labanotation, issue 8. London: Dance Books, 2002.

Hutchinson Guest, Ann, and Joukje Kolff. *Spatial Variations.* Advanced Labanotation, issue 9. London: Dance Books, 2002.

Hutchinson Guest, Ann. *Labanotation: the System of Analyzing and Recording Movement.* 4th ed. London: Routledge, 2005.

Hutchinson Guest, Ann. *Movement Alphabet.* London: Language of Dance Centre, 2006.
https://www.lodc.org/uploads/pdfs/MovementAlphabet.pdf

Hutchinson Guest, Ann, and Tina Curran. *Your Move.* 2nd ed. London: Routledge, 2007.

Knust, Albrecht. *Abriss der Kinetographie Laban.* Hamburg: Verlag Tanzarchiv, 1956.

Knust, Albrecht. *A Dictionary of Kinetography Laban (Labanotation).* 2 vols. Plymouth: Macdonald and Evans, 1979.

Laban, Rudolf. *Schrifttanz: Methodik, Orthographie, Erläuterungen.* Vienna: Universal Edition, 1928 (English and French editions 1930).

Laban, Rudolf, with F. C. Lawrence, *Effort.* London: Macdonald and Evans, 1947.

Marion, Sheila. "Pins/closed positions of the feet." Paper, International Council for Kinetography Laban (ICKL) Biennial Conference, Chantilly, France, August 13-20, 1979.

Wile, Charlotte. *Moving About: Capturing Movement Highlights using Motif Notation.* New York: Charlotte Wile, 2010.

Index

CPSIA information can be obtained
at www.ICGtesting.com
Printed in the USA
LVHW051207170622
721528LV00005B/175